Caring for Elderly Parents

Caring for Elderly Parents

ELEANOR DEEPING

Constable London

First published in Great Britain 1979
by Constable and Company Limited,
10 Orange Street, London WC2H 7EG
Copyright © 1979 by Eleanor Deeping
Set in Monotype Bembo
Printed in Great Britain by The Anchor Press Ltd
and bound by Wm Brendon & Son Ltd
both of Tiptree, Essex

Chapter 2 on Bereavement is reprinted
by kind permission of *Woman and Home*

British Library C.I.P. Data

Deeping, Eleanor
   Caring for elderly parents.
    1. Aged – Home care – Great Britain
   I. Title
   649.8   HV1481.G52

ISBN 0-09-462060-1
ISBN 0-09-462700-2 Pbk

In happy memory of my mother

Acknowledgment

I wish to acknowledge with gratitude all the help and encouragement given to me in the writing of this book by my Editor, Elfreda Powell.

E.D.

Contents

	Introduction	ix
1	Understanding ageing	1
2	Bereavement and widowhood	7
3	On their own	30
4	Nutrition	63
5	Financial problems of the elderly	72
6	Bringing an elderly parent to live with you	86
7	Illness in the elderly	120
8	Physical illnesses	126
9	Mental illness and impairment	170
10	Coping with stress	193
11	Nursing the elderly at home	217
12	Clothing and aids for the disabled elderly	246
13	Admission to hospital	260
14	Coping with terminal illness	274
15	The women who care	279
	Index	283

Introduction

Many people – mainly women – find themselves caring for elderly parents at some time in their lives. To respond to this need with love, or a sense of duty, or both, would seem to be the most natural thing in the world; but like many other natural things that happen to us in life, it can turn out to be not only right and rewarding, but occasionally anxiety-provoking, emotionally painful, and a real test of endurance.

There are seven million people over sixty-five in Britain today and the problems many of them have to face are highlighted by the results of a recent survey carried out by the census office. This shows that more than half of those in the sixty-five to seventy-four age group suffer from some disability which limits their activities, and 700,000 of them are unable to go out alone without assistance. So, encouraging as it may be to know that many elderly people are in fairly good health, the needs of those who are less fortunate are obviously great, and the job of meeting those needs invariably falls to their children.

Contrary to popular belief, based on the few bad cases of family neglect and rejection of their old people which sometimes receive wide publicity, most people want to do all they can to stand by their elderly parents when frailty overwhelms them. Often this just means giving them emotional support and making sure, as far as possible, that they are living in conditions where they can retain their own home and independence. But when it entails living together, both the carer and the cared for are presented with a very challenging situation, full of problems of all kinds: some big ones, but mostly small day-to-day ones, which if left unsolved can finally add up to the last straw that makes the weight of extra work and responsibility a crushing burden, instead

Introduction

of an experience through which new insights can be gained and strengths developed.

I know, because I was faced with just such a challenge myself. I was luckier than most though, because a long career in social work – much of it connected with the problems of the vulnerable elderly and their families – gave me a little more knowledge of the difficulties of ageing than I would otherwise have had. It taught me a few useful skills which I was able to use just when I needed them; although, like everyone else faced with the reality of caring, I learned most from my mistakes. I learned also that apart from actually experiencing old age, the best way to begin to understand it is to listen to what the elderly themselves feel about it – opinions that are often light-years away from some of the wishful-thinking theories many of us have while viewing it from a distance. And I have done a lot of listening.

This book makes no claim to be a guide for social workers or others already trained and experienced in caring for elderly people. They will already be well acquainted with all it contains. Rather it is an attempt to pass on to those closely involved in caring for their elderly parents some of the basic knowledge and problem-solving techniques that may help them to survive the sorrows and enjoy the rewards of what they are doing.

Note: In order to avoid the constant repetition of the words 'him and her', the parent being looked after is most often referred to throughout the book as 'her'. In most cases the reference applies equally to the case of men or women; where only women are referred to this is self-evident from the context.

1
Understanding ageing

Those who are caring for elderly parents, sharing their problems at close quarters and seeing all the changes that age can bring, are usually well aware that although their outward 'uniform' of life may be showing signs of wear and tear they are by no means a race apart, suffering from an illness called 'old age'. They are as different and individual in personality as the young, with all the same needs for love, self-expression and independence; even though they are involved in an increasingly uphill struggle to preserve their failing powers.

What exactly happens when people age has always been something of a mystery. Even the experts disagree, and theories still come and go. Some believe that the body cells, which build up and break down in cycles throughout life, gradually lose their power to perform this function efficiently, which leads to the ultimate breakdown of the whole human organism. Others say that we are all 'programmed' at birth, and that when our own particular programme has run its course there is irreversible failure of one or several vital organs, which brings life to an end.

All we know for certain is that the body and mind gradually run down and wear out, not necessarily in a steady decline, but in stages; and that when this process is nearing completion it brings about mental and physical changes. Some of these are of very little significance and do not affect the elderly person or his or her family to any great extent; others have a profound effect. So those who may be called upon at some time to care for an elderly parent need first of all to understand what bodily and mental changes in older people come within the normal range. These changes vary widely from one person to another and cannot be regarded as any form of illness, although some, at least, can prevent people from enjoying the robust health of their younger days, and impose certain limitations on their activities.

Bodily changes within the normal range can include loss of hair and of hair colour, thinning and wrinkling of the skin, wastage of muscles, shrinkage in height, brittle bones, changes in blood vessels, deterioration of sight, deterioration of hearing, lowered resistance to the effects of infection, tendency to breakdown or malfunction of several organs at once, inability of the body to control adverse physical reactions to hunger or fluid loss, and reduced physical ability to adjust adequately to heat, cold or excessive strain.

Mental changes within the normal range can (but do not always) include some decline in intellectual performance, deterioration of memory for recent events, difficulty in learning complicated new skills, difficulty in adapting to change, loss of flexibility in attitudes, increased self-absorption and varying degrees of decrease in sexual desire.

Not all these normal changes may apply to any one individual, of course, but some will apply to most of the elderly at various stages. A careful and imaginative study of them can soon dispel any illusions younger people might have that old age is a time of ease and replace it with an awareness that for some it is a time of considerable struggle to compensate for losses of almost every kind. Once we realise this, those of us who still have some way to go before we join the ranks of the elderly can begin to understand ageing in a new way. Such a formidable list of the changes they may have to face takes a good deal of the heat out of our occasional feelings of impatience with them. We realise, for instance, just how little instead of how much our elderly parents actually grumble about their aches and pains and limitations. We begin to wonder how we could ever have been less than generous in our judgement of people who have so many physical and emotional burdens; and we start to view them with the tenderness that great vulnerability always evokes. Few of us manage fully to live up to our good intentions to try to be more tolerant and understanding (and we forget how much *they* have to tolerate in *us*); but the more we learn about the facts of ageing, the better equipped we become to help our elderly parents with sympathy and insight, when the need arises.

It could be argued that the elderly are not the only group of people who have to cope with the stress of change. Other periods of life, such as adolescence and the menopause, bring their problems as well. But the difference is that the old are always aware that they are on their last lap, and that there are not too many tomorrows left in which it may be possible for life to surprise them with the fulfilment of a dream or the realisation of an ambition. This surely makes them something of a 'special case', and one can only marvel at the courage many show.

Perhaps the greatest aid to understanding ageing is to find out what our elderly parents themselves think about it, but that is not easy. Many of them are wary of giving a frank opinion, and not without reason, for society often regards any expression of negative feelings in the elderly as 'moaning'; and if they do not always appear to be growing old gracefully, they are frequently dismissed as being either sour or ungrateful for the (sometimes doubtful) blessing of longevity. But when we see the serious problems that age can bring, it is hardly surprising that at least some of the elderly subscribe to the view that 'whom the Gods love die young'! Those, however, who are willing to talk honestly about their feelings do so eagerly and with an obvious sense of relief, for they are anxious to be understood and to discuss the experience through which they are passing. Some of them tell us that they feel they have come to terms fairly well with the limitations of age and are quite contented now to live life in a different way, at a slower pace. These are usually people who have been fortunate enough always to have had an easy-going disposition and a philosophical outlook. Then there are the natural achievers who have retained their drive and desire to manage, perform or create, and have been lucky enough to find a satisfying niche for themselves to meet their needs, even in old age. They, too, tell us that life, for them, is still very much worth while.

Many others, however, may not be so lucky. They long for contentment and opportunities for further fulfilment, but they admit that they find old age a sad business. They faced retirement with high hopes. They were all bravely determined to look for new interests and experiences in their last years; then, through no fault of their own, they were attacked and overwhelmed by circumstances that robbed them of the independence and security that could have made it possible; and far too many say, understandably, that old age for them is a 'dead loss'. It is full of problems they cannot hope to overcome, such as deafness, failing sight, painful rheumatism and other disabilities (as well as shortage of money), that have led to a limited social life and loneliness.

The important truth that seems to emerge from everything the elderly tell us about old age is that unless people possess very rare spiritual qualities, happiness in the last years of life depends mainly on four things: good health, companionship, financial security, and an interest or occupation. These are, of course, ingredients for happiness for people of any age, but for the elderly the enjoyment of the quality of each one is much more dependent upon the existence in their lives of all the others.

Without good health, companionship may be difficult to find or sustain. Financial security, though obviously desirable, cannot compensate for pain or loss of mobility; and an interest or occupation of the kind the elderly person wants or needs may be unattainable.

Without companionship, good health can mean just 'existing' without discomfort. Financial security is no more than a useful protection against hardship, and gives no protection at all against loneliness in the true sense; and an interest or occupation can seem empty and purposeless with no one to share its pleasures and achievements.

Without financial security, good health can sometimes be undermined by anxiety. Companionship may be tested to the limits of endurance by the strains of poverty, and an interest and occupation most suited to the individual needs of the elderly may be beyond their reach, for money brings choice.

Without an interest or occupation, good health (and particularly good mental health) may collapse under the weight of boredom and depression. Companionship can cloy, and financial security can sometimes tempt the unoccupied elderly to an even greater withdrawal from the mainstream of life, into a position of emotional isolation.

This list for survival in old age sounds simple enough to those who already have these things; but sadly, by the time our parents need to turn to us for help, we know that, for them, supplies may already be running short. Their health may be failing. Bereavement will most likely have taken away their main source of companionship and we ourselves will have left home. Their income will probably have fallen disastrously; or circumstances generally may make it impossible for them to continue or start upon a special interest or occupation. This is the time when relatives who are ready to extend a helping hand to the elderly people in their lives come forward; while others, who have no intention of becoming involved, just make comforting noises as they keep well back. When such a situation of need confronts us and we begin to understand that ageing can for some be a sad and confusing time, we must face some big decisions. If we try to duck or dodge them, by taking the attitude that the problems of the elderly are best dealt with entirely by the State and its professional carers, not only are we turning our back on compassion, but we are giving our own children, who look to us for example, their first lessons in 'avoidance tactics' to carry with them into adult life. There may well come a point when our own turn comes, when they will know just how to deny any responsibility for us also.

If, on the other hand, we decide, when our elderly mother or father needs help, that we are going to give them our support, several things can happen. We may not succeed in our efforts. We may be putting our own way of life at risk for a time; or we may manage splendidly to enable them to live out the rest of their lives with some degree of security and contentment. But whichever way it goes, at least we shall know that we tried.

If we really want to know what growing old is like, we have to be prepared to look very directly at some fairly unpleasant truths, however depressing they may seem. We have, somehow, to find the courage to disregard the soothing voices of those refugees from reality who try to tell us what old age could and should be, instead of what it is for the majority – a long fight against a great variety of hard problems. If we can accept this, the last and most difficult fact of life, we are in a much stronger position to face up to it with the elderly in our care: to soften the blows for them, cheer them on, and help to make the fight worth while.

2

Bereavement and widowhood

Bereavement and the sorrow it brings is the price most of us have to pay sooner or later for the joy of loving, and it is a bill that the elderly have usually had presented to them several times in their lives in one form or another. They have lost parents, often a close relative or two and some of their oldest friends. Then comes the greatest loss of all: that of their marriage partner. Many men escape this, for most of them predecease their wives, but the majority of women have to face the crushing blow of widowhood. And so it will be mainly the plight of widows that we shall be considering here, although, of course, many of their difficulties are shared by widowers, some of whose slightly different problems will be examined later.

If you are caring for an elderly parent who is at some stage of grieving for a lost partner, whether she is experiencing the shattering despair that follows soon after bereavement, or the long sad loneliness and feeling of deprivation characteristic of its later stages, her deepest need will be for your practical and emotional support during her period of sorrow and adjustment.

If this is your first experience in the role of main helper to someone close to you who has suffered a major loss, and if you have not yet suffered one yourself, you may find the strange variety and intensity of her emotions and her need for long-term support rather daunting. If it is your own mother who is bereaved, the fact that you are grieving too will probably help you both a good deal, as you will be able to share your sorrow and comfort each other; though in some families shared sorrow occasionally leads to friction and unreasonable apportioning of blame for trivial or imagined omissions in the course of the terminal illness of the deceased. But when such rifts occur, they are not necessarily evidence of lack of love; they are more often due to the temporary emotional instability of the mourners, and usually heal swiftly, family unity being restored as the grief is worked through.

If the bereaved is your mother-in-law you have the problem of trying to help someone with whose personality and reactions you may not be entirely familiar; but you will have the advantage of being able to remain a little more detached from the throbbing centre of her pain and therefore freer to be objective in the help you give her, without in any way reducing the flow of sympathy and affection she will hope to receive from you.

The thought of entering the disaster area of an elderly widow's grief and shouldering some of the responsibility for helping her to bear it, and to rebuild what is left of her life, is enough to create feelings of anxiety in anyone; and admittedly this can be a very difficult assignment, for not only will you be well aware that you are unable to give her the one thing she really wants – the return of her husband – but you will feel, as we all do when faced with the bereaved, that their personality seems suddenly to have been crushed like a flower under the heel of a vandal, showing it to be so fragile and vulnerable that almost any attempt to revive it would seem to be doomed to failure. This is no time to hesitate, though, for however dazed, withdrawn, emotional, restless, irritable or distant she may seem, she is as urgently in need of help as someone who has just been badly injured in a road accident. She has, in fact, just been knocked down emotionally. She is in shock and in pain and requires an immediate transfusion of love and an injection of strength in the form of your quiet sympathy and understanding, and practical help with all the arrangements she has to make, as well as assistance with the simple routines of daily living; for even these may be too much for her to cope with alone while she is engaged in the important and necessary task of grieving.

You may feel inadequate at this point, because whatever you do for her will not seem to lift the cloud of her despair, but by being willing simply to *be* there and available in the background, accepting uncritically her inevitable mood-swings, and allowing her to talk, weep, or remain silent just as she wishes, you will be proving your concern for her; and loving concern and the right

Bereavement and widowhood

to grieve in their own way is what the bereaved need most of all.

If you lack confidence in your ability to give her the right kind of help and comfort, but really want to do so, you have nothing to fear, because this probably means that you are much better equipped for the task than you imagine. It indicates that you are unlikely to be a person who thinks she knows all the answers and would tend to overwhelm her with advice and urge her to 'dry your eyes and try not to think about it too much'; and best of all, you *care*. This gives you a head start, and if you are sensitive to her changing needs as she goes through the grief experience you will learn your role and recognise your cues as you go along.

It is important to have some clear basic understanding of the nature of bereavement and the grief that follows it. There are many people, though, who cannot bear to delve too deeply into this vast and painful subject, although they are anxious to know enough about it to enable them to act wisely when called upon to support and console a relative who has suffered a major loss. If you are one of them, do not worry, or fear that you will be handicapped as a helper and comforter. Just accept it, remembering that an ability to show true sympathy and the courage to 'stay the course' with the bereaved, as they go through their sorrow and their search for a new identity, are the most important qualifications. If you possess these, you will not find it difficult to bring yourself to learn the simple arithmetic of grief, its common pattern and some of its variations, and you will find that as your knowledge increases your fears will decrease. You will become more objective and in control of the situation, and in time you will gain sufficient confidence to begin to understand and deal with some of its more complex problems as they arise.

Begin by listening carefully to how the bereaved speak about their loss. Many of them so often quite rightly describe what has happened to them as a deep wound resulting from the blow they have received. Some of them say, 'It has been a terrible blow', or 'It's like a gaping wound', or 'I feel torn apart. It's as though I'm bleeding inside'. This gaping wound that bereavement inflicts on the emotions will react, and should be treated, very much like a physical wound. There will be shock – usually the haemorrhage of tears, followed by temporary loss of normal function because of depression; then, if all goes well, and the wound is 'nursed' with care and patience, it will finally heal, the severed edges uniting to produce a strong and healthy scar. But as with physical wounds, it can sometimes run into complications caused by careless handling or the existence of unfavourable external or internal conditions which may delay recovery; so the main concern of those caring for the bereaved should be to try to create the best possible conditions in which healing can take place, in which they feel loved and safe, and are permitted to take their time to absorb the fact of their loss and come to terms with it.

Understanding bereavement
There is no set pattern for grieving, for just as no two people love in the same way, no two people grieve in the same way. But there are certain feelings and reactions in bereavement that are common to much of the animal kingdom, including the human race, and all who are caring for the bereaved need to be aware of them, as well as being ready to accept the tremendous range of responses that people can produce from time to time in their efforts to deal with their painful situation.

Strange as it may sound, there is such a thing as 'successful' grieving. This is the normal way of gradually and painfully realising fully that a loved companion has gone, never to return: recognising what has happened and letting them go. Not rejecting them, not ceasing to love them, but slowly building up a new role and identity which no longer depends upon their presence for its satisfactory functioning. And finally, it is the ability to open the arms of memory to welcome them back as a valued part of the whole life experience, with which it is possible to live at peace, without pain, and with a sense of completeness at last; and when this has been accomplished the bereaved are ready to embrace life again.

There are those, of course, who for various reasons become 'stuck' at some point in the grieving period and become chronically depressed, sometimes for years. This is often the result of lack of ability or opportunity to express their sorrow, or avoidance of the realisation of their loss. Such people can be a great trial and anxiety to their family and friends, but they suffer very badly and may need psychiatric help before recovery takes place. Fortunately, though, they are very much in the minority. Most bereaved people soon begin to discover that grief does not settle in their life like a gravestone, permanent and immovable: it lives, moves and changes, like all great emotions, and they finally emerge from it not crippled, but stronger in many ways than they were before, in spite of their loss.

It is a hard road to tread, though, for major loss means a frightening separation from that which gives life meaning, satisfaction and purpose, and it often brings other losses in its train that continue to bludgeon the spirit and create feelings of anxiety and insecurity. Your elderly widowed parent may not only be losing her close companion, friend and confidant (and, if she is still sexually active, as some woman are, well into the sixties and beyond, her lover), but also the one she depended upon for financial advice, physical protection in an increasingly violent society, and transport if she does not drive herself or can no longer afford to run a car. Unless she is very fit, able to care for the garden and do decorating and other jobs of that kind around the house, she will miss his support in this way too. Relatively unimportant as these smaller losses may seem compared with the main one, together they may add up to a total picture of her life which she feels has been shattered overnight by a single blow. She may also have to face a serious reduction in income, which might necessitate the sale of her house and the loss of her settled way of life by a move to another neighbourhood and to a smaller home, or into yours if that is to be the arrangement you both decide upon.

The change of status, too, from 'wife' to 'widow' is felt very keenly by most women as a loss of considerable significance, which indeed it is; for without a partner, a woman who has been married for some years may, unless she already has well developed interests outside her home, find that her social life is suddenly transformed in a very disturbing way. To begin with, it is a sad but true fact that society as a whole does not welcome the widow, however sorry they feel for her. One reason for this is that many people have a fear which they cannot conceal of anything or anybody who reminds them of death; knowing that contact with a grieving widow will exacerbate these fears they tend, after expressing their sympathy by word or letter, and sending flowers to the funeral, to withdraw to a safe distance 'to give her time to get over it' just when she needs them most. Subtle changes take place, too, in the attitudes of some of her friends to whose circle she belonged when her husband was alive, which may lead her to feel rejected at a time when she needs to be accepted in her new role and to have her self-esteem strengthened. Some of her married friends will still invite her to their homes, but her ties with others will be weakened. They begin to feel that 'three's a crowd', and finally so does she. She has to look for new friends amongst the ranks of the unattached like herself; and until she has recovered sufficiently to become interested in organising her social life to the best advantage, her opportunities to continue to enjoy the pleasures of mixed company may be very limited.

Grief is not only a reaction, though, it is a process, so your bereaved parent will need your help through all its various stages of numbness, yearning, quiet or vocal distress, anxiety, depression and adjustment to her new situation; and the way she behaves during the grief process will depend very much on her personality type, her previous life experiences and the strength of the tie that has been severed, as well as the amount of support you can give her.

No one is ever fully prepared for bereavement, and even if her husband's terminal illness was one from which she had known he could not hope to recover, his death will still have come as a shock to her which may create a feeling of numbness and unreality: a difficulty in 'taking in' what has happened. This defence may last for days or for weeks, but usually the funeral begins to make it all real to her. She may start to release her emotions fully during or after the service, or she may go through all the ritual connected with it in a daze, but sooner or later it can be expected that the flood-gates of her grief will open and she will then begin to work her way through the multiplicity of problems that lie ahead of her.

If she has always been an outgoing person, her grief will probably be expressed in painful episodes of weeping, punctuated by the need to 'talk it all out' over and over again in great detail to you and to other sympathetic relatives and friends, and you will help her a great deal if you are a patient listener. The fact that you will find it difficult to know what to say to her, except that you understand how she must feel, will not matter at all. If you are a shoulder to cry on without fear of being shrugged off, that is all she will want from you at that stage. Do not be surprised though if, following one of these episodes, she suddenly picks herself up temporarily and shows a marked increase of physical activity and busyness, which may include such things as arranging to have some redecorations done in her home or changing all the furniture around. This should not be interpreted as lack of real feeling or a sign that the end of her grieving is in sight. It will all be a part of it, her way of coping and trying to damp down her feelings of despair.

If, however, she is a more inward-looking person, she may show few of the usual signs of distress connected with bereavement, but she will be dealing with it internally and suffering just as much. As she may not be a particularly gregarious person she will experience great loneliness after her husband's death, and her need will be for the company of her family and a few special friends to see her through this difficult period.

If her personality tends to be an obsessive one – if she is excessively devoted to tidiness and perfect order in every part of her life and home, a great maker of 'lists' for everything and a habitual 'double-checker' in all her activities – you may find that although she is grieving deeply, she may throw herself with remarkable zeal into the business of 'tidying up' her husband's financial affairs and concentrating even more strongly on getting everything in the house cleaned and polished; for this is the method used by most people who are inclined to be obsessional, to control their anxiety. They feel that the more control they can exercise over their surroundings, the safer life will be for them. If she reacts in this way, it will be best not to try to interfere or worry about her tiring herself out with too much activity, as this may be even more disturbing for her. She will be working out her problems in her own fashion and should be allowed to do so.

It is the anxious and emotionally immature women who suffer most in widowhood, and if your elderly parent falls into this category her reaction to her loss may be very trying for you. Often such women have been married to strong, protective men who accepted and possibly even fostered their childish and dependent attitudes to everything in life, and when this support is suddenly withdrawn they feel completely lost. The temptation to put some kindly pressure on them to become more responsible and independent as quickly as possible is always great, but it has to be remembered that the habits of a lifetime in a basically anxious personality cannot be changed overnight. If she is ever going to learn to stand on her own feet finally, when her grieving is over, she will need your acceptance, for the time being, that what she is experiencing now is something like the intense suffering of a child separated from the security of its mother's presence, with all the feelings of fear and panic that brings. Her best hope of surviving it successfully lies in *your* maturity and willingness to act as a temporary crutch for her and as a quiet stabilising influence until she learns how to walk alone and unaided. There will, of course, be reasons why she has never 'grown up' emotionally, and most of them will be no fault of her own. If you can bear this in mind and be gentle in your judgement and handling of her, you will find you will be under much less strain yourself in what may be a very stressful situation.

Those who are caring for the bereaved need to be prepared to expect all kinds of strange reactions and uncharacteristic behaviour from them occasionally. They should try not to worry too much about it, knowing that it will pass. Some widows, for instance, show signs of bitterness and anger, particularly during the first year of bereavement. These may be triggered off by someone who tries unwisely to hurry the widow into the full realisation of her loss before she is ready to accept it. She may experience a crisis of disbelief in her religious faith, or direct her anger towards the medical or nursing staff who cared for her husband, for failing to save his life; or she may blame family or friends and have feelings of guilt and anger against herself for things that were done or not done during his lifetime. She needs to find someone or something to blame for the catastrophe that has overtaken her, so she looks for reasons, because she may not yet be ready to face up to the extremely anxiety-provoking fact that life itself is unpredictable and the world is an insecure place. She finds it easier to say to herself, 'He might never have died, if only . . .'. This is not cowardice, but a part of the grief experience for some people, which should be understood and dealt with patiently. It is equally possible though that she will show no signs whatever of anger in her grief and instead may become apathetic and drained of all energy and normal drive for a time.

She will almost certainly have some kind of disturbance of her normal health during the early months of mourning. There may be loss of sleep, nightmares, loss of appetite and consequent weight loss. Aches and pains of various kinds may occur, some of which may mimic the symptoms of her husband's last illness, and her general health may deteriorate, because at first she will be so absorbed in grieving and a kind of mental 'searching' for what she has lost that she may tend to neglect her bodily needs.

Some widows become so restless and panic-stricken in the early months of bereavement that they fear they may be going mad, and you may find yourself having to give your parent strong reassurance on this point, to help her to deal with this common anxiety.

Finally, you may expect her to go through a period of depression when she is ceasing to try to avoid the reality of her loss. This will be painful for her to endure, and for you to witness, but under normal circumstances it will pass. She will gradually adjust to her new role and begin to feel that life may still have something worth while to offer her.

The widow whose marriage was unhappy

If your widowed parent had an unhappy married life, you will have a rather different problem on your hands, for hers will be a special kind of bereavement which will need great understanding and respect for its reality, which sometimes such widows do not receive. Some of her family and friends who knew that her marriage was unsuccessful may assume that her feelings about her husband's death could only be those of relief that their life together is over at last and that she is now free to seek a better future for herself; not realising that if a woman has lived with a man for many years, unless he has treated her with extreme cruelty, and shown her no love at all throughout the whole of their marriage, some kind of bond is bound to have existed between them, and that even if he left her with only a handful of good memories of times they spent together, it is likely that she may want to hold on to them, cherish them, and even build upon them.

Friends may refrain from expressing any sympathy because they feel that it might be inappropriate and embarrassing for her, and she may be feeling that people will regard her as a hypocrite if she gives way and weeps, although she may need to do this for a variety of reasons, one of them being not so much for what she has lost, but for what she never had. You may need to allow her to feel very free to express mixed feelings of grief and anger too within the safety of your confidential relationship.

She may know that she is not going to recover from the blow of widowhood any sooner than other women do, many of whom at least have a large legacy of happy memories upon which to draw in the years ahead of them. To her it may seem that not only was she robbed of happiness during her marriage, but that she is now also being denied the right to grieve as well, for there will be those who will be expecting her mourning to be nothing more than a brief bow to convention, followed by a fairly speedy rise in spirits and return to normality. This may make her feel that society regards her as a second-class widow, and you may need to help those who come into contact with her to understand how important it is going to be for her future adjustment for them to treat her just as they would any other bereaved person.

Her grief will be particularly hard to 'work through', for to some extent it may always be open-ended. She may, for years, have nursed the hope that one day her relationship with her husband would improve. Now that hope will have been taken from her, leaving her feeling that they have unfinished business, which (unless she believes in life after death) will remain unfinished for ever. Nor will she be able to look forward to that sense of completeness when her grieving is over which is experienced by the widow whose marriage was happy, and she will have some difficult emotional adjustments to make in order to come to terms with her situation, in which both love and life seem to have betrayed her. If she discusses feelings of this kind with you, perhaps the best you can offer her, apart from a sympathetic ear, is to try to assure her that love freely given is never pointless and never lost. It may be rejected or abused but it cannot be devalued, and if she can bring herself to look ahead without bitterness it can still bear fruit in her own life. It will be important too to let her see that you understand her special kind of grief and respect it. You will realise that words of comfort like this can solve no problems for her; they can do no more than bathe the wound she has sustained, but she will be badly in need of something to cling on to and because they are spoken by someone who loves her they may be exactly what she wants to hear when she is trying to reassemble herself and face the future.

In time she will find her own way of dealing with her pain. She may even do this by denying the bad experiences in her marriage to herself and to others, remembering only the good times, however few they were, and concentrating her thoughts on the positive aspects of her husband's personality. Some widows in this position transform their lost husband in their minds into the man they wish he had been, and finally live at peace with a dream instead of in conflict with reality. Who is to say that they are wrong, if it helps them to live out the rest of their lives in a happier frame of mind? This is always a surprising development from the point of view of those close to her, but if you are faced with this reaction in your elderly parent, or any other that seems strange but harmless, tread softly, and accept the fact that she must be allowed to grieve and to adjust in her own way.

The widower

Broadly speaking, a man's experience of grief when he loses his life-partner is similar to a woman's; but there are one or two important differences worth bearing in mind if you are caring for an elderly parent who has become a widower. Although the effects of loss vary from one individual to another, on the whole it seems that men tend to fare a little better in bereavement than women, and fewer of them are found to be in need of psychiatric treatment for chronic grief and depression. There are several reasons for this. Clearly many men are as capable of deep love and attachment as women, but usually more of their emotional energy is invested in their world of work outside the home, and unless a woman also has an outside career role and some interests separate from his, she relies much more on her husband for her happiness and fulfilment than he does on her. Byron may have been exaggerating a little when he wrote, 'Man's love is of man's life a thing apart, 'Tis woman's whole existence', but obviously there is more than a grain of truth in it, and not necessarily a painful or unacceptable one either. In a strange way it can actually contribute to the success of many marriages, for not every woman wants to spend her life with an eternal Romeo.

Society in general is kinder too in its attitude to the widower, and is prepared to draw closer to him to give him help and support as he does his grief-work. It sees the widow as the creator of life who has suddenly become the symbol of death, and who also, as an unsupported woman, may be an expensive burden on the rest of the 'tribe' for the remaining years of her life. The widower strikes no such fear into the heart, even though, in reality, he may turn out to be just as big a responsibility. But these are primitive feelings and run very deep. Fortunately for him, he is more often seen as the 'little boy lost' (which is often just how he feels, so his suffering is considerable), for apart from his obvious grief and loneliness, who now will cook his meals and iron his shirts? Usually it is not long before the female members of his family, and the wives of his friends and neighbours, come to his rescue to 'mother' him through the period of his grieving and depression, and some, whose children have grown up and left home, will find great pleasure in doing so. A widower can become something of a 'cause' to those living in the same street or block of flats, whereas a widow, although not shunned, may be to some extent avoided by all but the most caring individuals in the early days of her bereavement.

The widower will receive many more invitations out to meals in other people's homes in the early days too, and he will have the advantage of never having to feel trapped in the isolation of an empty house in the evenings; for if his emotional condition after his wife's death is reasonably steady and he feels the need of company, he can always stroll out to the local pub for a drink, where he can remain in complete control of the amount of conversation he wants, or can endure, and can head for home again just when he feels like it. In fact social life in the evenings will be easier in every way for him to find than it is for a widow, who cannot go out alone at night without some feeling of apprehension, and who would generally anyway feel out of place sitting on her own in a saloon bar. There are other places she could go to, of course, but so many of them would be clubs in which she would be expected to communicate and contribute at a time when all she wants is occasionally simply to be 'with' people and to be able to depart when she wishes without giving offence or disturbing the gathering. Special clubs for widows can sometimes be a great help, but not to everyone.

One of the big problems the widower does have is that he does not feel so free to express his grief to others by weeping when he talks of his wife, their life together and the events that led up to her death. He may need to do all this, and to ventilate his fears of a future without her; but he has probably been told since he was three years old that 'boys don't cry', and that men must always show courage and maintain the stiff upper lip, so he may deny himself the relief of lowering his defences and 'letting go' which society expects the widow to do quite naturally. This is an important area in which you can help him a great deal if you can make him feel that with you open grieving is permissible.

Although he may receive more help in the first few months than the widow usually does, he may find that his sudden change in life-style is a considerable shock. For her, there is some slight security in the continuity of attending to all the basic daily household tasks as she has done for many years, but when his 'first wave' of helpers begins to depart he will have to learn to do much more for himself to keep his home going, which will be an added burden to those he is already carrying. So unless he is coming to live with you, this will be the time for you to begin to show him how to cope alone. This will have to be done very tactfully, though, for men find it much harder than women to admit how dependent they have become on their partner. Their instinct is to try to hide this for fear of being thought weak or inadequate, and this, in part, contributes to the fact that although their overall experience of the distress of bereavement may be slightly less than that of widows, many men take longer to recover fully. It should be remembered that generalisation about bereavement or any deep experience in life can be dangerous if carried to extremes, and if you are caring for an elderly parent of either sex who has lost his or her partner, you will have no idea of just how painful their sorrow is for them, so it will be wise simply to assume, whatever their reaction may be, that they are going through a very bad time indeed. Every scrap of understanding you can glean about the dynamics of bereavement will, of course, be valuable; but never try simply to 'play it by the book' – this or any other, for in the long run it will be the way you use your heart, not your head, that will count most. Their overriding need will not be for advice, but for love and support, and if you provide this you will not fail them.

Ways of helping the bereaved

IMMEDIATE SUPPORT

You will probably have been giving your elderly parent emotional support all the way through the anxiety of her husband's terminal illness, unless his death was sudden and unexpected. But when it actually occurs, whether her reaction is one of numbness and shock, or of anguish more openly expressed through episodes of weeping and talking freely about her feelings, you will need to brace yourself to catch her as she falls into what will seem to her to be the bottomless pit of her sorrow. Yours will most probably be the arms she needs at this point, and the best thing you can do for her is to show that you share her grief, and that as far as possible you are going to be the rock on which she can lean while the sands of her life are shifting so frighteningly beneath her feet. How you do this will depend upon your own personality and your relationship with her, but however it is done, the message she will be hoping to receive through your words and actions will be that you care, you sympathise, and that you are going to stand by her and give her all the help and comfort you can in the months that lie ahead. Having done this, you can begin by making sure that she is not left alone at all at first in her emotionally collapsed condition, unless she clearly indicates that she wants a period of solitude. In this case you should make sure she has all she needs, including easy access to you by phone, and you should keep in daily contact with her.

She will probably welcome your offer of help with such matters as the registration of the death, notifying distant friends, putting an announcement of death in local or national newspapers if she wants this, and dealing with kindly enquiries from neighbours in a tactful way, so that they understand that she may not be feeling like having too many callers at first but will greatly appreciate their help and sympathy in a few days' (or weeks') time; and making arrangements for the funeral and any family gathering that is to take place afterwards. If she wants to do any or all of these things herself, though, she should be allowed to, and her own wishes in everything at this time should be respected.

THE FUNERAL

The funeral itself will be a painful but important occasion for her, as this, and all the ritual connected with it, will be her first big step forward into the grieving process which is to lead on to final recovery. It will begin to 'make real' the fact of her husband's death and permanent departure from her life, so everything possible should be done to give the occasion dignity, beauty, and a feeling of thanksgiving for his life; for this is a memory she will carry with her always, and it is one from which most widows can draw some comfort if it has been an uplifting experience shared with her family and friends. This does not necessarily mean spending a great deal of money on it, but careful and considerate plannning of the whole day.

If she has a religious faith which enables her to believe that death is not the end and that she and her husband will be re-united one day, she should be supported and encouraged in this, as it is something really positive on which she can begin to rebuild the rest of her life.

Although the whole family will be mourning, this should be

regarded very much as 'her' day, and her wishes should come first. If she dislikes all outward signs of mourning, wanting people to wear their normal clothes and for the proceedings to be very quiet and simple, that should be for her to decide, but if she is of the old school, who prefer mourners to dress rather sombrely, you should try to persuade the rest of the family to do so whatever their personal opinions may be; although care must be taken not to cause friction over this or anything else which may sour the family gathering. The form of service and the choice of hymns, if any, should be your parent's, and if she is hoping to see her husband's coffin surrounded by flowers on its last journey, nobody should suggest to her that she should instead consider asking relatives and friends to send donations to a suitable charity, for this may upset her deeply, and if she gives in to it, it may become a burning resentment in her later on. Many people now regard the sending of flowers to a funeral as an inexcusable waste of money, arguing that since they cannot possibly help the deceased, it is better to help the living. But they forget that flowers are sent not only as a mark of respect for the dead, but also as a gesture of sympathy to the living, suffering widow, to bring some of the hopeful beauty of nature to soften the bleakness of one of the saddest days of her life, and to show her how much the one she loved was also loved by others.

If she would like the family and close friends to gather together for a meal or light refreshments after the service and committal, you will of course have prepared for this beforehand. Many widows like to stay in the home of a family member for a few days or weeks afterwards, but if she is going to return to her own home at some time, this should not be delayed for too long. When she does so, you or another relative could suggest staying there with her for a day or two until she is ready to face the loneliness she has to learn to live with. If she is to come to live with you, or someone else in the family, consideration should be given to arranging this along the lines mentioned in Chapter 3.

SAFEGUARDING HER HEALTH
The bereaved often show signs of ill-health, which is not surprising since they usually feel quite ill in their minds and crushed

by the burden of their sorrow. You should, as far as possible, make sure that the widow is having a nourishing, if light, diet and proper exercise, and seeing her doctor if she has any special problems. If she is severely disturbed emotionally, above the level normally expected in bereavement, and if she cannot sleep, he may prescribe tranquillisers and a night sedative; but this will usually be only for a limited period to help her over a particularly bad patch, as he will not want her to become addicted to these drugs, which if taken for too long may delay the normal grieving process which she will need to experience if she is to make a satisfactory recovery.

Some widows who have been moderate social drinkers begin to drink more during bereavement, in order to take the edge off their emotional pain; but this of course creates more problems than it ever solves, so you should never encourage your elderly parent to start taking 'tonic' wine for her 'nerves' or a tot of whisky at night to help her to sleep, for you may be helping her to establish a habit that can easily get out of control and become very hard to break. Your aim should be to see that she does not suffer long periods of loneliness and that she feels so well cared for that she can manage to endure her period of sorrow without too many crutches, until life becomes worth living again.

PRACTICAL HELP

You will no doubt have been assisting her in basic matters connected with the running of her home while she is still in a state of shock following her husband's death, for at this point even the most capable women sometimes find day-to-day planning and decision-making very hard to cope with and need to be eased gently back into their normal routine.

She may welcome your help with some of the business matters she has to deal with, too. The first essential is to see that she has a good solicitor to advise her and sort out her husband's affairs, making sure beforehand what his fee will be for the work he is going to do for her. She may wish you to accompany her to his office or to be present if he is to visit her in her home, and he will be pleased to have your co-operation.

Apart from dealing with the matter of the will if one was

made, it may be agreed, if your parent wishes, that he should also take on the responsibility for contacting various persons and organisations: the bank, to arrange for money to be available to her pending the settlement of her husband's affairs; her husband's employer and Trade Union branch secretary, or the secretary of any professional association to which he belonged; his insurance company; the Department of Health and Social Security, to obtain forms for claiming the death grant and the widow's pension; the Inland Revenue, if her husband was still paying income tax; the Building Society, the mortgagor (or landlord if she and her husband lived in rented property) and any other person or organisation concerned. He may suggest that you might like to undertake some of the less complicated tasks on your parent's behalf if she wishes. If so, he will advise you what to do, but you may also find it helpful to obtain a copy of a booklet entitled *Caring for the widow and her family*, published by CRUSE (The National Organisation for Widows and their Children, Cruse House, 126 Sheen Road, Richmond, Surrey TW9 1UR), which gives a great deal of useful information on all these subjects and many others connected with widowhood.

In all your efforts to help her at this crucial time the most important thing to remember is to try to reduce her anxiety by being as relaxed and quietly optimistic about her future as you can, and to restrain her from making any major decisions hastily, regarding such matters as the disposal of property or moving house, as she may regret this later on when she is feeling less depressed.

When she feels ready to contemplate it she may also want your help in the sad business of disposing of her husband's clothing. She may like to give this to the WRVS or Oxfam, who would be happy to collect it if necessary, as would 'Help the Aged' and many other organisations. He may also have had expensive tools or special equipment of some kind, or a car or boat which has to be sold. Here you can do much to protect her interests at a time when she is very vulnerable by making sure that they are first valued by an expert before being advertised, for widows are often 'conned' into selling their husband's valuable possessions very cheaply to unscrupulous people, simply because they are feeling too low in spirits to resist any offer to have them removed speedily and without fuss.

You may find that she will need to lean on you a little for several months to speak and act for her in matters she cannot give her full attention to, because she will be quite rightly absorbed for the time being in grieving, which is mentally and emotionally very hard work indeed. You have no need to worry, though, that this situation will be a permanent one, for as she recovers she will gradually want to take over the reins of her own life again.

EMOTIONAL SUPPORT

Practical help and emotional support of the bereaved are of course interwoven, but from the purely emotional standpoint it could be said that their greatest needs are for loving concern, good listening and patient understanding of their need to work through their grief in their own way at their own pace.

Ideally the support of the bereaved should be a team effort, and the choice of captain of that team should be left to the widow herself, for she will need one special person to whom she can turn with confidence in any circumstance. This will most probably be you, but try not to feel hurt if she chooses someone else. You will still have a very important part to play. Each member of her family and each of her close friends will have different strengths upon which she will need to draw, and together you should try to form a bridge over which she can gradually cross from the barren wasteland of her sorrow back into society where her new role awaits her. It will be a slow journey, in which progress will be seen to be made in stages rather than continuously.

In the early months of her grief, you and her other helpers may need to listen endlessly and give her quiet comfort during her episodes of extreme anguish and emotional excursions into the past. You will also have to be prepared to overlook sudden flashes of anger or periods of irritability which may seem to be aimed at you but which are much more likely to be an expression of her natural resentment of the disaster that has befallen her. She will, at this point, be a very disturbed person indeed, but it is a condition that will pass, so you should show generosity in your acceptance of any unusual behaviour within reason.

When she has, through the process of grieving, faced the reality of her loss, you will need to be very patient with her through the period of depression that will follow, in which she may feel slowed up and extremely lethargic because, for a while, life will appear to her to have no further meaning or purpose. She may find it difficult to concentrate or interest herself much in anything or anybody. She may appear to become quite self-centred, and those who have been doing all they can to help her may become exasperated and tempted to hint that it is time she tried to 'pull herself together', for by then they too will be feeling the strain. On the other hand, she may show signs of a kind of restless agitation which can be equally hard to handle. But if she is allowed to go at her own pace, without criticism, while she is dealing with the chaos within, you will find that her mood will gradually become more optimistic and her feelings of despair less frequent.

A time will come when you will know that she is no longer saying to herself, 'If I can't have him, I don't want anything'. She will be preparing to face the future, having come to terms to some extent with the loss of her previous expectations concerning it. This may be a good moment to indicate to her very gently that she has grieved well and long, and that if she is beginning to feel that her period of mourning is nearing its end (even though you appreciate that she will always carry the scars of her sorrow), you are ready to give her any help she needs to adjust to her new and different life. If she responds favourably to this (which, if you are wise, you will have conveyed more through your attitudes than your actual words), you and her other helpers should try to create various circumstances or events which may stand a chance of helping her to break the habit of mourning: an interesting holiday, perhaps, or some new and mildly challenging experience which calls for her to look beyond herself to someone else in trouble, who will make her feel 'needed'. These or other events in her life at this time, even the sad ones like the passing of the first anniversary of her husband's death, may be the key that will open the door for her to freedom from the prison of grief where she has finished the hard labour of bereavement. But remember that these stages on her journey to the position where she can love and remember her husband without pain, and without being emotionally tied to him, will only be acceptable to her when she is really ready for them. Her recovery could take anything up to around two years to be complete, according to her personality and the strength of the bond that existed.

Helping an elderly woman to adjust and to find a new identity is never easy, but it can nearly always be achieved if she is shown that she is still loved and needed, by her family and friends. Contact also with organisations for the assistance of widows can be useful to some women, and one of these, CRUSE, which has already been mentioned, runs groups and an excellent counselling service. They tend to cater mainly for the under-sixties, although they are always willing to do everything they can to help the older widow too. But the best form of support for her is of course to be found in the framework of an affectionate and united family who will make sure that she is not too lonely and can help her to rebuild her social life.

If you have a really warm relationship with your elderly parent and the two of you communicate well, you may also be able to help her a good deal by occasional discussions on attitudes generally in bereavement and the more positive aspects of what has been such a tragic and painful experience for her; steering her tenderly towards the realisation that what she now has is not only what Dylan Thomas's wife described as 'left-over life to kill', but left-over love to *give*, which is a very different thing. When at times she is feeling particularly low and bereft, you might also remind her gently that although it seems that love has departed from her life altogether with the loss of her husband, this is not so. Since she was capable of loving so deeply, she can still, if she chooses, remain in the business of giving and receiving love for as long as she lives, for although she may feel that she is no longer everything to anyone, she can still mean a great deal to a number of people. She may also be helped to understand that if she is willing to try to spread the love she once gave to one person around to others who may be badly in need of it, she will move into an entirely different dimension emotionally: one that will provide her with new satisfactions and in which she will discover that the lovers of this world are not only those who enjoy a close and exclusive relationship. They are to be found everywhere, even among the old, the disabled, the celibate, the deserted and the bereaved – in fact, all those who have learned to value and use left-over love. So she can still be one of them.

If she is very apprehensive about how she is going to manage her role in society as a woman on her own, you could remind her of something she has probably completely forgotten: that she coped with life quite adequately as a single woman, before she met her husband, so there is no reason to suppose that she cannot do so again, and possibly even better now because of the love they shared and her greater maturity.

If your timing is right, positive ideas of this kind may well give her hope and encouragement, but they should not be introduced too early in the grieving process, or she may regard them almost as an insult to the depth of her sorrow at a time when she is not yet ready to look to the future. So choose your moment carefully.

Even if she is not someone who could easily enter into discussions of this nature, in which her feelings are explored, it is possible that she could benefit considerably from advice and comfort delivered to her in a less personal way through the pages of a book. Amongst the many excellent and well researched books that have been written on the subject of bereavement the following are outstanding in their capacity to help those who have suffered a major loss: *Grief and how to live with it* by Sarah Morris (published in 1971 by George Allen and Unwin); *A grief observed* by C. S. Lewis (published in 1961 by Faber and Faber) – of particular interest to widowers – and *Bereavement. Studies of grief in adult life* by Colin Murray Parkes, MD, DPM (published in 1972 by Tavistock Publications).

If, of course, her grief becomes prolonged and it seems that she is making no headway towards adjustment, it will be advisable for her to see her doctor, but this rarely happens.

Helping an elderly parent through her sorrow can be a long, hard haul, but very rewarding in the end – not only in terms of her recovery, but also because, if you find yourself in the same position in later years, you will look back on this experience you shared with her and find that it has left you with a far deeper understanding of grief, and a greater confidence in the healing power of time to see you through your own period of adjustment to loss.

Bereavement is the one battle in which people dice with a death that has already occurred in order to survive all the dangers of the loss and deprivation it brings, and it takes courage to stand shoulder to shoulder with someone who is in the thick of it. But fortunately the dice are almost always loaded in their favour, and if we decide to fight with them the end result, for them and for us, can be that 'Out of this nettle, danger, we pluck this flower, safety'.

3
On their own

'I'd rather stay under my own roof. When I leave here it will be feet first!' A courageous and independent elderly woman once said this to me, and I understood and respected her feelings; for few elderly people want to give up their own home and go to live with relatives. Some years later, when her health and strength failed her, she found that she had to; but when that day came, she packed her courage as well as her clothes into her suitcase. She knew that she would inevitably be just exchanging one set of problems for another when she moved in with her daughter and son-in-law and the grandchildren, but she had taken her time and come to the decision in her own way, and finally managed to make a very good adjustment to an entirely different life in a busy household. She was one of the lucky ones.

Elderly people should never be persuaded against their will to move out of their own home, unless their mental or physical health or living conditions are so deplorable that they are a danger to their own or other people's safety. An elderly parent living alone invariably has problems to cope with, though, in some area of life, and ideally the people to help them should be members of their own family; people who know their character and understand their needs, those they do not have to make an effort to relate to and trust, and who can move around freely in their homes, to sort through the various 'pockets' of their anxiety more easily than any stranger can do.

If everyone could look after their own, there would be far fewer people like social workers running around looking after other people's own. Unfortunately, in modern society, our 'own' are rarely living in the same town or even in the same county as us, which makes the ideal situation very difficult to achieve. The large extended family, with its reliable supporting cast of aunts, uncles and cousins, as well as sons and daughters, all willing to help older members to remain happily in their own homes for as long as possible, is a thing of the past. The responsibility now usually rests heavily on the shoulders of one or, with luck, perhaps two relatives, and they will often need all the help they can get from the local social, medical, nursing and voluntary services.

Some people are 'naturals' when it comes to helping the elderly, because they are affectionate, imaginative and capable. Others, who are just as willing, have great difficulties in trying to understand them and meet their needs without appearing to intrude, or deprive them of their independence. The mere fact of having been cast in the role of daughter, daughter-in-law, son or son-in-law does not automatically endow any of us with the ability to play that part to perfection, particularly when it begins to need more than smiles and pleasantries at family gatherings, and demands qualities of patience, perseverance and insight, and the regular visiting of a lonely and possibly disabled old person. Those who do their best but, for reasons for which they may not be to blame, are not temperamentally suited to deep involvement in the special problems of the elderly, may have other talents for caring. They may, for instance, be capable of rising magnificently to the occasion when a neighbour's sick, deprived, or even delinquent child needs help, or they may be wonderful wives, husbands or parents and do much useful voluntary work in the community, and yet lack the particular type of emotional muscle required to support old people. If the challenge comes, though, they will usually do what they can, however inadequate and apprehensive they feel. What they need, apart from encouragement, is a little practical know-how about the job they are taking on, to enable them to tackle it with confidence.

The first thing to do, if you are embarking on helping an elderly parent who lives alone, is to make sure that she (or he) knows that you have a genuine desire to assist her in every way possible; and then respect her right to make either a positive or negative response to your overtures. It is always best to dip a toe in the water first, rather than plunging in with a programme of hopefully helpful ideas for the improvement of her life and comfort. The need for independence, linked with the need for love, are amongst the last treasures of old age, and should be treated with great delicacy.

Obviously, not all elderly parents who live alone are in need of a greal deal of assistance: they just like to know that it would be available if they wanted it. If they are still in good health and spirits, they are often busy helping other people – including their own families – and living a full and satisfying life, continuing to manage and run their home and all their affairs quite efficiently. There are also those who have been rather self-sufficient all their lives, who really like living alone, enjoying their own company and quiet pursuits. No two old people will react the same way, so no standard procedure can be recommended. However, most of them do need our help in various ways when the going gets rough, and it is their needs that we are mainly examining here.

Most elderly parents who are living alone will be widows or widowers, and the understanding of their feelings of loss, and ways of helping them to cope with bereavement, were discussed in Chapter 2.

Visiting

Visiting should be tailored not only to the needs of the elderly person but also the amount of time you can reasonably spare from other family responsibilities. It is important to make a definite decision about this right from the start, without letting her feel in any way that she is being given a weekly or monthly 'ration' of her family's free time, as a duty rather than a pleasure. Some elderly people who have always been very flexible like being 'popped in on' without prior warning, but most people as they grow older much prefer all the events in their lives to be regular and predictable. Old people are, of course, entitled to the same social courtesies as we are, and it can be very irritating for them if they are made to feel that they are regarded as has-beens who have nothing better to do than to sit around waiting to be visited at our convenience. Even though they are no longer working or bringing up children, their time is as precious to them as ours is to us. It may, according to circumstances and the personalities involved, be best to fix a regular mutually agreeable day for visiting, so that it is something to be looked forward to and prepared for. Alternatively, if they are on the telephone, a call, well beforehand, to ask if it is convenient is usually appreciated.

You need to remind yourself that a visit paid to an elderly relative living alone is a very important occasion, although of course the atmosphere should be relaxed and happy. If you are really fond of her, then you know that you will both give each other pleasure simply by being together for a while, but you must be prepared to give much more of yourself to the conduct of those few hours than you probably would in other social circumstances. She will be able to give you a great deal too, if you are prepared to open your mind to her memories and experience of life, realising the significance of her 'past' to your 'present'; and when you understand that the old are by no means always on the receiving end of their relationships, then you are ready to assemble the love, time, patience and energy you have to offer, and decide on the best way of presenting them. Even love itself is better for being carefully 'gift-wrapped' sometimes, when the recipient is elderly, and fearful of the slightest hint of patronage or pity.

Preparing yourself for a visit to an elderly parent who may not be exactly on your list of favourite people is quite another matter. If you are sure she wants to see you and you feel that you should go, your only hope of making the visit a success is not to drag yourself with a reluctant sense of duty to her front door, groaning inwardly at the thought of it. You will find it much easier if you can bring yourself to take the very positive attitude that today the two of you are going to share just a few hours of life together: time that can never come again. So you are going to give all you have got, and try to make something good out of it.

If your elderly parent is, by nature, affectionate and demonstrative, always kiss her warmly on arrival, and when you leave; for many old people are greatly deprived of essential physical contact.

If she lives on her own and poor health has robbed her of a normal social life, it is to be expected that her loneliness may have created such a build-up of unexpressed thoughts, feelings and opinions that she may need to talk herself to a standstill before she is ready to converse with you, and interest herself in anything you have to say. You just have to be patient and allow her all the time she wants in which to 'say her piece'.

Bearing in mind that the elderly often most enjoy visits that are on a one-to-one basis, during which they can ventilate their anxieties and have the undivided attention of a sympathetic listener, it is not always a good idea to arrive with several young children in tow, if they can be happily parked elsewhere. Most old people love children, but usually in much smaller doses than their parents realise, and more often in your home, where spills, sticky fingers and noise are more easily dealt with, than in theirs.

The most popular visitors to old people are the good listeners, who concentrate with interest on what they are saying, making the occasional encouraging comment. It is unfortunately very easy sometimes to let the eyes wander – and the mind as well – if an elderly person is running the gamut of a whole list of troubles, some of which may seem more like minor irritations. Sometimes, too, it is possible to make the mistake of thinking that she is expecting us to come up with all the answers when, often, all she wants is the opportunity to state the problem to someone who understands and will not criticise her. This is not mere grumbling or sourness, but a perfectly normal reaction to her circumstances. She needs to unburden, and good listening is not only good therapy, it is probably the most important contribution anyone can make to the happiness of the elderly who live alone. You do not have to be clever, or to know all the right psychological approaches; you just need to be kind, and to care, to become a sanity-saving safety-valve in someone else's life.

Many elderly people have a wide range of interests, maintain them – if only through reading – right on into old age, and still enjoy the cut and thrust of discussion and debate; but we have to accept the fact that for some, the main topics of conversation will be their own and other people's health, past reminiscences, and family matters. When this is so, a visit will always go well if they are allowed to make the running. Health matters will usually come first, and then talk either of family news or of their past lives. This is a topic that some who visit the elderly find extremely boring, just as others find it fascinating. But those who hate the nostalgia of the elderly should remember that one of the reasons why they want to talk so much about the past may be that, for them, the present is unbearable, and the future unthinkable. An understanding of this can do much to damp down the fires of impatience, and kindle those of tolerance in younger people, for 'Granny's old stories'. To show enthusiasm for a glance with them through the pages of old photograph albums, can often give immense pleasure; and half an hour spent like this can mean more to them than a whole evening of television, for they are warmed by memories of happier days. It is naturally important to them that their children and grandchildren should know what life was like when they were young, and although younger people may not realise it at the time, a knowledge of their own family history and the characters that made it can be valuable to them, too, if they are to understand themselves and their own lives.

When passing on to them family news, which they are usually anxious to hear, remember that the time for leaning on them with your more serious troubles is now past; so unless there is some inescapable reason for giving them bad news, try to protect them from it, for they will probably be worrying about it in isolation until your next visit. It is much better only to tell them of the happier events in your life: the progress the children are making and the amusing things they say, descriptions of family outings and news of old friends and neighbours. An effort should be made, however, to make them feel that they still have a strong role to play in your life, and that their opinions are still valued and respected. This can be done by making a point of asking their advice on small matters, which cannot create any anxiety in them.

Some elderly persons are very inward-looking and completely uninterested in the lives of others, even those of their close family. They have usually been inclined to be rather self-centred all their lives in a quiet way, and this tendency has become overt and accentuated in old age. If so, it is really useless to try to change them, however maddening their attitude may be. It is far better, for the sake of peace and quiet, to 'give them their head' within reason, without allowing them to get a total stranglehold on your time.

If, on the other hand, your elderly parent shows a quite uncharacteristic withdrawal from her normal concern for you and for others and is totally obsessed in an agitated fashion with herself and her own troubles, over a long period, you should begin to wonder if, in fact, she is suffering from a true depressive illness and may be in need of medical help. It should be remembered, however, that all old people tend to become a little more self-centred as the years go by. They need to be, in order to survive. Their bodies require more careful maintenance to keep functioning, and to some extent they have to protect themselves from too deep an involvement in the problems of others as their own emotions become more frail.

When you are visiting an elderly parent you will probably notice that there are times when they do not feel particularly like either talking or listening. This will often be just after a meal, when they are feeling drowsy. But this, of course, does not mean that they are not enjoying your company, if you show that you are quite happy just to sit quietly with them, looking through a newspaper or reading a book; for silence is for sharing too on the right occasions.

Most elderly people like to make a cup of tea for a visitor, and this should always be accepted with pleasure; for eating and drinking with somebody else is another of life's important shared experiences, of which they are deprived if they live alone. Also it is something *they* can do for *you* and gives the visit a sense of occasion.

Some visitors never learn how to come and go with grace, and clock-watching, when the time for departure is drawing near, should be carefully avoided. Old people are no fools, and can easily be hurt; so however many things you have on your mind to be done when you get home, never leave them feeling that you have given them time that you have grudgingly spared. Never greet them with 'Hello, how are you? I'm afraid I can't stop long', or leave them with 'Well, I *must* go; I've got *such* a lot to do'. Both may be statements of truth, but they are bad statements because they can make an elderly person feel how unimportant she is in your life, even though you may not mean to convey this.

If you are under pressure in your own life, with heavy business or family responsibilities, and find that, much as you would like to do so, you cannot spend a whole day, or even a whole evening with your parent, there are several ways of coping with this, according to your circumstances. One is to telephone, or write to her beforehand, saying that things have been so hectic at your end recently that it seemed at one point that you might have to postpone your visit for a week or two, but that you are so keen to see her that you are absolutely determined to 'make it' somehow, even if it has to be just a 'flying visit'. Another is to ease her gently into the awareness that your visit will be shorter than usual, doing so some time *after* you have greeted her affectionately on your arrival and listened patiently to her news, views or troubles. Then give her a definite reason for the necessity of an early departure (not just general 'busyness'). It may be an appointment to meet a business colleague, or a promise to collect the children from a party so that they do not have to walk home in the dark. If you are being honest with yourself and with her and you really are terribly pressed for time, you will never be short of concrete reasons to give, and she will find these much more acceptable and less hurtful than vague excuses, provided, of course, that your overall treatment of her is one of care and not neglect.

A very clinging and demanding elderly parent presents a much greater problem. If you are faced with this, the only thing to do is to refuse to be drawn into any fruitless arguments, but stand firm in your resolve to leave when you feel you must, assuring her of your affection and concern for her and your intention to visit her again as soon as you can. Obviously there are no simple solutions to a difficult relationship with a demanding parent, but it can often be kept ticking over on a mixture of kindness and firmness and a refusal on your part to come out of your corner for a fight every time she chooses to ring the bell.

It is clearly very important to make sure that at least some of your visits are completely unhurried and timed to suit her convenience, for to many elderly people a few hours relaxing in the company of a son or daughter they love can be an oasis in the desert of their week if they live alone.

Gifts
It is never difficult to think of suitable gifts to take to elderly people who live alone, but apart from the obvious ones it is worth remembering that things like home-made cakes, biscuits, jam or marmalade which they may no longer bother to make for themselves are particularly appreciated. They have the added advantage too of being evidence of the kind of affection that is willing to spend time and energy as well as money. Fresh fruit is valuable also for its high vitamin C content, but plums should be avoided unless they are made into jam, as they sometimes tend to cause diarrhoea in the elderly if too many are eaten in one day.

Birthdays
Old people either dislike having a great fuss made of their birthdays or they love every minute of it. If your elderly parent is in the second category, this event always provides a valuable opportunity for the family to make every kind of affectionate and celebratory gesture that says, 'We're glad you're still around'.

Social life
The possibilities for an active social life for those living alone will obviously vary according to age, health, personality and mobility. Many elderly people are quite capable of maintaining old friendships, making new ones and keeping themselves interested and involved in life around them without any help from their children. Others, particularly the bereaved (whose special needs were examined in Chapter 2) may require a little tactful help and encouragement when they are ready to face life again. Those who are newly bereaved and naturally dread the loneliness of returning to an empty house should be visited frequently in their own homes; and when you are able to persuade them to get out of their own four walls as much as possible for fresh air and

exercise and to meet others and visit relatives, it can be a considerable help if you can bring them home and go in with them for a cup of tea or a chat, even if it is only just for a quarter of an hour.

Some elderly people can find pleasure in joining with others in their age group in various kinds of purposeful activity or service to the community. Alternatively, membership of one of the many different kinds of clubs that exist to suit all interests, or attendance at a Day Centre may be the answer for them, and we shall be examining some of these possibilities in detail later.

If there is a marked resistance on the part of a lonely, but fit and mobile elderly person to consider any ideas for the possible improvement of her social life, and if gentle persuasion is of no avail, you may be justified in suspecting a condition of hidden depression. In this event, she should never be nagged or criticised. She has a right to do what she chooses with her time, and interference often makes matters worse. Your best course is to keep visiting her, if she will have you, with patience and understanding and watch how the situation develops. If she shows signs, after a while, of sliding into a depressive illness, it may be wise to have a quiet word with her doctor.

Even if they are not visibly disabled, some elderly people reach a stage in their lives when slight muscular weakness and general frailty, combined with a natural anxiety about crossing roads or being jostled off their feet in crowded places, makes going out difficult for them. Many of them struggle on bravely and still manage to take a limited amount of daily exercise, but sometimes a point is reached when they are no longer able to go out alone at all to enjoy any kind of social life. If they also happen to be living alone, we can make all the difference to the monotony of their existence by arranging to take them out regularly. When this is suggested, the invitation should always be along the lines of: 'I'd love you to come out for a run in the car with me some time. Will you?' rather than, 'Would you like me to take you out for a run in the car some time?' The first is a request for the pleasure of their company while the second implies slight patronage, and highlights their inability to go out on their own and their need now to be 'taken'.

Where you take them should, within reason, be left entirely to them. Many elderly people still enjoy a visit to the cinema, the theatre or a concert. Some just long for a slow 'mooch' around a department store. Others love a day by the sea or an afternoon in the country; and many most enjoy being taken to the homes of relatives or friends for a meal. Wherever you take them, though, try, if it is possible and the weather is good, to arrange for them to spend some of the time out of doors – for the housebound elderly are often short of vitamin D, which most of us get from natural sunlight (as well as certain foods) and this deficiency can lead to the painful condition of osteomalacia, in which there is rarefaction of the bones.

If they are churchgoers, but unable to go out alone, it is usually possible to organise lifts for them in the cars of other church members to Sunday services as well as week-day activities. Other ways of making life more interesting for the housebound are the occasional holidays in the homes of various members of the family; also offering to help them to entertain their friends in their own home to more than just a cup of tea, by arranging to take a pre-cooked, easily served meal round to them beforehand.

Domestic chores
Many elderly people can remain in their own homes even if they are living alone, provided that they can get adequate help with some of the heavier and more awkward chores: cleaning high up, or low down, under furniture or in corners which have become inaccessible to them. Jobs which involve using heavy domestic equipment, or climbing steps and taking down curtains can be a real problem, and the thorough spring-clean they always used to do becomes a complete impossibility if they happen to suffer from one of the common disorders of old age, such as arthritis or heart trouble. So they worry, and look back with longing to the good old, bad old days, when there always seemed to be a kind and sturdy neighbour nearby who was willing to pop in to lend a hand to the elderly and disabled, in the closer-knit communities of their youth.

The maintenance of proper standards of cleanliness in their

homes is very important to most mentally unimpaired old people. If the home starts 'going to pot' they often feel that it appears that they are 'going to pot' with it.

Much anxiety may be avoided for your elderly parents if you can organise yourself and other members of the family to help them regularly with the jobs they cannot cope with – anticipating their needs rather than waiting to be asked. Many old people tell their elderly friends, in confidence, that although they worry sometimes about various things in the house that need attention and are beyond their capabilities, they don't like to keep mentioning 'this and that' to their children when they visit, as they are only too delighted to see them and feel it is a bit hard to put them to work as soon as they arrive. This is why it is so valuable to arrange with them that certain visits will be regularly earmarked for 'odd-jobbing'. You can arrive wearing suitable clothing, on a day when you have not tired yourself out cleaning right through your own home. They can have all the cleaning equipment ready for you, tidying and moving any light objects, as necessary, as their contribution to the exercise before your arrival, and then when the work is completed they will usually be very pleased if you have allowed time to sit down and have a cup of tea or a drink with them for a while before you leave.

If for some reason it is impossible for you to give them the help in the house they need, a Home Help can be provided by the local authority social services department. These are usually strong, friendly, competent women, employed to undertake a variety of household tasks, including some shopping, washing and ironing if necessary. Unless there is exceptional need they only work from Monday to Friday, and as the service is very short-staffed in many areas most people can only receive a few hours' help a week; although in special cases daily help can be arranged. Elderly people pay for this according to their income, which has to be declared in full, but those on very small incomes may have nothing to pay at all.

It is possible for them (or for you on their behalf) to make application direct to the social services department. It may be done through their general practitioner, or, if they are being discharged from hospital and obviously need help in the home, it may be arranged by the hospital social worker. The Home Help Supervisor will then call to see what type and amount of help is required, and assist them if necessary to complete the forms on which the assessment for payment will be made. This is usually a very pleasant and reassuring interview for a worried old person, who can be helped to feel that much of the anxiety about her heavy housework is going to be taken off her hands; and the supervisor then tries, as far as possible, to choose just the right member of her staff to suit the needs of the applicant.

Many Home Helps become very fond of the elderly people they visit, often doing all kinds of extra jobs for them when they have the time, and the moral support they give to lonely old people is invaluable. Most social workers who are in touch with the elderly disabled living alone hear the praises of their Home Helps sung time and time again: 'She's like a daughter to me', and 'I don't know what I'd do without her'. These women, often with family responsibilities of their own, do a heavy and demanding job with great generosity of spirit.

Domiciliary medical and social services

The most important person employed by the State to supervise the health and care of the elderly at home is the general practitioner. A good general practitioner keeps an eye on the health of his elderly patients, knows the score, and can conduct the whole orchestra of welfare on their behalf when they need it. He is the one with the knowledge and power to bring in the right instruments at the right time, often just by raising a hand to reach for his telephone. He should never be regarded as someone only to be approached when a prescription is required or when some serious breakdown in health occurs. The emphasis with the old, as with any other age-group, should be on prevention before the need for cure arises, and some elderly people suffer quite unnecessarily from the 'silent' types of illness which show no dramatic symptoms in their early stages (such as anaemia), and which might well be diagnosed if they visited their doctor at six-monthly intervals when feeling at all 'off colour'. Even if they feel quite well, an annual check-up after the age of sixty is a sensible idea.

If your elderly relative is unfortunate enough to be registered with a doctor who is impatient with the older patients on his list and not particularly interested in geriatric medicine, the best thing to do is to try to get her transferred to the list of another doctor in the area whose attitude towards his elderly patients is known to be more sympathetic and thorough. Advice on whom to choose can usually be obtained through the local grape-vine of elderly neighbours and old people's clubs and organisations. Instructions as to how to change one's doctor will be found on your elderly parent's medical card and the procedure is simple. No reason has to be given either to her present doctor or to the one to whom she wishes to change, but undoubtedly it can facilitate the change-over and make the new doctor more likely to be willing to accept her if she has some sensible but low-key reason ready should there be any query. This could perhaps be that the new doctor's surgery is nearer, or easier for her to get to, has less steps to climb to the front door, or that she has a neighbour on his list who would accompany her to the surgery. Of course if her doctor has been guilty of serious neglect, you and your parent may decide that you should lodge a complaint with the local Community Health Council, whose job is to represent to the Area Health Authority the interests of the public in the district in which it operates. However, if it is just a matter of not liking the doctor, or of finding his attitude casual, there would be no point in exposing your elderly parent to the trauma of a 'post-mortem' on the death of their doctor/patient relationship. The main thing to aim for is simply a change of doctor as soon as possible. In the meantime, until this can be achieved, if you are worried that your parent is not receiving proper medical attention you should start to make a polite nuisance of yourself by frequent visits to the surgery to impress upon the doctor the fact that you consider there is real cause for concern about the state of her health and ask if he could arrange for a 'second opinion'. Very few doctors will resist constant requests for this from close relatives.

Fortunately most old people do get a satisfactory service from their general practitioner, finding that he will go to great trouble to see that they get all the medical and social help that is available to them. This can include district home nurses if the need arises, the vital service of chiropody and even a visit from a National Health Service dentist in certain circumstances if they are ill and housebound.

He will also be in touch with all the local voluntary services for the elderly and disabled, whose help he can raise. Most important of all, he will have good liaison with the local social services department, who can draw all the threads together and link his elderly patients with the organisations that can best meet their needs. Regular visits from a social worker can be of immense value to old people living alone, particularly if their family lives some distance away and cannot do all that they would wish for them. The social worker will be like a skilled 'friend' to them, who can help them in many areas of their life, perhaps by suggesting ways of overcoming loneliness by putting them in contact with the type of activity, club, Day Centre or workshop that would interest them, and arranging suitable transport for this; or, if they are not particularly keen on group social activities, sometimes by finding individual volunteers to visit them and take them out; although it should be remembered that no social worker or voluntary visitor can ever be a real substitute for care from their own family.

The social worker can, also, in co-operation with the social services occupational therapist and physiotherapist, arrange for them to be supplied with any special aids they need for safety and mobility, and adaptations to their home. Elderly people can turn to the social worker as well for advice on their financial problems and welfare rights. The social worker can give them emotional support too, strengthening any network of support that already exists from relatives, friends and neighbours, or trying to form one for them if they are in a position of isolation. The modern social worker's role is an enabling one, helping elderly people to make the best use of their own inner resources as well as the many social services available, and to retain some independence for as long as possible.

Elderly people and their families who wish to 'go it alone' so

On their own

far as obtaining outside help is concerned are, of course, quite at liberty to do so, and four of the large organisations who can give advice on a great variety of problems are:

> The National Council of Social Service,
> 26, Bedford Square, LondonWC1B 3HU.
> Age Concern, 60, Pitcairn Road, Mitcham, Surrey CR4 3LL.
> The National Association of Citizens' Advice Bureaux,
> 26 Bedford Square, LondonWC1B 3HU.
> Help The Aged, 8–10, Denman Street, LondonW1A 2AP.

All these agencies have local offices in many areas of the country, the addresses of which can be found in the telephone directory or the local public library.

There are many other groups and councils which provide services and information for elderly people throughout the country. Details of their activities can be found in the *Social Services Year Book* in public libraries.

Reliable young people who belong to local groups of Community Service Volunteers can often also be very helpful to elderly people who have no one to assist them with gardening, heavy house-cleaning and decorating. A phone call to the local authority social services department should produce the right contacts for this, if there is such a group functioning near them.

Errands

Many elderly housebound people living alone feel the loss of their independence very keenly and fear becoming a burden to others. Some of them are reluctant to ask visiting relatives, who may already be doing shopping for them, to run extra errands, such as taking prescriptions to the chemist or clothes to the launderette or dry cleaners, changing their library books and collecting their pension; so it is always as well to check to make sure that you are meeting these needs, or arranging for someone else to do so.

Diet

Cooking for one can sometimes be a dreary business, and many elderly people on their own do not eat the right types of food to maintain health. If they are frail or disabled and housebound they often become members of the tea-toast-and-tinned-soup brigade, and develop various kinds of vitamin-deficiency diseases.

If you find this happening to your elderly parent, try to help her to reorganise her eating habits. This is never easy, and she will only respond if she feels that your suggestions spring from real affection and concern for her and are not just an attempt to dominate or to 'bully' her into a new regime. A change in diet, like any other change in the lives of the elderly, has to be introduced gradually to succeed.

Sometimes the Women's Royal Voluntary Service 'Meals-on-wheels' service can help if old people cannot prepare food for themselves and are unable to get to one of the many luncheon clubs they run. A good hot meal is delivered to their home (the number of meals per week depending on the staff and resources in each area) and a modest charge is made for them. They should eat a proper breakfast and supper as well, though, since the meals have to be kept hot *en route* to the recipients and some of their original vitamin content can be lost.

If the frail or housebound are to eat properly, it is essential to see that they have help with their shopping, for carrying or pushing heavy baskets soon becomes an impossibility and very few shops now deliver goods. Once that problem is solved, the next hurdle is to put forward some practical suggestions on how they might improve their diet. These should be few and simple, and must certainly not involve them in any anxiety, or a sharp increase in effort or expenditure.

A plan that sometimes works very well – after their kitchen equipment (which should include a refrigerator) has been checked – is to start them off with a 'gift' for their larder of a small box-full of a variety of inexpensive sauces, seasonings and flavourings, which can be used to add interest to very simple meals. These can be packed, almost as an afterthought, beneath a nicely arranged selection of fresh fruit, which is presented ostensibly as the main part of the gift. These will probably be things that they would have kept as a matter of course in their store cupboard in earlier days, but have gradually dropped off their shopping list as they grew older and only had themselves to cook for; so there is no question of giving them new ideas – only trying to revive old ones, which may tempt them to prepare more varied and nourishing meals to achieve a balanced diet. The delicious and time-consuming dishes and sauces they used to make may no longer be possible for them, for many reasons, so there should be no hesitation in trying to interest them in some of the tinned and packet products which may be just as good for them if fresh milk has to be added.

Unless your elderly parent is known to be both very slow to take offence, and also to be a great lover of 'lists' for everything in life, it would be useless and irritating to her to be presented with a series of sensible menus to follow. But if you are tactful in your approach in this touchy area, you may be able, slowly and patiently, to build up for her a picture of a sample programme of meals for a seven-day period that would be low in cost and effort but reasonably tasty and nutritionally adequate. Ideas for this may be found in Chapter 4. A firm, but not frightening, explanation of what dietary deficiency can do to the health of old people can often work wonders in stirring them into action, too.

Another point worth remembering is that it is important to make sure that your parent's larder is well stocked with the right kind of non-perishable foods to deal with any emergency such as extreme weather conditions, or times when you may be unable to visit her because of illness or holidays, unless a neighbour is doing her shopping for her. You should also make certain that she has a good tin-opener which she can use without difficulty.

Financial problems
Some elderly people who are living on reduced incomes have good reason to worry about money, particularly when they live alone. But even those who are reasonably secure financially often experience more anxiety over money matters in old age than at any other time in their life. They feel that the 'rainy day' for which they have worked and saved for so long has now arrived, and they fear that they may, at any time, have to dip into what-

ever nest-egg they have tucked away for emergencies. Retaining this nest-egg of savings untouched, however small it is, is of the greatest importance to the elderly.

Many have a dread of something happening that will plunge them suddenly into a situation of near-poverty, and a few also unconsciously use their financial problems as pegs on which to hang their much deeper fears concerning their health and their future, which they may find hard to face. In all this, as in everything else in their lives, you can help them best by listening with patience and sympathy, never dismissing their anxieties – however unreasonable they may seem to be – simply by telling them not to worry because you will always see that they are all right. This can be comforting to them to some extent, but what they really want to hear is that you will not only see that they are cared for properly for the rest of their days, but that you will help them to remain in control of their own finances and to be as independent as possible.

The next step is to ensure that they are receiving all the State benefits to which they are entitled (a subject we shall be examining in more detail later in Chapter 5) and that any capital they have is being invested wisely and safely.

Communication

To be alone is one thing, but to be alone and to have no means at all of shattering the shell of silence around you to summon the comforting sound of a human voice is quite another. To have no line of communication to your own kind available can turn a tolerable solitude into a state of intolerable isolation; and yet thousands of elderly people, who live on their own and are too frail to go out, are in this position. Fortunately, many of them know that their relatives and friends will be calling in to see them from time to time; but 'from time to time' does not take care of those long days and nights in between, when, apart from their often desperate need for company, they feel frighteningly cut off from the world of people who would come to their aid at once if they fell ill, if only they had the means of contacting them.

Of course, there is always the milkman: one of society's frontline social workers, who has saved the lives of countless elderly people by noticing that there is something amiss and alerting neighbours or the police. Sometimes his willingness to raise the alarm is literally the only thing that stands between an old person and the possibility of a lonely and lingering death following a fall or sudden illness. One would think that an old person would have to be living in an isolated cottage, in the heart of the countryside, to be so out of touch with the world; but sadly we know from the frequent reports in the newspapers that such tragic loneliness can exist right in the heart of our towns and cities, and that the old have sometimes remained undiscovered for weeks and months after they have died in their own homes.

Obviously one of the most important lines of communication for the elderly is the telephone. If they cannot afford to have one installed, this should be regarded as a first priority and paid for by their children if they can afford it, which is often quite possible if there is a willingness on their part to make some small economy in their own spending each month. However, if your elderly parent has no telephone and neither of you can pay for one, you should contact the local authority social services department, who are empowered to provide assistance towards the cost or, in some cases, free telephones for disabled housebound elderly people and others, under the Chronically Sick and Disabled Persons Act 1970, although the extent of need is determined by the local authority in the light of resources. This, in reality, may mean very long delays before an instrument is installed, if at all. All social services departments are being hit by inflation and are short of cash and staff with which to meet the many urgent requests for help from all sections of the community. Most of them do all they can for the elderly with their limited resources, but if your parent is badly in need of a telephone and there is no way of your managing to install it for her, you should bring every possible pressure to bear to produce some speedy action on his or her behalf; for sudden illness, and the need for medical attention, does not wait for lengthy negotiations and committee work to rumble on indefinitely before it puts in an appearance. With very few exceptions, blaming individual social workers for delay in providing any particular service is usually an unfair and useless exercise, for they are only part of a large organisation and if things go wrong an approach to the local Director of Social Services is the best course of action.

The bedside table is usually the best place for the telephone if the bedroom is properly heated. An extension in the living room is useful too, but an expensive extra. When a telephone is installed, it is possible to have a very long flex put on for very little extra cost, and it can then be carried to any room, but you should consider the advantages and disadvantages of this carefully before coming to a decision to have it done, as it has been known to be the cause of accidents to some old people. If they are arthritic, their sight is poor, or they are subject to dizzy spells they may trip over the flex. Also many frail but not necessarily disabled elderly people feel the need to steady themselves by touching various pieces of furniture with one hand as they move around their homes, and for them, carrying a telephone and manoeuvring the flex from one room to another may have its hazards. For the younger and fitter elderly person, though, the long flex is a very good idea.

Telephoning the elderly who live alone needs even more care and tact than talking with them in the course of a visit. To you, the phone call may be just one of many activities packed into a busy day; whereas to them it might be the main event. When you replace the receiver after calling them, you get caught up at once by all the other pressing demands on your time, while they, in some cases, may be left sitting in a silent room, turning over everything you have said, and sifting it eagerly for confirmation of your real affection and concern for them.

The old and lonely are very vulnerable, and if you have sounded detached, preoccupied, or hurried during the conversation they can easily feel hurt and rejected; and that hurt can be like an emotional graze that will remain painful until you are able to see them again and heal it.

The most welcome caller is not the one who rings up with a carefully arranged bouquet of words delivered 'at the double'; it is the one who calls to enquire, to listen, and to sympathise when necessary, leaving the elderly person feeling warmed and cared for. There is a tendency of course for some old people to expect to have long telephone calls of even an hour or more with their children at very inconvenient times, both at home and at their place of work, and this can be a big problem. If your elderly parent is in the habit of doing this, the only way around it is to tell her quite frankly, as kindly as possible (even at the risk of giving some offence), that there are certain times of the day when it is very difficult for you to make or receive phone calls except in an emergency. So far as shortening or terminating a conversation is concerned, your ability to do this without upsetting her will depend very much on both your personalities, the warmth of your relationship, and the extent of her tolerance and sense of humour. One woman with this problem, whose rather self-absorbed elderly mother used to keep her on the telephone for hours with doom-laden conversations, solved it by telling her that she had developed migraine which was always triggered off by holding a phone to her ear for more than a quarter of an hour at a time! Another, a business woman, often under considerable pressure, managed to come to an arrangement with her voluble but good-humoured mother, that she could terminate any of their telephone conversations speedily if necessary, without giving offence, simply by saying, 'Well, I'm afraid it's all action stations here now, so I'll have to say goodbye'; and it worked remarkably well. She had found a good quick way of conveying the fact that something had arisen suddenly at her end that must claim her immediate attention; a summons to go to the boss's office, the arrival of someone with whom she had an appointment, or letters to be signed to catch the afternoon post. Sometimes, of course, all that had arisen was a lump of anxiety in her throat at being interrupted for so long in the middle of work which required a high degree of concentration and often had to be done to a deadline. Her mother never knew this, though, and because she had agreed to accept that the words 'action stations' meant that there was an urgent and valid reason for the conversation to be terminated she felt no sense of rejection. This arrangement was kept going very nicely by her daughter (who had a real affection for her) reminding her occasionally that although she sometimes had to cut their conversations short, she never cut her out of her thoughts when she put the phone down.

Visits from a local authority social worker can also do much to open up other lines of communication for the old and lonely; and it can be helpful too for any elderly person who is housebound and not within easy calling or tapping distance of her neighbours, to have a large clear HELP notice to put in her window, and a loud bell to ring in an emergency if there is no telephone.

The elderly and their animals

The company of a dog or cat can mean more to an elderly person than perhaps we can possibly imagine. It may be a poor substitute for human companionship, but the fact that it is a living creature who needs her and responds to her affectionate care brings a great deal of pleasure and interest into her life. Owning an animal also makes it easier for her to make new friends and contacts, particularly children. Many elderly people become so deeply attached to their animals, however, that when they lose them they go through a very real and depressing bereavement experience; so every effort should be made to help them to keep their animals properly fed, groomed and exercised when they begin to find this difficult to cope with themselves.

Improvements and alterations in the home

It is rare to find an elderly person's home that could not be made much more comfortable, convenient and secure for her by a few carefully planned improvements and adaptations. The extent of the work that could be undertaken would depend not only upon her willingness to consider it, but also on the finance available from the elderly person herself, her family, or the local authority, who are able to make grants for this purpose in suitable cases.

In order to avoid disappointment and the frustration of delays, it should be clearly understood from the outset that obtaining grants from local authorities is by no means an overnight business. Many conditions have to be fulfilled and eligibility established, which can take a considerable time; so if you can improve the living conditions of your elderly parent yourself, without undue hardship, you would be well advised to do so. If, however you are going to help her to seek a grant for home improvements, a visit to the local authority environmental health department can be useful, as you and she can receive there an explanation of all the different forms which may need to be completed, and your queries can be answered. A Department of the Environment leaflet called *Your Guide to House Renovation Grants* can also be obtained from the local council offices, or Citizens' Advice Bureau. This should be read carefully before making an application, and no work should be started until an application for a grant has been approved.

Local authority grants for improving homes to a good standard are at the authority's discretion, but houses built after 1961 are not normally considered unless the applicant is disabled. The applicant must be a freeholder or have a lease with five years or more to run, and will be required to sign a form to say that she intends to live in that dwelling as her only or main place of residence for at least five years after the work has been completed. This does not mean that the applicant cannot let the house, but if she sells it, or simply uses it as a second home, she may have to pay back the whole or part of the grant with interest. Usually the grant is paid to the applicant when the work is finished to the satisfaction of the council's inspector, but sometimes it is agreed that the council will pay for it in instalments. Occasionally the local authority will be willing to do the work and then charge the applicant for the cost of it, less the amount of the grant. Another point to be taken into consideration is that grants are only made to applicants whose homes are below a certain rateable value, which varies in different areas of the country, and that, when the work is completed, the home must be regarded as a suitable dwelling for occupation for at least another thirty years.

The types of work for which grants may be given are: the provision of a damp-proofing course, dealing with dry or wet rot, repairs or renewal of faulty floors, ceilings or roof, installing a hot and cold water supply, adding or installing a bathroom if one does not exist in the house, installing an inside lavatory with proper drainage, extending a very small kitchen, improving the heating system (with in some cases a grant towards the cost of installing central heating), and roof insulation.

Improvement grants may also be given towards the conversion of a house into flats.

Intermediate grants may be given on which there is no rateable value restriction, for any missing standard basic amenities such as a bath, shower, wash-basin, lavatory, sink and hot and cold water supply.

Grants of any kind are usually only given for a proportion of the cost of the work to be done, but when necessary, local authorities can make loans for the balance, on which interest has to be paid.

If an old person is also disabled and requires special adaptations or improvements to her home, careful study of a booklet entitled *Housing Grants and Allowances for Disabled People* (from The Central Council for the Disabled, 34 Eccleston Square, London SW1V 1PE) can be very helpful, as it goes into great detail on the subject. But anyone wishing to apply for any type of house renovation grant should be sure to consult the local council at the outset for advice.

It is clear, though, that if you decide to help your elderly parent or parents to apply for local authority grants, you are probably going to need to have great determination and infinite patience, and in the meantime there is a great deal you could do yourself to improve their comfort and living conditions in small but important ways.

Remembering that the elderly often become quite anxious and upset at the prospect of any change or disturbance of their normal routine, however pleasing the end-result promises to be, you will need to take anything they may regard as an 'upheaval' very slowly. In fact, before you even begin to discuss the possibilities, it will be better to make a private room-by-room list of things that might be done to increase their comfort and safety. Then you can begin to introduce new ideas gradually, one by one, being willing at the same time to take 'no' for an answer if they are definitely opposed to change of any kind, since this is their right and must be respected. Tactful handling of the matter rarely provokes outright opposition, though, particularly when their advice is sought, their choices accepted all along the line, and assurances given that any alterations will be carried out quietly, with a minimum of fuss and disruption.

The main areas for consideration should be: security measures against intruders, insulation, heating, lighting, safety of floor coverings, the easy moving of furniture, improvements and adaptations to the kitchen, improvements and adaptations to the bathroom and lavatory, the safety of halls and stairways, the safety and functioning of all equipment, improvement in garden planning.

This could form the basis for a more detailed check-list which might read as follows:

SECURITY MEASURES AGAINST INTRUDERS
Front *and* back doors should be of heavy quality. *Both* fitted with a five-lever mortice dead-lock, a bolt at the top and three-quarters of the way down, a strong door-chain and a 'visitor viewer' spy-hole. All windows should be fitted with locks.

INSULATION
Homes, like teapots, can be kept much warmer by the addition of a 'cosy' and heating bills can be greatly reduced by installing efficient insulation. A good deal of heat is lost through the roof of a house, a bungalow, or a top flat in a block, so this should be insulated by a layer of not less than three inches of insulating material. This can be done by a handyman, although if the roof is a flat one and not already insulated, special insulating tiles should be fixed inside, which will usually need to be done by a professional. A thick lagging jacket should be put on to the hot water tank. The thin, cheaper ones are a poor economy.

Thick fitted carpets with a good underlay are ideal, but if these cannot be afforded, plenty of newspaper under the carpet will help to insulate the floors.

Unused fireplaces should be blocked off, but the material used must have a number of good sized holes in it for ventilation.

Copper or plastic draught-strip (which requires no maintenance) should be fixed permanently round the front and back doors and, if necessary, plastic foam strips around draughty windows. Heavy lined curtains are also an excellent way of retaining heat in a room, although double-glazing is the most effective way of cutting out draughts. It also reduces a certain amount of heat loss, as well as cutting down traffic noise. Unless you intend to fit double-glazing yourself (and even 'Cling-film' can be very effective), it is best to get brochures and free estimates from several of the largest and longest-established firms in this field before making any decision, as there are numerous small firms selling sub-standard products at high prices. Small reliable local firms whose work you may have seen in other people's homes are of course worth considering. Some of the best-known big firms have special discount offers for those who are willing to purchase their double-glazing during the summer months.

Wall cavity insulation can also reduce heat loss and could be considered, but only after expert advice has first been taken from an independent builder or surveyor as to the suitability for the type of home occupied by your elderly parent. Then, if you decide that it would be a good idea, here again it is safer to approach several of the largest firms for free estimates.

HEATING

Central heating which provides safe, controllable background heat, plus a well guarded electric or gas fire which gives some form of instant extra heat when required is ideal if it can be afforded. If central heating is to be newly installed, it should be borne in mind that people who have two different forms of heating are at an advantage during a power failure or power cut if there is a strike, also that gas- or oil-fired central heating depend upon an electric pump.

Some elderly people still prefer (or have to make do with) an open fire, but this often presents problems if they have no one to carry coal for them and help to clear out the grate if it is of the old-fashioned type. If an open fire is to be used, you should see that it has a good fire-guard.

By law, all gas and electric fires have now to be fitted with a fire-guard by the manufacturers, and when helping an elderly person to choose one it is wise to encourage her to buy one with the on/off control switch on the top or high up on the side, to avoid unnecessary bending. Paraffin oil heaters, although now much improved in design for safety and ease of filling, can be a hazard for some of the frail elderly, and should not be used by them if any other form of heating is available.

It is important for the elderly to have heating in their bedroom because of the risk of hypothermia, and it is also essential to make sure that they are living in a home that is well ventilated as well as warm. There must be some movement of fresh air for their health's sake and to prevent condensation, which can create a damp atmosphere and in some cases wall fungus.

LIGHTING
Poor lighting is poor planning when it leads to accidents. Halls and stairways in particular should be well lit; and these are just the areas in which many old people feel that they should economise.

Each room should have a centre light which can be switched on before entering it, as well as table lamps, and there should be no trailing wires or flex that the elderly person could trip over.

Power points should be raised to waist-level by a qualified electrician, as this makes plugging in lamps, vacuum cleaner and other equipment much easier.

Finally, an emergency lighting kit should always be ready in an accessible place, in case of a sudden power failure. This should include a torch (the batteries of which should be checked regularly for deterioration), a box of nightlights, which are safer for the elderly than candles, and a box of safety matches.

SAFETY OF FLOOR COVERINGS
Serious accidents amongst elderly people in the home are often caused by worn carpets or small rugs or mats. Many of them wear slippers around the house, and if they tend to shuffle a little as their joints stiffen, rugs become dangerous obstacles to their safe movement from room to room. Loose or worn stair carpets are another common cause of falls.

If the money is available fitted carpets are a good investment, particularly those that are patterned in a mid-shade of the colour most favoured by the elderly person, as this will not show either marks or dust so much as a plain light- or dark-coloured carpet does. Their other advantages are warmth and ease of cleaning with a carpet sweeper or vacuum cleaner.

Kitchen, bathroom and lavatory floors should be covered with one of the easily cleaned vinyl-type floor coverings, preferably patterned in a mid-shade of the chosen colour. Fitted carpets, though warm, are not a good idea for the bathroom and lavatory of an elderly person who may have minor 'mishaps' and spillages which they cannot easily deal with as they advance into old age.

THE EASY MOVING OF FURNITURE
The elderly heart and spine should never be subjected to the tremendous effort required to move heavy furniture and equipment in order to clean under and behind them. Mini-castors, which can be bought at all good hardware stores, should be fitted to every piece of furniture that will take them except chairs, which can be fitted with small metal domes so that they slide gently and slowly. Sets of bars and rollers can be bought from hardware stores for the heaviest furniture and kitchen equipment.

IMPROVEMENTS AND ADAPTATIONS IN THE KITCHEN
Kitchen equipment – cooker, refrigerator, washing-machine and spin-drier – should all be checked to see that they are functioning well and safely.

Many elderly people who suffer from backache and stiff joints find bending and stretching difficult, so it is important that the cooker, sink and work-tops should be at the correct height for them, and that cupboards and larder shelves that are in daily use should not be too high or too low for them to reach without strain.

The use of steps or step-stools by elderly people living alone is dangerous and should be discouraged if possible, as their grip and balance are often impaired; but a one-step, non-slip footstool, with four legs and a chrome-plated tubular steel handrail at the front to hold on to, is very safe and stable. It can also be very useful for an elderly person to keep an aid called a 'helping hand' (long length) in the kitchen. This is a stick-like instrument, light in weight, with an end designed to pick up light objects and a magnet for very small objects as well. It will also lightly grip a cleaning cloth for wiping out difficult corners in the kitchen or other rooms. To have one standing in the corner of every room in the house is a tremendous help to an old person who cannot bend; although, of course, one will suffice, as it can be carried from one room to another when it is needed. (Details of these aids will be found in Chapter 12.)

Kitchen curtains which need to be washed fairly frequently can often be hard for an elderly person to reach to take down and to re-hang; so one of the easily wiped vinyl-coated roller blinds is an excellent idea. They can be bought at most large hardware stores and fixed by a handyman. If they are purchased through a large department store, the shop will send an expert to fix them for a small extra charge.

The kitchen should be well ventilated, and an extractor fan is an efficient way of doing this without creating draughts.

IMPROVEMENTS AND ADAPTATIONS IN THE BATHROOM AND LAVATORY

For the elderly who have some form of infirmity, the normal daily routine of keeping the body clean and disposing of its waste products can be exhausting, hazardous, and, in some cases even painful when the back must be bent and the limbs slowly manipulated into the appropriate positions to get in and out of the bath, and down and up from the lavatory seat. There are many ways of solving these problems for them, though, by quite a small initial outlay (which the local authority social services department may meet in some cases).

A good non-slip rubber bathmat with suction caps underneath it is the first essential. A bath safety-rail made of chromium-plated tubular steel makes getting in and out of the bath much easier and safer; and a bath seat with a back support eliminates the need to sit right down in the bath (see Chapter 12). Chromium-plated hand-grips which are an integral part of some modern baths also help the elderly to rise more easily.

For those who cannot get down into a bath at all (as is the case with many back-sufferers and arthritics), a shower fitment at one end of the bath, with nylon shower-proof curtains to pull round inside the bath, is one of the best answers. A shower that is thermostatically controlled is ideal, but the reliable and efficient ones can be expensive to buy and to install, and a mixer system working off one large hot and cold mixer with two tap controls can be very satisfactory for all but the very severely disabled.

These are adjusted by the user to obtain a flow of water at the desired heat before stepping into the bath, and the shower can be started as soon as the curtains are pulled round. A separate shower cabinet may be more convenient to step into for those with much arthritis in the hip and knee joints, but the cabinets of superior quality, which are not too small, are the only ones really worth considering for a disabled person, and they are fairly expensive. Here again, if any particular type of equipment is absolutely essential in the bathroom, and finance is a problem, the social services department of the local authority may be able to help, and it is worth approaching them *before* anything is purchased or installed.

Some old people living alone, who are very frail, are unable to expend all the energy required to take a bath or shower unattended every day, and if their standards of personal hygiene have always been good this can be a real worry to them. Their problem can be partly solved by the use of a portable plastic bidet that can be filled at the washbasin, placed over the lavatory and emptied into it after use (see Chapter 12). The feet can be washed in an oblong, straight-sided plastic household bucket filled with about six inches of warm water and a few drops of mild disinfectant, while sitting on a bathroom stool (or using the lavatory as a seat). An Addis plastic linen-box with solid sides, and a lid with top ventilation, in which to store both bucket and bidet out of sight, can be kept in the bathroom. The bidet can be ordered through any local chemist selling medical and nursing aids and the plastic bucket can, of course, be purchased from a hardware store.

If the lavatory is too low for an elderly person, a raised polypropylene toilet seat which fits over it, but is easy to remove and to wash, can be very useful, and a chromium-plated hand-grip fixed very securely to the wall at the side of the lavatory can also be helpful. (Further details of these and other aids will be found in Chapter 12).

THE SAFETY OF HALLS AND STAIRWAYS
Having accepted the fact that good lighting, unworn carpeting (fitted if possible) or non-slip vinyl floor-covering and an absence

of rugs and odd mats is essential, a check should be made on the positioning and stability of the handrail the elderly person will depend upon for going up and down stairs. The hall should have only a minimum of furniture in it, and nothing too near to the bottom of the stairs which could increase her injuries if she fell.

THE SAFETY AND FUNCTIONING OF ALL EQUIPMENT
All gas and electrical equipment and appliances, wiring, lamp holders, power points and plugs, and particularly electric blankets should be checked for safety and efficiency, and taps, pipes and tanks should be looked at also to see if they are in need of attention.

IMPROVEMENT IN GARDEN PLANNING
If the upkeep of a garden is getting too much for an elderly person, and finance and willing helpers can be found, a suggestion that it should be paved, with a few easily managed tubs of flowers and shrubs at a convenient height, is often an acceptable idea. Otherwise arrangements can sometimes be made with a reliable local resident, who has no garden of his own, to grow flowers and vegetables in it and share the produce with her. This can work very well in many instances, for it is not only means a supply of fresh vegetables, but a friendly link with the family of the man growing them.

Preparation for possible urgent admission to hospital

If sudden illness overtakes an elderly person living alone and she needs to be admitted to hospital, she sometimes becomes very agitated and distressed. This can be reduced a little if she goes in with all she needs for the first few days: a clean dressing-gown, slippers, a change of night clothes and bedjacket and all the toilet articles and other small items she is likely to want. This avoids the extra worry of having to give friends or relatives last-minute instructions about where to find everything in a hurry.

A sensible way for her to prepare for such an eventuality is to keep a small case already packed and labelled with her name and address in her wardrobe or in a corner of her bedroom where it can be got at easily (see Chapter 13). This has to be suggested to her with some care, without giving her the impression that you think her sudden collapse into illness is in any way imminent or inevitable; and it should not be suggested at all if it is felt that it might upset or frighten her. Fortunately most old people are all in favour of precautions of any kind, and if, in addition, you can tell her truthfully that you have just such a 'hospital case' packed for yourself at home, for an emergency, she will probably go along with the idea very willingly.

Most people try to do all they can to help and support their elderly parents and other relatives who live alone. If they are what one might call the 'young' elderly, who are still keeping afloat very happily in the mainstream of life and enjoying their independence, the problems are few. In fact, they may be helping you with yours! But for those in the older age-groups, whose health and strength may be failing, things are very different. Unless they, and you, wish to join forces under the same roof, you may often be very conscious that their biggest problem, that of loneliness, is beyond your reach. You come and go with your offerings of help and affection, knowing that what they really need is a constant presence, and sometimes this knowledge can be as painful for you as it is for them.

If you know they have always enjoyed close companionship until they finally had to live alone, it is not difficult to imagine what it must be like for them to have no one to share their life with any longer, and no hand to hold as their step becomes less sure. Yet many of them come to terms with it magnificently, trying so hard not to add their pain to that of their children, in a situation that sometimes neither of them can alter.

4
Nutrition

It is not the intention here to go into great detail on the subject of nutrition, but rather to give a simple guide that may be useful to those who want to make sure that the elderly parent in their care is being properly nourished.

An adequate, well-balanced diet is one of the most important factors in the maintenance of health in older people, and the lack of it is responsible for many preventable illnesses. Many more of the elderly population are under-nourished than their relatives realise, and there are several reasons for this:

The ageing body does not absorb and distribute food as efficiently as it used to do.

In some cases, a low income is not keeping pace with the rising cost of food.

Physical disability makes shopping difficult, and sometimes forces the elderly to rely entirely on the good but fairly limited range of foods that can be delivered to their door by the milkman.

Sometimes there is apathy and lack of incentive to prepare varied meals to be eaten alone, particularly when age has blunted the taste-buds.

Some old people have ill-fitting dentures which make them change to a 'soft' diet of bread, jam, cakes, biscuits, tinned puddings, and other convenience foods which do not supply all their dietary requirements.

Depression, which is a very common cause of loss of appetite, often reduces old people who are living alone to a tea-and-toast-type diet, on which they soon become ill.

The basic constituents of food

The basic constituents of food: water, proteins, carbohydrates, fats, minerals and vitamins, all play an important part in the 'upkeep' of the body and we should make very sure that our elderly relatives are not missing out on any of them in their diet.

PROTEINS

Protein is found mainly in meat, fish, chicken, rabbit, cheese, eggs, dried beans, peas and lentils, baked beans and milk, and in smaller quantities in other types of food. An elderly person should try to eat approximately half a pound of protein in some form in her diet every day. This could be made up, for example, of 4 oz. of lean meat, fish, chicken or rabbit, plus 2 oz. of cheese and one pint of milk OR 3 oz. of cheese, 3 oz. of beans, one egg and one pint of milk.

CARBOHYDRATES

Carbohydrates are found in flour, bread, cereals, cakes, biscuits and most sugary foods. Since these are fairly cheap to buy and easy to prepare, the elderly rarely go short of them. The problem more often is to see that they do not come to rely upon them almost exclusively, as a high intake of carbohydrates can lead to obesity.

FATS

Fats exist in certain quantities in many of the foods normally eaten by the elderly, apart from the obvious ones of butter, margarine, milk and cheese, so most old people on a varied diet are consuming adequate amounts.

MINERALS

Iron is the most important mineral to be concerned about in an elderly person's diet. It is found mainly in meat, eggs and vegetables. Some elderly people suffer from iron deficiency due to a very slight, and sometimes unrecognisable, blood loss from such conditions as piles, diverticulitis, hiatus hernia – and occasionally bleeding from the stomach, if they have been taking aspirin for rheumatism daily for long periods, and this may cause anaemia.

Nutrition

Calcium, which is found in cheese and milk, is also vital for an elderly person, for a lack of it can cause bone troubles and a type of 'old age rickets', and this can be one of the causes of severe backache in later life.

VITAMINS

Vitamin A This vitamin is found in fruit, lettuce, carrots and green vegetables.

Vitamin B Vitamins of the B complex are found in cheese, fish, eggs, wheat-germ, meat, liver, lentils, beans and peas.

Vitamin C This vitamin is present in fresh fruit, particularly orange and grapefruit, and vegetables, including new potatoes, but it can be rendered useless by long storage or over-cooking. It should be taken in some form every day.

Vitamin D This vitamin is found in margarine and butter (although margarine is a richer source). It is also present in milk and eggs, and the body takes it in from exposure to sunshine as well, which is one reason why it is so important for the elderly to take outdoor exercise.

Vitamin deficiency Vitamin deficiency can only be properly diagnosed and treated by a doctor, but there are certain fairly obvious signs which should be noted, bearing in mind that an old person who is obese can still be suffering from malnutrition and vitamin deficiency through eating the wrong kinds of food. The corners of the mouth may be cracked and sore and the tongue unusually red. There may be diarrhoea, tingling in the feet and hands, swelling of the abdomen, legs and ankles, and breathlessness. Small bruises may appear for no apparent reason under the skin, and the skin itself can become hard and have a tendency to crack.

There is no need to become over-anxious about the subject of diet for the elderly. We simply need to keep a careful eye on things, to see that they are eating a good variety of food which includes plenty of protein, dairy products and fresh fruit and vegetables, together with some roughage, which is often best taken in the form of a bran cereal, and which will, in many cases, completely eliminate the problem of constipation and ease that of piles. Sometimes, if elderly relatives are living at a distance, it is not possible to be certain, in spite of advice from us, and help from neighbours with the shopping, that they are eating properly, but if they can only be persuaded to drink a pint of milk every day and eat some fresh citrus fruit, wholemeal bread, cheese or eggs, margarine or butter and a bowl of bran cereal, we shall know that they cannot come to any serious harm from a dietary point of view, even though a much more varied diet would be more suitable. They should be reminded too that canned baked beans in tomato sauce are highly nutritious and can be a quick and convenient addition to many main meals or can even make quite a good meal on their own if they are served on buttered toast.

The question of diet generally for elderly people has already been mentioned in Chapter 3, and all who are trying to ensure that an elderly parent (particularly one who is living alone) is eating sensibly know what a difficult problem this is. Most of them have managed their own homes and catered for their families efficiently for many years, and even elderly men know a little more about cooking than their fathers did. Understandably, women in particular resent advice on how to feed themselves in their old age; but there are some women (and even more men) who will welcome help in this respect if it is given tactfully. They want to feel that they are eating the kind of food which will add to the chances of their remaining in good health, but often they cannot see how they can do so if their income has been drastically reduced. Also many of them have little inclination to cook much for themselves when they usually have to eat alone, and they prefer to use the smallest possible number of cooking utensils, pans and dishes which have to be washed up afterwards. Bearing all this in mind, it may be helpful to those who are still open to suggestions to try to work out with them some very simple menus for a seven-day period; meals which will suit their pocket, entail little expenditure of energy, but at the same time cover all their basic dietary requirements, and which can be made tasty and interesting by the addition of some of the sauces, seasonings, and flavourings with which you can supply them.

Something along the following lines may be worth considering, and of course many other simple dishes could be introduced according to their taste, provided each day's food is well balanced from the point of view of the nourishment elderly people require. As well as their daily pint of fresh milk taken in one form or another, if they can be encouraged to cook themselves some fresh green and root vegetables several times a week, so much the better, but these menus are designed primarily for old people who dislike spending much time on the preparation of their food and are unlikely to be persuaded past a certain point of effort.

MONDAY
Breakfast Bowl of cereal (preferably All-Bran for roughage) with milk. Wholemeal toast with Flora margarine or butter and marmalade or honey. Tea or coffee.
Lunch Two slices of toasted wholemeal bread spread thinly with Flora margarine and topped with 2 oz. grated cheddar cheese. Browned under the grill and served with mustard, chutney, or a bottled brown or tomato sauce. Followed by one fresh orange. Tea or coffee.
Tea/supper Half of an 8-oz. tin of shoulder ham (or corned beef), the other half to be put into the refrigerator for the next day. Two tomatoes cut in half and sprinkled with a little castor sugar. Mayonnaise. Mustard. Two cream crackers with Flora margarine, followed by one fresh apple diced and eaten with the skin on if possible after it has been well washed. Tea.
Evening drink Cup of Complan (flavoured or plain), Cocoa, Ovaltine or malted milk.

TUESDAY
Breakfast As Monday.
Lunch Half of the 8-oz. tin of shoulder ham or corned beef left over from Monday. Lettuce or watercress. One tomato. Mayonnaise. A portion of instant potato (the type with added vitamin

C) creamed with a small knob of Flora margarine and salt and black pepper. Followed by a small tin of creamed rice (hot or cold) with a teaspoonful of strawberry jam. Tea or coffee.
Tea/supper Boiled egg with wholemeal bread and margarine or butter. (It is not necessary to avoid butter completely because of the connection between high levels of cholesterol and heart disease, but merely to cut down on it.) Fresh grapefruit. Tea.
Evening drink As Monday.

WEDNESDAY
Breakfast As Monday.
Lunch 8 oz. minced beef cooked slowly and thoroughly in a small saucepan with a level dessertspoonful of dried onion, a little black pepper and a Swiss Knorr beef stock cube, dissolved in a quarter of a pint of hot water from the kettle. Thicken towards the end of cooking if necessary with plain flour mixed with a little water and a few drops of bottled gravy browning. Transfer mince to a small warmed ovenproof casserole dish. Top with instant mashed potato and brown under the grill. Serve with tomato sauce. Followed by one fresh orange. Tea or coffee.
Tea/supper 1 oz. of cheese with lettuce (left over from Tuesday's lunch). Wholemeal bread with Flora margarine or butter. Followed by one grated apple. Tea.
Evening drink As Monday.

THURSDAY
Breakfast As Monday.
Lunch Three pork sausages (out of five bought from a butcher who will sell small quantities. Cook all five of them and keep two in the refrigerator to have cold for Friday's supper). Small tin of spaghetti or baked beans in tomato sauce. Followed by one grated fresh apple topped with a quarter of a pint of vanilla-flavoured custard (make half a pint of custard, adding a little extra sugar and a few drops of vanilla essence, and save half of it in the refrigerator for Friday). Tea or coffee.
Tea/supper Scrambled egg on wholemeal toast. One apple, orange, or pear. Tea.
Evening drink As Monday.

FRIDAY
Breakfast As Monday.
Lunch Small packet of frozen fish fingers (grill for 4–5 minutes each side). Serve with bottled tartare sauce or a squeeze from a plastic lemon. Potato crisps or sticks and one slice of wholemeal bread with Flora margarine or butter. Followed by one fresh orange, peeled, sliced and served topped with a quarter of a pint of vanilla custard (left over from Thursday). Tea.
Tea/supper Wholemeal bread spread with Flora margarine and a small jar of ham paste and topped with two sliced cold pork sausages (left over from Thursday) with mustard. Followed by one fresh apple. Tea.
Evening drink As Monday.

SATURDAY
Breakfast As Monday.
Lunch Belly of pork. Four thick slices cooked slowly in the oven in a small covered pyrex casserole with salt and black pepper. Sage and onion stuffing. Mix half a packet of stuffing as directed but adding a little extra dried sage and dried onion and a good pinch of salt. Remove lid from casserole when pork is cooked; grease it lightly with Flora margarine and use it to cook the sage and onion stuffing. Increase oven heat to crisp the pork and cook the stuffing for about twenty minutes. Cook a 4-oz. pack of frozen peas or runner beans and serve with an uncooked grated sharp-tasting eating apple to save the trouble of making apple sauce. Followed by a fresh grapefruit. Tea or coffee.
Tea/supper Wholemeal bread spread with a small jar of anchovy paste and topped with a chopped hard-boiled egg. Followed by a sliced banana in banana-flavoured instant whip. Tea.
Evening drink As Monday.

SUNDAY
Breakfast As Monday.
Lunch Roast leg of chicken. Parsley and thyme stuffing. Bread sauce. Potato crisps. Small tin of garden peas. Loosen the skin from the flesh of the chicken by gently inserting a finger between them. Push slivers of Flora margarine under the skin so that the

flesh is prevented from drying out as it cooks. Also rub a little Flora margarine over the outside of the skin and sprinkle with salt and pepper. Wrap loosely in foil and place the leg on a flat enamel pie plate and cook in a pre-heated moderately hot oven. Mix half a packet of parsley and thyme stuffing as directed, but also adding a good squeeze of lemon juice from a plastic lemon and an extra sprinkling of dried thyme. When the chicken leg is cooked, cook the stuffing by the side of it on the same plate, according to the instructions on the packet. Ten minutes before the end of the cooking time, open the foil covering the chicken to allow the skin to brown, while you are making a small quantity of (packet) bread sauce in a small saucepan, and heating the tinned peas in another. Serve with potato crisps. (In this way, the washing up for this modest roast dinner can be kept down to the absolute minimum.) Followed by one fresh orange. Tea or coffee. *Tea/supper* 1 oz. of diced cheddar cheese mixed with one diced fresh apple. Wholemeal bread and Flora margarine or butter. Tea. *Evening drink* As Monday.

Not exactly Cordon bleu! – but easy, adequate, and not too expensive, and no doubt you and your elderly parent would be able between you to work out many alternatives to these suggestions. If however a special diet has been recommended by the doctor, you should of course see that it is possible for her to adhere strictly to this, and if she is amongst those who enjoy various products from Health Food shops she should not be criticised for having fads. The only important thing is to see that she is eating wisely. Make sure, for example, that if she does not eat meat, she gets sufficient iron through other foods such as eggs, lentils and a variety of vegetables, so that anaemia is avoided. When you are considering the problem of diet for an elderly parent it would also be helpful to have a copy of *Easy Cooking for One or Two* (published by Penguin), by Louise Davies, who is a dietician.

Elderly people should be invited to eat meals with other members of their family as often as possible, for not only will they enjoy their meals more, but this is a mark of their continuing membership of, and acceptance by, the 'tribe'. There are, however, several small points worth remembering when eating either at home or in a restaurant with older people. Most of them prefer to sit with their backs to the light. They sometimes have problems with the control of their dentures when eating certain types of food, and some have slight difficulties with swallowing as the muscles get weaker (or if they have at some time suffered a small stroke), so they dislike being watched. We should also try to eat at their pace, not ours, and not allow them to feel that they are holding us up.

The elderly do not always want to be on the receiving end, and any gift of food they offer us, whether it is a meal or just a pot of home-made jam, should be accepted with appreciation, for all such gifts are a part of the pattern of love in which they still wish to be involved.

5
Financial problems of the elderly

Money matters a a great deal to the elderly. They know that it is not as important as good health, a contented mind, or that gift that the poet Ruth Pitter said was the one she would choose, above all others, to bestow upon a child at birth – 'love in old age'. But money matters because it enables the elderly to continue to retain the power of choice in many areas of their lives, to defend themselves to some extent against the 'slings and arrows of outrageous fortune' and to enjoy a well earned retirement with dignity. Unfortunately, most elderly people have to suffer a considerable drop in their income after retirement, and careful planning and budgeting is required to maintain a reasonable standard of living. Usually they are quite capable of doing this for themselves, but if your elderly parent turns to you for advice on financial matters your main aims should be: 1. To make sure that she is receiving all the State benefits and pensions to which she may be entitled. 2. To see that she is receiving the correct amount of occupational pension (if any) that is due to her. 3. To ensure that any capital she may have is being invested wisely. 4. To see that she is being taxed correctly by the Inland Revenue. 5. To see that her financial affairs as a whole are being managed properly for her, according to the law, if she is mentally incapable.

The financial problems of the elderly differ from one person to another as widely as do their health problems, so it is not possible to lay down any hard and fast rules, or to produce any magical solutions. Each case is different, and it will be for you to decide upon what action you should take to try to improve your parent's situation in the light of your knowledge of her circumstances.

Financial problems of the elderly

Since the rates of State benefits and income from various types of investments change so frequently, there is little point in quoting figures, but it will be important for you to know how to gather the up-to-date, accurate information. Many people know very little about the benefits that can be claimed by the elderly and those who are looking after them, or the free services to which they are entitled, so they often fail to claim something that is their right.

State pensions and benefits

Anyone who is caring for an elderly mother or father would be well advised to visit the local office of the Department of Health and Social Security and ask for a complete set of leaflets on this subject which will explain what financial help is available, apart from the State Retirement Pension, both for their parent and for themselves. These should include the following: NP27, 'Looking after someone at home'. NI106, 'Current rates of all benefits'. SB1, 'Supplementary benefits'. NI212, 'Invalid care allowance'. NI205, 'Attendance allowance'. NI13, 'Widow's benefits'. NI9, 'How a stay in hospital can affect your social security benefit'. HB1, 'Help for handicapped people' (which gives detailed information about other benefits and services which may help your elderly parent). NI211, 'Mobility allowance' (but this at present is not payable after pension age, i.e. 65 for men, 60 for women), and NI49, 'National insurance death grant'.

In these leaflets the benefits available to both men and women are clearly explained. They can be studied at home and if you feel you need clarification on any of the points in them, the Enquiry Clerk in the same office is available to answer questions and give guidance.

DETAILS OF SOME OF THE STATE BENEFITS OF MAJOR IMPORTANCE TO THE ELDERLY AND THEIR CARING RELATIVES

The supplementary pension A weekly supplement which can be added to the basic State retirement pension for those in financial need (see leaflet SB1).

The supplementary allowance A weekly allowance that can be made to those in financial need who are not in receipt of a State retirement pension (see leaflet SB1). All people of pensionable age have a right, under the Supplementary Benefits Act 1966, to a guaranteed income. This is not an income that allows for any luxuries. It is simply a figure calculated by the government to meet the basic needs of rent, food, clothing, heating and day-to-day expenses, plus, when necessary, payments for what are called 'exceptional needs', such as the renewal of bedding, furniture or household equipment, and payments for 'special expenses', such as extra heating, special diet, or essential domestic help (see leaflet SB1 for details of current scale rates laid down by parliament, and other information).

Although supplementary pensions and allowances ensure that basic needs are met, those who are entirely dependent upon them certainly suffer some degree of hardship compared with the standard of living of the majority of citizens, and strenuous efforts are being made to raise the level of the government's 'guaranteed income'. Those whose entitlement is established, however, will find that not only the first few pounds of some other form of income they have may be disregarded, but the value of a house they own or occupy is not counted as part of their income. Capital of less than £1,250 (and any income it produces) is also ignored when the amount of the supplementary pension or allowance to be granted is worked out by the Department of Health and Social Security.

Many elderly people who are in need fail to apply for a supplementary pension or allowance, because they are inclined to regard it as some kind of charity (a much maligned word) – which of course it is not, and there should be no loss of pride or dignity for those who apply for it. To do so is simple. Leaflet SB1, which is obtainable not only from the Department of Health and Social Security but also from the Post Office, incorporates an application form, and there is also an application form in the back of every State retirement pension book. Applications should be sent to the local office of the Department of Health and Social Security. The form allows applicants to state their choice between going to the local office of the department for interview, or having one of their officers call on them at home. A home interview for this is usually preferable and more convenient for the elderly, as they can feel more comfortable and relaxed in their own surroundings, and there they will be sure to have all the papers connected with their financial affairs to hand.

The purpose of this interview will be to assess the elderly person's financial needs, the income she has from all sources, and her capital (if any), and to establish whether she is entitled to receive a supplementary pension or allowance. Most elderly people find that the visiting officers are friendly, patient, and helpful, and although it is not necessary for a relative to be present, no objection will be raised to this if the elderly person wishes it. She will need to have certain documents available for the officer to see, such as a rent book and details of any savings, but she can be sure that the information she gives will be treated in strict confidence.

She will be notified of the decision on her claim as soon as possible, and if by any chance she is not satisfied with it she has the right of appeal to an independent Appeal Tribunal, by writing to the Social Security Office within twenty-one days of its receipt. If the claim goes through satisfactorily, the supplementary pension or allowance that has been granted can then be drawn weekly at the Post Office.

The Department of Health and Social Security are concerned that all elderly people who are in need should receive the appropriate help to which they are entitled, and the visiting officers are always pleased to explain what other benefits a successful claimant may have automatically, but even if a supplementary pension or allowance is not granted, if their income is below a certain level some of the extra benefits such as free dentures, spectacles, hospital fares, and rate rebates (this last is not usually granted to those on supplementary pensions) may be available to them.

Attendance allowance For full details see leaflet NI205. Attendance allowance is a tax-free cash benefit for people who are severely disabled physically or mentally and who need a lot of care. For those who require attendance both by day *and* night there is a higher rate allowance. For those who require attendance either by day *or* night there is a lower rate allowance. Before the allowance can become payable the requirements must be satisfied for a period of at least six months (this can include periods in hospital).

The medical requirements are: *By day*: frequent attention throughout the day in connection with bodily functions *or* continual supervision throughout the day in order to avoid substantial danger to the disabled person or others. *At night*: prolonged or repeated attention during the night in connection with bodily functions; *or* continual supervision throughout the night in order to avoid substantial danger to the disabled person or others.

The higher rate can be paid if one of the day requirements *and* one of the night requirements are satisfied.

The lower rate can be paid if any one of the requirements is satisfied either by day *or* at night. Claims should be made by completing the claim form at the back of leaflet NI205.

If your parent receives this allowance it can only continue for up to four weeks after admission to a National Health Service hospital (unless he or she is a private patient).

No member of the family has to give up work before the allowance can be claimed and this extra income can sometimes enable a caring daughter to continue in her job if it is used to pay for help at home.

Invalid care allowance For full details see leaflet NI212. Invalid care allowance is for people of working age who cannot work because they are staying at home to care for a severely disabled relative. The benefit counts as taxable income, but it is not meanstesetd and there are no National Insurance contribution conditions. In general, married women cannot qualify for the allowance, but there are some exceptions to this rule, so if in doubt enquire at the Department of Health and Social Security.

The allowance carries with it a Class 1 contribution credit for the recipient's National Insurance record, and if there are serious financial difficulties the recipient may also be entitled to supplementary benefit allowance.

Those who give up their employment to care for a disabled relative may also have their pension rights protected by the Home Responsibilities Protection Regulations which came into effect in April 1978. Claims should be made by completing the claim form at the back of leaflet NI212.

If *you* are admitted to hospital for in-patient treatment, your allowance can continue for up to twelve weeks. If your invalid parent is admitted, however, and payment of the attendance allowance is withdrawn, your invalid care allowance will have to be withdrawn at the same time, and you should immediately notify the Invalid Care Allowance Unit, Department of Health and Social Security, North Fylde Central Offices, Norcross, Blackpool FY5 3TA.

Benefits affected by admission to hospital For full details see leaflet NI9. If your elderly parent is admitted to hospital or an old people's home under the National Health Service, there may be a reduction in, or a withdrawal of, certain State benefits (but this will not apply if she enters a charitable home or has treatment as a private patient). It will be very important for you to study the leaflet mentioned above carefully to discover exactly what your parent's position will be, and if you are in any doubt, ask for an interview with the Medical Social Worker at the hospital or see the Enquiry Clerk at the local Social Security Office.

The Department of Health and Social Security should be notified immediately of your parent's admission to hospital so that the appropriate adjustment to his or her State pension or other State benefits or allowances can be made, but the pension book should be retained. The pension can be drawn in full for the first eight weeks in hospital, after which your parent will be notified that it will be reduced by a few pounds (for the exact amount of the reduction see the current issue of leaflet NI9). The pension book must then be returned to the Department of Health and Social Security, where it will be adjusted and then sent back. After a year in hospital the pension may be reduced still further, but if your parent is treated as having a dependant this will be taken into account. Supplementary benefit or supplementary pension or allowance may be affected immediately on admission or after eight weeks, according to circumstances, and widow's pension and some other State pensions and benefits also after eight weeks. Attendance allowances will be withdrawn after four weeks.

If your parent's pension or benefits are reduced and she is worried because she has rent, mortgages, or other commitments to meet, special allowances can be given in the form of supplementary benefit, and you should discuss this with the hospital's

Medical Social Worker or the Enquiry Clerk at the Department of Health and Social Security. If this help is given it will be for three months in the first instance and the position will be reviewed from time to time after that.

If your parent is allowed home from hospital (or other National Health Service accommodation) for a few days occasionally you should notify the Department of Health and Social Security, as she may be entitled to her pension, benefits or allowances at the full rate for that period.

If your parent is incapabable of acting for herself, discuss this with the hospital Medical Social Worker or the Enquiry Clerk at the Department of Health and Social Security, and arrangements may be made for you or some other relative to be appointed to act on her behalf and to receive payment of the benefit or pension. If no relative or other person is willing to be appointed, the benefit is payable to the hospital authorities to be used for the patient's comfort and enjoyment.

Immediately an expected date of discharge from hospital is known, inform the Department of Health and Social Security so that any pensions, benefits and allowances to which your parent is entitled may be restored to the normal level as soon as possible.

Death of the parent

If your parent dies no further orders should be cashed from the pension book. It should be sent (or preferably taken) as soon as possible, together with the free death certificate (Form BD8) which you will have been given by the Registrar of Births and Deaths, to the local Social Security Office, and as in most cases there is an entitlement to a National Insurance death grant, application can be made for this at the same time. Full details of this and the documents that will be required can be found in leaflet NI49. If at this distressing time, however, you feel unable to study this, simply take the death certificate and the pension book to the Social Security Office and one of their officers will be glad to help and advise you. If your father dies and you are helping your widowed mother with these matters, you can assure her that not only will she not lose her own retirement pension, but that it may be paid at an increased rate after her husband's death. She need not send in her own pension book, but should have it with her if she is able to go with you to the Social Security Office. If this visit is not possible, she should fill in section B *or* C (as well as section A) on the back of the death certificate (Form BD8) issued by the Registrar and send it to her local Social Security Office without delay, and they will send her a claim form; or she may just write to the local office asking for a claim form for widow's benefit.

If your mother dies and your father needs your help, you should see that he returns her pension book together with the free death certificate (Form BD8) to the local Social Security Office and assist him to apply for the death grant. There will, of course, be no change in the amount of his retirement pension.

The value of visiting rather than just corresponding with the Social Security Office when a relative dies cannot be emphasised too strongly, as this enables any problems to be discussed and dealt with speedily.

Occupational pensions

It is very rare for government departments, the armed services, or commercial or industrial undertakings to make errors in calculating the pension of a retiring worker. If, however, your parent thinks that some mistake has been made and cannot sort it out, you can easily contact the pension fund headquarters on his or her behalf and ask for details of how the amount has been arrived at. If you are not satisfied with the reply, the trade union or professional association to which your parent belongs may be able to go into the matter further. Failing this, a local solicitor operating under the Legal Aid Scheme could be asked to advise if your parent's income is low.

Income tax

The Board of Inland Revenue issue a very helpful free booklet entitled *Income Tax and the Elderly*, which can be obtained from any Inland Revenue office. It should also be remembered that the Inland Revenue officers are always willing to give advice, and even to assist an elderly person with the completion of their income-tax return if necessary.

A few of the main points worth bearing in mind when discussing the subject of income tax with your elderly parents are as follows:

TAX POSITION ON THE NATIONAL INSURANCE RETIREMENT PENSION
Tax is not deducted from National Insurance retirement pensions, but they are taken into account when deciding how much tax is to be paid on the elderly person's income as a whole. However, the basic National Insurance retirement pension by itself is not enough to bring her above the point where tax begins to be charged, so if she has no other income apart from this, she will not be asked to pay tax. But she may be liable for some tax, if, in addition to the basic retirement pension, she is getting a graduated pension, or an additional pension for working past retirement age. (A supplementary pension payable under the Supplementary Benefits scheme is not taxable, nor are voluntary payments made to her by you or other relatives, for which you can claim tax-free allowance. See section on 'Other forms of income' later in this chapter.)

TAX PAYABLE ON OCCUPATIONAL PENSIONS
The elderly person's former employer will deduct tax from her occupational pension under Pay As You Earn (as he did from her salary or wages) if her income from pension and other sources is big enough to make her liable for tax.

TAX CODES
If, when your parents begin to draw a National Insurance retirement pension, they go on working, or their former employer is paying them a pension, their code will need to be changed so as to take into account the National Insurance pension. The right code can only be issued to them if the tax inspector knows about their National Insurance pension; so it is very important for your parents to let the Tax Office know in advance if they are going to receive a National Insurance retirement pension. If they delay they may fall into arrears with their tax and later be faced with having to pay tax for past years.

Financial problems of the elderly

TAX PAYABLE BY A WIFE WHO ALSO HAS A PENSION

A wife's pension is liable to tax and, like any other income she has, it is added to her husband's in arriving at their total income. But there may not be any tax to pay on it if the pension comes from a former employer of hers, and if she has a National Insurance retirement pension from her own contributions the special 'wife's earned income allowance' will be due. If she exceptionally draws a pension by virtue of her husband's insurance in place of a smaller one by virtue of her own insurance, the special allowance will be due on the smaller amount.

TAXING AN ANNUITY

If an elderly person buys an annuity out of her own capital, part of it will be treated as a repayment of capital, and so not liable to tax. The remainder will be treated as investment income, which is liable to tax. The amount of the annuity that will be taxable will depend mainly on her age when she buys the annuity. There are rules for deciding how much is taxable, and these should be explained to her by the insurance company with which she is dealing.

HOUSE TAX

Although the elderly do not have to pay income tax on the value of a house which they own and occupy, if they let any part of it, furnished or unfurnished, the income they receive from the letting must be included in their tax return.

SAVINGS INVESTED WITH A LOCAL AUTHORITY

If your parent has savings invested with a local authority, from which tax is deducted at the basic rate, she can only get some of this tax back if the tax, together with any other tax that is paid (e.g. under Pay As Your Earn), comes to more than the proper tax on her total income. Normally if tax is paid under Pay As You Earn, the tax deducted at the basic rate will be correct. If she thinks she has a claim on this account, though, she should get in touch with the Inspector of Taxes.

TAX ON THE INTEREST ON MONEY IN A BUILDING SOCIETY
Building society interest is taxed under a special arrangement, and basic-rate tax does not have to be paid on it, but a tax refund cannot be claimed. The interest is, however, taken into account when determining liability at rates in excess of the basic rate; also when calculating total income for the purposes of the special allowance for the elderly (see below).

The amount of building-society interest actually received is regarded as what is left after tax at the basic rate has been deducted from a larger amount. It is this larger amount that is taken into account for tax purposes.

When filling in the income-tax return, building society interest must be included by entering the amount actually paid or credited.

OTHER FORMS OF INCOME
There are special arrangements for taxing the dividends on shares, war widow's pensions, ordinary deposits in the National Savings Bank, and deposits in the ordinary department of a Trustee Savings Bank, all of which are discussed in detail in the Inland Revenue booklet, *Income Tax and the Elderly*, which needs to be studied carefully for each individual. Some forms of income, however, are not liable to any tax at all. These include: attendance allowances payable by the Department of Health and Social Security, wounds and disability pensions of former members of the forces, and disablement pensions under the National Insurance (Industrial Injuries) Acts. No tax is payable on the interest on National Savings Certificates, nor on the bonuses payable on Save As Your Earn contracts and index-linked Retirement Certificates. Nor are voluntary payments made to the elderly by relatives liable to tax.

SPECIAL ALLOWANCE FOR PERSONS AGED 65 OR OVER
There is a special allowance for people aged 65 or over with modest incomes. This is given in place of the ordinary single or married allowance, and is called 'Age Allowance'. It is designed to help the less well-off, and details of the scheme are covered in depth in the Inland Revenue booklet *Income Tax and the Elderly*.

Financial problems of the elderly

This also gives information and current figures for other types of allowances which elderly people may be able to claim, such as those for the registered blind, allowances for the cost of a resident housekeeper (relative or non-relative), and allowances for elderly people who are maintaining a daughter who has to live with them to care for them because of their age or infirmity.

Rent and rate rebates

Before considering making an application to the local council for a rent or rate rebate, an elderly person who is hard pressed financially should consider first whether her income is so low that she might do better to make an application for a supplementary pension, which brings with it other benefits (previously described). If in doubt, an interview with an officer from the local social security office would help her to make the most advantageous decision. If she is sure that she would not qualify for a supplementary pension and wishes to apply for a rent rebate or allowance, an application form, and the information leaflet *There's Money off your Rent*, can be obtained from the local authority Housing Department. For a rate rebate, an application form may be obtained from the local authority Treasurer's Department, together with the information leaflet *How to Pay Less Rates*.

Assistance with rent and rates for people on a low income is available not only to council tenants, but also to tenants or private landlords, those who live in housing association accommodation and owner occupiers.

The safe investment of capital

If your elderly parent has a family solicitor who knows her and her circumstances well, he will be the best person to give expert advice on the investment of her capital, but if she prefers to rely solely upon your advice you should encourage her to put safety first in this matter, for unless someone is very wealthy, and can afford to lose money occasionally, playing the stock market is a foolish and risky game in later life.

One of the best things she can do is to invest as much as possible, up to the maximum of £500, in the government's index-linked Retirement Certificates, which can be purchased at the Post Office, where information leaflets are available. These protect the purchasing power of savings in a way that no other completely safe investment can do, and they are free of United Kingdom income tax and capital gains tax. This is the best 'bargain offer' pensioners have ever had, and any woman over 60 or man over 65 should take advantage of it if possible.

Other safe forms of investment which could then be considered for any capital your parent may have could also include the building societies, local authority bonds (if she is prepared to leave her money untouched for a year or two), National Savings Certificates, Post Office Savings, the National Savings Bank and Trustee Savings Bank. The most obvious choice for most elderly people of modest means is the index-linked certificates, with the rest of their small capital in a building society, but the decision must be tailored to their requirements.

For some elderly people who have no family or who (quite reasonably) do not feel that they need to hang on to capital to pass on to relatives who are themselves well provided for, the purchase of an annuity can be an advantage. Very careful thought is needed, though, before taking the big step of spending a large sum of money to purchase a regular income, for there can be snags, and it is wise to get quotations from several of the major insurance companies, and the advice of a solicitor, before proceeding. The purchasing of an annuity may certainly be an excellent idea for some elderly people (and the older they are, the better will be the terms offered to them), but independent expert advice should always be sought first.

The management of the finances of the seriously ill

If the occasion arises that your parent is seriously ill and wishes you (or some other relative or close friend) to act for her and have access to some of her money so that you can pay her bills and buy her anything she needs, she can grant what is known as 'Power of Attorney'. This should be done through a solicitor on a form drawn up, signed, registered and stamped. Your sick parent must be mentally fit to make this decision of her own free will, and it does not rob her of the right to make her own decisions as to the spending of her money or her free access to it.

Financial problems of the elderly

She may also cancel the arrangement whenever she wishes.

If, however, your parent is so seriously ill physically or mentally that she is no longer capable of dealing with her own financial affairs at any level, arrangements can be made by her solicitor for these to be dealt with by a government department known as the Court of Protection, and you should discuss this matter with the solicitor.

In everything you do and say connected with helping your elderly parent with her financial problems, your aim should be, as far as possible, to advise tactfully but allow the actual decisions to remain hers.

6
Bringing an elderly parent to live with you

The big decision
When people of different generations decide to live together, because the older of the two is in need of care, they are making one of the major decisions of their lives. To give or receive help, perhaps over a long period, which inevitably involves some self-sacrifice on the one hand and some loss of independence on the other, is a very big step. It should never be taken hastily or immediately a crisis arises in the life of an elderly person, such as bereavement or a sudden illness or depression, for grief usually passes to some extent after a period of supported mourning. A cause and a cure can be found for some of the illnesses of old age, and depression often responds to suitable treatment and sympathetic handling.

If elderly people are persuaded to uproot themselves in a hurry at the first sign of trouble, making major decisions at a time when they are not emotionally stable enough to think them through, like selling their homes and moving away from old friends and familiar surroundings into the different world and routine of a younger household, they sometimes regret it, and much unhappiness ensues for everyone.

It can be equally disastrous for them and for others if they make a permanent arrangement on impulse and encourage a relative or friend to give up their own home and move in with them because they are under stress and feel that they may not be able to continue to live alone.

If your elderly parent is faced with this problem, the most sensible first step towards a solution will be for her to spend a longish 'holiday' in your home before making a final decision, or for you to make an extended 'visit' to her if you are thinking of going to live in her home. This can meet her need temporarily when she is at some crisis point, providing, for all concerned, a trial period of living under the same roof, in this tactful guise of a holiday – without commitment on either side. During this period, both she and you need to consider very carefully all the possible gains and losses of a decision to live together permanently. You have to ask yourselves some searching questions, particularly about the quality of your relationship prior to the present state of emergency. Has it been a happy one that augurs well for the 'marriage' of your two households? Or has it been difficult and full of 'needle' and misunderstanding? Most important of all, are you able to accept each other as equal, mature individuals, or has the parent/child relationship never been outgrown, so that one of you may feel the need to dominate, and the other will begin to lose confidence?

The fact of being 'family' is no guarantee that people can live together happily on a long-term basis, and almost any other good 'care' arrangement that can be made for an elderly person is better than a cat-and-dog life with relatives, where there is no common ground for agreement, and constant quarrels make home life a misery. But if the decision *is* made to share the same house, and it looks like a viable proposition, then planning should begin optimistically and without fuss, having due regard for the needs of all parties.

Living with an elderly parent in their own home

A daughter (or more rarely a son) who has never left the parental home, or who has returned after widowhood or divorce to stay on indefinitely to care for an elderly parent or parents, does not make this choice automatically. Some families take it for granted that the elderly are the natural responsibility of the unattached, but this is not so. The daughter at home has her moment of decision to face too: when she has to make the choice between committing herself, or taking flight, which in these more liberated times is almost always possible. Such is the remarkable sense of loyalty of millions of these women, though, that they usually decide to stay and see it through.

It is always dangerously easy to write superficially about human relationships, particularly this one of the mother and daughter living together in old age, picturing them enjoying endless winter evenings by the fire, with never a cross word, and long summer afternoons in a garden of roses, sitting in deckchairs on a lawn that never needs mowing. But they deserve more honest treatment, and who wants fairy stories? Certainly not the mature women who are caring courageously, and quite alone, for the elderly. They know the truth: that life with an aged parent can be a strange mixture of joy and sorrow, and all they ask is for that fact to be accepted, not glossed over by their family and society, and then to be offered some practical ideas on how to make the best of a good job, which they consider to be well worth doing.

Some of the information in other chapters on nutrition, health, financial problems, and coping with stress may be useful for the daughter at home, but if you are such a daughter there is something else you need too – a healthy determination to protect your own right to a reasonable way of life, while striving to improve that of your parent. There are very few 'angel' daughters or 'monster' mothers around: just millions of women, both young and old, living and giving, to the best of their ability, under the same roof, sometimes beset by problems of herculean proportions which are none of their making. This is not to say that there are not many households where there is peace and contentment, when the old person is fortunate enough to keep well in mind and body even when she becomes frail, and where the daughter prefers to remain at home, and is able to make a satisfying life for herself. But these cases do tend to be the exception rather than the rule, so it is sensible to consider, briefly, some of the negative aspects that can sometimes be a part of the 'caring' situation. To face every possibility, however remote, is the surest way of arriving finally at a position of strength, with the ability to cope, come what may. Any emotional pain, sense of frustration, or loss of freedom cuts both ways in this relationship, as it does in many others. A mother who loves her daughter can experience real anguish on her behalf if she becomes totally dependent upon her, and recognises the limitations this imposes on her social life and activities. And however much she loves her mother, the daughter who has undertaken to care for her in her old age is, in some instances, taking on one of the toughest and loneliest jobs on earth. If, at first, she is able to continue with her career, she is in some respects in the same position as the working wife and mother, who has the strain of two heavy areas of responsibility: her home and her job, but with several important differences. She is not operating within a hopeful situation of growth and development, in which she will see the fruits of her work in terms of certain ambitions fulfilled for herself and her family, with the love and companionship of a husband to support her. For her, apart from the rewards of her job (which she may plan to give up anyway when her parent becomes more dependent), her life is centred on a household where she knows she may have to deal with a slow decline in the health and strength of her relative, with all that implies for both of them in the future.

When she arrives home in the evening, she knows she will have no stimulating exchange of news to look forward to with a husband and family. Unless she is very lucky, she will be the one who will be expected to provide the stimulation, for her elderly parent may have been alone since breakfast-time, and will be waiting to be 'cheered up' by stories of all she has been doing during the day. Only they will probably both know that these must not include anything too worrying or controversial, which could create the type of tension and anxiety that can so easily build up in the elderly, particularly in the many who suffer from circulatory troubles, or who have a naturally anxious personality which has become even more vulnerable with age. So there is none of the relief of a true unburdening, and the discussion of problems that characterises the homecoming of someone to a companion who is close in age as well as relationship. Even where deep affection remains unaltered, the gap between them often becomes a chasm as years go by. So she learns to give all her stories happy endings and take her troubles to bed with her – after she has cooked, cleaned, washed and ironed and prepared for another day.

This is the way life is for thousands of working women living with elderly relatives, running a home that the parent is no longer able to manage, as well as giving her care and emotional support, and often feeling too exhausted to be able to organise any reasonable social lives for themselves. They hold down their jobs somehow for a certain length of time, if they have good family back-up, kindly neighbours to 'pop in', and various types of help from voluntary and statutory social services in their locality. But when their parent can no longer be left alone and they decide, as many of them do, to leave work in order to care for her full time, their major problems begin. Some will be connected with the parent's needs, but others will be personal to them; psychological, social and financial.

A daughter who has given up her career will undoubtedly feel the loss of her previous role in the working world. She will no longer be Miss, Mrs or Ms Jones, secretary, teacher, nurse, or producer or seller of merchandise. She will have become one of that great army of 'daughters at home' who have to fight hard to establish an identity for themselves other than that of 'head cook and bottle washer'. Her new role may, in fact, call for a much wider range of skills, both mental and physical, than did her previous one; but however well she develops them, they will go largely unnoticed by society. The work she does will be taken for granted by nearly everyone, except the relative she is caring for, and there will be no prospect of promotion either, unless it be from housekeeper to nurse.

She may look back with longing to the coffee-breaks and lunch hours she used to share with colleagues at work, which may seem in retrospect to have been so full of interest – and best of all, laughter, forgetting any strains that existed in her job. She will try to accept the fact, as she takes her mother's 'elevenses' in to her, that any attempt she may make to start a discussion of something that might not be of immediate interest to her mother may be turned off suddenly like a switch, and will plunge her temporarily into an emotional darkness in which she will feel very much alone. She may understand that this habit is one that develops in many otherwise unselfish old people when their powers of concentration begin to weaken slightly, just as a child tosses an unwanted toy out of its pram, and that no hurt is intended. But it *will* hurt, and each time it happens, it will feel like a shock, and a sad renewal of the realisation that a loved companion is beginning to drift away from her, and that there is nothing either of them can do about it.

People will say, kindly, 'What a good thing you have each other' – assuming that the single, widowed or divorced daughter would be very lonely on her own; and of course, if it is a loving relationship, these words will find a genuine echo in her mind. She will dread the thought of that final parting, which must come in time. But she will probably already be experiencing more loneliness than they imagine, for much as she may enjoy her parent's company, she will also have a need for other friendships and contacts with the world outside the home, and these may be very difficult for her to achieve.

Whenever she wants to go out, she may have to arrange for someone to come and 'sit in' if her parent cannot be left alone; and suitable 'mother-sitters' are always much harder to find than 'baby-sitters'.

If you have embarked on this decision, entertaining friends at home may became increasingly difficult too, for your parent may look forward always to being present on these occasions, without realising for one moment that her daughter needs the opportunity sometimes to be able to relate to her friends alone, so that she can project her personality freely and share confidences and opinions with people of her own generation.

In some cases another problem can arise. Elderly parents may begin to feel tense and unsure of their previous social skills and ability to sustain long conversations with visitors, or may tire very quickly, which may lead them to start placing obstacles of one kind and another to people coming to the house at all. The fact that any extra emotional effort makes them anxious and exhausted is often too painful to admit, even to themselves, and their pride prevents them from beating a perfectly acceptable retreat to their own room for 'a rest' when visitors are expected. Consequently the daughter is left to pick up the pieces of the havoc caused by the strain of raised blood-pressure and general anxiety the next day.

A gradual reversal of the parent/child roles may have to be adjusted to, as the elderly parent moves further on into old age and becomes more dependent in every way, and sometimes the inner fears and insecurities of an old person express themselves in jealousy, possessiveness and resentment of the daughter's contacts with other family members or friends, which can create many embarrassing situations, and the need for small deceptions to keep the peace.

Many daughters who are caring full-time for a parent or parents at home have financial worries too. Loss of earnings and career prospects can be a serious matter for someone who knows that she is going to have to support herself for many years after her parents have gone; and unless the home in which they are living is owned by them, and left to her in their will, she is also going to have to provide accommodation for herself when they die.

This rather gloomy picture of the troubles of the daughter at home obviously does not apply in every case. There are many parents who remain in good health both mentally and physically to the day of their death, even if their physical strength is reduced, and it becomes no longer desirable for them to live alone; and there are many daughters who share their homes in an atmosphere of personal freedom, happiness and fulfilment, enjoying their companionship right to the end. They can look back on the last years they spent together as some of the best in their whole lives. But the fact has to be faced that these are a minority, for the trials of old age can have a crippling effect on some relationships, and it is the various problems of the majority that we are examining here.

So how can you as a daughter find a way through the maze of difficulties that confronts you when you undertake the care of an elderly parent? What practical steps can you take to ensure that you can carry out the task you have undertaken with advantage to your parent and without damage to yourself? And what kind of attitudes can you learn to adopt that are likely to make this possible?

A good starting-point would be for you to get in touch with The National Council for the Single Woman and her Dependants, 29, Chilworth Mews, London W2 3RG, by writing (with a stamped addressed envelope enclosed) for one of their information leaflets. There are just over 300,000 single women in Britain living with elderly parents, and this organisation, which has branches in many parts of the country, can be extremely helpful to them. It can give moral support and advice on numerous problems connected with your and your parent's rights to various types of State benefits and services, the support that may be available to you from voluntary bodies, and help in planning ahead for accommodation if this proves necessary when your parent dies. They will also be able to supply you with a list of suitable short-term homes for the elderly in your area, to which your parent might consider going for a few weeks each year in order that you may have a holiday, if there is no other member of the family who could take over your responsibilities in your absence.

The way you manage to cope with all the problems that life with an elderly parent may present will depend not only upon their magnitude, or the help you receive from others, but also on your attitude towards them, and your determination to live life just a day at a time, thus breaking your stress up into smaller and more manageable 'sections'.

The most valuable resolve anyone who has decided to care for an elderly relative can make is to give her all the love and loyalty you can but without becoming a martyr in the process, for martyrdom in such circumstances often breeds repressed resentment, which eventually boils over into words and actions that are later bitterly regretted.

You have to be determined to pay attention to your own needs as well as those of your parent. If you don't, your emotional strength will gradually be sapped, to the point when you will no longer be able to give her the support she requires, and the whole arrangement may collapse around you. Sometimes this means taking a very definite stand on certain issues, but it has to be done for both your sakes. It helps if you can bring yourself to take a very positive line of thinking about each problem as it comes along, being as practical and objective as possible, for sometimes the limitations of home life with an old and possibly infirm parent may seem to close round you like a prison. If this happens, you can respond in one of three ways. You can become resigned to the monotony of captivity and give up the struggle to maintain your own interests and identity. You can revolt against it by a breakdown in health or morale, going what the Americans call 'stir-crazy'; or you can accept it calmly, as just a temporary 'pause' in your normal way of life from which you intend to extract some good for yourself and others, keeping active, keeping your eyes on the world beyond the bars, and planning and preparing yourself for your ultimate return to it. Like all prisoners of circumstance, you will probably reflect a good deal on the whole subject of 'time' and of its strange habits of hanging, dragging, or running out too quickly, but if you decide to use and dominate it, instead of allowing it to dominate you, you will inevitably come to the conclusion that it is only wasted if it is thrown away, never when it is offered freely, as a gift of love.

In considering ways of keeping emotionally fit enough to continue to give your parent the care she needs, try to maintain and, if necessary, improve the quality of your own life. To this end it can be quite a good idea to sit down and make a list of all the social activities you would like to enjoy if you were free to do so – such as visiting and entertaining friends, going to the theatre, cinema, concerts, evening classes, study groups, church activities and special interest clubs, as well as the occasional holiday. Then decide what positive action you could take to achieve at least some of these goals, without neglecting home responsibilities.

If visiting or entertaining friends is difficult, this is the first and most important problem to be tackled, because maintaining (or restoring) this particular activity will do more than almost anything else to keep life in balance. It may mean some gentle but very straight talking, if your parent does not realise your need to have time alone with your friends, but if you cannot bring yourself to establish this right, you will have precious little hope of organising any other social activities that will give you a break from daily routine.

If the bedroom you occupy is large enough to be turned into a comfortable bed-sitting-room, or if you have your own private sitting-room in the house, you can avoid trouble and confrontation by entertaining friends there, and that will be the end of it; but if not, after a tactful explanation of your needs to your parent, you should get to the point of suggesting clearly that she might agree to retire to her room for a few hours sometimes when your friends come to the home (after you have all shared a meal together first, if she wishes). You should also have set an example for this beforehand, by sometimes making yourself scarce when your parent's friends come, without being in any way unsociable or unwilling to prepare food and drink for them.

You may have to face up to a display of feelings of hurt or rejection; but if your parent is a naturally unselfish person (and not mentally impaired) who had simply failed to realise your need for this degree of privacy and emotional 'living-space', she will probably be only too anxious to co-operate. If not, you may have to steel yourself to deal with surprise and indignation from her. If that is the case, and she becomes upset, you could be very tempted to drop the whole issue, feeling that it is just 'not worth the candle'. But this is one candle you cannot possibly afford to extinguish in your life, for without it you may lose much of the valuable to-and-fro of friendship, which can protect you from isolation, and act as a safety-valve when you are under strain.

Your parent's agreement should be obtained too, if possible, for arrangements to be made for someone suitable to come and spend a day or evening with her regularly so that you can go out. Once this has been settled and accepted, the next question is – how do you find such people? Obviously if you have family living near enough, they would be the first to turn to for help of this kind. Failing this, a fit elderly neighbour may be willing to come, either voluntarily or for a small payment, which would be useful to them if they are living on a small pension. If they would be offended by an offer of money, the occasional (money-saving) gift to them might be very welcome. Younger neighbours may be glad to 'sit in' for one evening a week too, if you can give them some service in return, such as looking after their child for a morning while they go shopping, although of course there are people who will help with no expectation of reward, if you make your need known to them – perhaps more of them than you imagine.

Volunteers can also be contacted sometimes through the local authority social services department, and the local branches of the Women's Royal Voluntary Services, the National Council of

Social Services, Age Concern (Old People's Welfare) and the National Council for the Single Woman and her Dependants, whose addresses can all be found in the telephone directory or at the public library. When someone has been found, if they are strangers, it is sensible to invite them first to drop in for a cup of tea, to make sure that they can establish a good rapport with your parent, and that the two will get along well together.

A break from the cares of caring is essential sometimes, if you are to keep going year in and year out. At least two holidays a year, of a fortnight each should be planned if possible, when you can get away on your own, or with friends. You will find little pleasure and relaxation in it, though, unless you are sure that your parent is happy and in safe hands. The ideal solution is for her to go to stay with other members of the family to be cared for in their home, or for a relative to come to take over in your absence. If this is not possible, your parent might be willing to consider going for a temporary period into one of the short-term homes for the elderly known to the National Council for the Single Woman and her Dependants, or into a home for the elderly run by the social services department of the local authority, while you are away. If she needs nursing care, arrangements can sometimes be made for her to be admitted for a few weeks to the local hospital on medical recommendation. Private nursing homes are another possibility, but these should be ones that are known to your general practitioner as being reliable, and fees are usually fairly high. A living-in housekeeper or nurse can also be arranged in some circumstances, and lists of suitable agencies can be obtained from the Elderly Invalid's Fund (Old People's Information Service), 10 Fleet Street, London EC4Y 1BB. But here again the cost may be considerable.

Financial problems can become an added burden and anxiety to the daughter at home. If you have worries of this kind a visit to the local office of the Department of Health and Social Security, plus an interview with a social worker at the local authority social services department, is a very wise move. In these two offices all your rights, and those of your elderly parent, to State benefits, pensions and special concessions and allowances can be explained, as well as ways in which you may apply for grants and other forms of help in some circumstances from various voluntary organisations. Although the range of benefits to which the elderly and those caring for them are entitled is still inadequate to meet every need, it is wider than some realise. Many people are not aware of the existence of some of them or of their own eligibility to make a claim, so are not taking them up; and you may find that you are one of them. Sparing the time to make these two visits may show ways of substantially increasing the household income, and reducing its outgoings on rent, rates, prescription charges and many other expenses for which you may not have realised there is help available.

Financial problems are examined more fully in Chapter 5 but as each individual case is different the visits suggested above should be carefully considered.

If there are likely to be difficulties about accommodation for yourself as the daughter at home, after your parent's death, contact should be made well before this event is imminent with the Housing Manager of the local council for advice, and you might write also to the Housing Corporation Head Office, Maple House, 149 Tottenham Court Road, London W1P 0BN, who will send a free directory of registered Housing Associations and other housing schemes in the area of your choice, so that you can begin forward planning. The enclosure of a large stamped addressed envelope will of course be appreciated by any of the organisations you may wish to write to for information, booklets or advice on your own problems or those of your parent.

Anyone who is carrying someone she loves, who can no longer walk unaided through the minefields of old age, knows that there are times when she comes close to losing her nerve – and times when it shows. When you are feeling particularly tired, you may occasionally become very irritated and verbalise your frustration, but if you care enough to want to keep going, the one you are supporting will know it, and forgive you, as you must forgive yourself.

Inviting the elderly to live with you
If inviting an elderly parent to come to live with you in your own home seems to be the best way of helping her in her last

years, the first overtures you make to her on this subject need to be very tactful, bearing all the hallmarks of a really welcoming invitation. The right approach might possibly be along the lines of: 'How about the family closing ranks and getting together now that you need a little help?' or 'Give us the pleasure of doing something for *you* for a change.' These are warm and positive. The wrong approach would be something like: 'Obviously you can't look after yourself any longer. You'd better let us look after you now,' or 'We've talked it over, and we've decided to offer you a home with us.' This is cold, negative and grudging, but unfortunately not altogether uncommon. It treats the elderly relative like a stray domestic animal, to be 'looked after' rather than 'cared for', and 'offered a home' rather than a share in the life of the family, as someone who has something important to contribute.

MAKING PLANS

If an elderly parent is giving up her home to move into yours it can be a very traumatic experience for her, even though you are 'family' and she wants to be with you. So each step has to be planned patiently with her, so that this big change in her life can take place as smoothly as possible.

She may have a house to sell, or a tenancy to terminate, and she should be made aware of your willingness to help her with this, if she wishes, and with everything else connected with the move. There will be many things for her to think about and remember, at a time when she may be feeling quite disturbed emotionally, and you can do much to ease the strain of it all for her. Arrangements will have to be made with a suitable removal firm if she is going to bring some of her furniture with her, and she may need help in finding the best dealers or auctioneers to take the items she wants to dispose of. Then there will be many people and organisations she will need to notify of her date of removal and her new address, such as the Gas and Electricity Boards; the Department of Health and Social Security, for the transfer of the drawing of her pension to the post office near your home; the local rates office, income tax office, and television rental office; the bank manager, and building society or other

Bringing an elderly parent to live with you

places where she may have invested her savings; her insurance agent, the headquarters of any pension fund to which she may belong, the telephone manager, and the post office for the redirection of her letters (for which a form has to be completed and a fee paid). Her milk and newspapers will have to be cancelled as will any services she is receiving, such as home help, meals-on-wheels, or visits from social workers or home nurses. You may also need to help her to transfer to the list of your own general practitioner, if she and he are both agreeable to this; and of course she must be assured that you, or some other member of the family will be with her on the actual day of the move or, if she wishes, take the responsibility of it off her shoulders completely.

You should both know exactly where you stand on all the major issues of planning, right from the start, so that mutually acceptable decisions can be made well ahead of time. What type of accommodation will you be able to offer her? Is it to be the often ideal arrangement of a 'granny-flat' extension to your house, in which she will have her own bed-sitter with kitchen, bathroom and lavatory? If so, this may take some time and finance to organise, and planning permission may have to be obtained from the local authority. Or is it to be a bed-sitting room, or just her own bedroom? Will she need to have any adaptations made if she is infirm, or special aids installed? If so, all this should be done before she moves in, and her room or rooms redecorated in colours of her own choice if possible.

If, as is the case in most households, only one room can be spared for her, it will be greatly to everyone's advantage if it is big enough to take her bed, wardrobe and dressing-table, and other necessary items of furniture plus two comfortable armchairs and a television set and radio, so that she can be on her own when she likes, with her favourite programmes (which may not always be yours) and able to entertain a friend in the privacy of her own small domain when she wants to, with familiar things around her which help her to preserve her identity and links with the past. Some people who have an elderly parent to live with them are heard to say, 'We're very fond of her of course, but the trouble with Mother is that she's always there!' Yet they may have made no effort to give her anywhere she can go to, having allocated a large bedroom to one of their small children and relegated her to the tiniest bedroom in the house, to which she can never withdraw unless she actually gets into bed. So everyone is unhappy and, what is worse still, the children are being brought up to believe that the old should always be given second best and be prepared to shrink into the smallest 'shell' that is offered to them.

Broad agreement has to be reached, too, on how she will be able to fit in happily with your particular routine of family life, and this can only be decided after very frank discussion of her needs and yours. This is no time for pretending that all will automatically be sweetness and light, just because you have a deep affection for each other. Living under the same roof permanently will need working at, and sacrifices will have to be made on both sides if it is to succeed. The likeliest battleground will be the kitchen. If she is very advanced in years and no longer interested in cooking, she may well be happy to stay out of it completely, apart from making the odd cup of tea or coffee, and be pleased to have her meals prepared for her. If so, there is no problem. But if she wants to get her own food, or offers her help to you with the family cooking, all this will have to be sorted out very carefully. It would be heartless to deny her the pleasure of feeling that she is making a useful contribution to the preparation of meals, but it would be equally unkind not to make it clear to her from the beginning just who will be in charge and wearing the chef's hat! Usually a compromise can be reached when there is good will and honesty on both sides. Sometimes very small things can help to preserve an elderly person's feeling of value and self-esteem, like encouraging her to make some special dish or cake (for which she has long been praised in the family circle) once a week, or on birthdays. In some families, of course, where the mother is working all day outside the home, a willing and efficient granny in the kitchen, who loves cooking, can be a real advantage, and then you have to be very careful not to exploit her good nature and allow her to work too hard – which she may tend to do.

For some families breakfast can be a time when they are on a very short fuse and tensions abound, so if you can persuade her to have hers on a tray in bed, many problems may be avoided. Again, in the evening, times of meals and who is to share them should be decided before she moves in. The need for a husband and wife to have some part of the evening alone should be discussed openly and accepted as being important, for this is another 'danger' period when tensions can build up between in-laws. The company of some elderly relatives can only be enjoyed for a limited period at the end of a busy day, and long evenings – every evening – spent together can be a strain on all concerned in different ways. One woman whose mother was coming to live with her and her husband solved her problem by saying quite firmly beforehand, 'Now Tom and I like to eat supper alone and have a couple of hours' quiet talk together in the evening before we settle down to watch television, Mother. I'm sure you and Father probably felt just the same, so you'll understand, won't you?' – blunt perhaps, but honest. Fortunately 'Mother' did understand. She had her own meal early, around six, then watched some television on the set she had in her room, and came down later for a chat with the family when everyone was feeling relaxed.

Things do not always work out as simply as that, of course, but knowing the rules and drawing clear lines before the game starts are essential if misunderstandings are to be avoided.

The question of annual holidays will also have to be raised. Will she be going away with you? Or will she stay with relatives or friends, or take a holiday away with them? If none of these ideas is possible, would she be willing to spend a few weeks each year in a home for the elderly or, if she is infirm, in a nursing home or a local National Health Service hospital? Many elderly people do this each year if it is not suitable for them to go away with their family, and they understand the need those who are caring for them have for a complete break. Often their own need for a change is equally strong too, and if the arrangement is made through a social worker from the local authority social services department in whom they have confidence, they go with no fear of not being allowed to return when the holiday period is over.

Financial arrangements have to be discussed as well, and the matter of her contribution to the household expenses has to be agreed upon, making sure that she is left with enough money each month for her clothing, personal expenses and pocket money. It should also be remembered that anyone, married or single, who is maintaining or accommodating a dependent relative over 65 (or a mother or mother-in-law on her own) is entitled to claim a tax allowance.

Settling in
The departure from her old home and her arrival in her new one will be a tremendous double adjustment for her to make, so you should try to give it a sense of occasion. You will also need to realise that she will be particularly sensitive and watchful at this point for any signs of rejection by her in-laws, whose home she may feel she is 'invading'. If you have children, it will be sensible to tell them how lucky they are to have Granny coming to live with them, and they should be encouraged to give her a warm welcome. Small gestures will help too, like flowers in her room and a special, but quiet celebration meal on the day of her arrival, with the whole family present.

It will be a time for you to use all the imagination of which you are capable, to try to think how you would be feeling if you were in her shoes, and to handle her fragile emotions very gently. According to her personality type, she can be expected to react on this first day with anything from brave smiles to tension and tears, but this will be quite normal.

You must not worry too much if she seems a bit depressed during the first few months, instead of being a 'sweet and grateful granny'. You have to accept the fact that she will not be feeling she has too much to be grateful about, when she ruminates on the loss of her home and some of her previous complete independence. She will need time to grieve inwardly a little over these losses and gradually come to terms with them in her own way, so you should not assume that any moods of depression or irritability she has in those early months are a reflection on the efforts you are making to help her to feel 'at home'. Unless there is some other underlying reason or hidden illness it will pass in time, as she adjusts to the change.

In the meantime, you should quietly do all you can to help her to feel a part of the life of your local community. She should be introduced with an air of pride and affection to your friends and neighbours if she does not know them already, accompanied to all the places locally which will be of special interest to her in the future: the public library, the shopping centre, the best places to go for morning coffee, and any small parks where she might like to walk or sit in the fine weather. If she is a regular churchgoer her previous vicar, minister, priest or rabbi will probably have put her in touch with a place of worship near to your home, and whether you are churchgoers or not you should make every effort to enable her to remain active in church life and enjoy all the organisations connected with it, in which she will make friends. Tasteless ridicule of her religion should be absolutely forbidden in the family circle; not only has she a right to her own beliefs, but an attack on them would be an attack on something that gives her strength and comfort and, best of all, hope as she nears the end of her life.

You should make it clear that she is welcome to entertain any of her friends at home at reasonable times, and help her to cater for this if necessary. She should also be encouraged to have as many outside interests as possible.

If she is fond of animals, providing her with a cat or a small dog of her own, if she can look after it (and if your household as a whole would find its presence acceptable), may make a tremendous difference to her life. It will give her something of her own to love and care for which will return her love, and help to reduce any feelings she may have of being 'odd man out' in the home.

You should be prepared for the fact that some of her views and opinions will be rather different from your own, remembering that they were formed in an entirely different social climate. If you find it difficult to understand some of the feelings she expresses, you have to realise that she has reached a stage in life's journey of which, as yet, you know nothing at all, and until you stand where she is standing now you are in no position to pass any judgement on her attitudes.

A classic example of this is the need some elderly people have to talk about death – often their own death in particular, even to the point of wanting to discuss very freely the kind of arrangements they would like to be made for their funeral: how it should be conducted, what hymns should be chosen, and who should be invited to it and to the family gathering afterwards. Sometimes younger people consider this to be nothing more than morbid indulgence, and refuse to listen, mainly because it is a subject they do not care to think about. They fail to appreciate that all elderly people are constantly aware that they are approaching the last great event in their lives: their own death. And just as those who are young feel the need to talk about and prepare for earlier important events, such as their wedding, or their children's christenings, it is quite normal and not at all macabre for some old people to want to look ahead and plan for the ritual and display of family love and unity that will take place on the day of their departure from this world.

Life with mother (or mother-in-law)

If we apply the yardstick of affection and respect to all our dealings with the elderly and they feel this in everything we say to them, most of the small problems which are bound to arise when we are living together stand a reasonable chance of solution. Provided they are not mentally impaired, and we are able to exercise tact, the truth, spoken in love, will always achieve more than saying nothing in order to 'keep the peace', and harbouring resentments which fester in the mind and inevitably make us bad-tempered towards them for reasons they do not understand. Even if, in the end, we have to agree to differ on some matters, grievances should be discussed, not camouflaged.

If the elderly relative is your own mother, frank discussion of problems is usually (but not always) easier than it is with an in-law. Even if tempers do get frayed occasionally and harsh words are exchanged, if there is love and close kinship 'making up' is not difficult when you have both cooled down, and the memory of such little 'spats' is quickly erased. On the other hand, your patterns of behaviour and response to one another will have deep roots reaching right back into your childhood, and you may both have to work very hard now at becoming adult 'friends', respecting each other's status and individuality. She may find it difficult not to regard you still as the child who would do her bidding without question; and you have to learn to see her, not just as your mother, but as a 'person' too, with good and bad traits in her chacter just like everyone else – not expecting silver-haired sainthood from her simply because she gave birth to you. If you can get this right, the maturing of your relationship will be an interesting voyage of discovery.

If she has any problems in her relationship with the man you married, she should feel able to talk about these privately with you, knowing that because you love them both you are prepared to accept her negative feelings, and to try to help her to understand his personality and attitudes better, in the light of your knowledge of him, his family, his upbringing, and the events that have shaped his life.

If it is your mother-in-law who has come to live with you, even greater efforts will usually be required on both sides if there is to be peaceful co-existence, for this is always a challenging relationship (there are not too many Ruths and Naomis around). But some in-laws do manage to get along remarkably well together, even when they have to spend a great deal of time in each other's company. When this happens, sometimes it is because they are fortunate enough to have similar interests and standards of behaviour, plus warm, easy-going personalities, with a good tolerance of other people's ways and opinions. Occasionally it can be achieved by two very different people who may not see eye to eye on a lot of things, but who are determined to try to respect and understand each other for the sake of the man they both love.

If you are the daughter-in-law in this situation, you need to accept the fact that most of the problems that arise have their roots in hidden jealousy (including your own). Since jealousy has its roots in emotional insecurity it is these feelings, so often experienced but not recognised, that you must try to treat with sympathy and imagination; remembering that you, one day, may feel just as your mother-in-law does. As 'number-one woman' in your husband's life you are in a strong position, and can afford to be very generous to her, especially in the all important matter of making sure that she is often able to spend time quite alone with her son. Many mothers of sons never see them to talk to on their own from the day they marry, because their daughters-in-law always expect to be present on every conceivable occasion, and this is something that can build up a very understandable resentment. They never have the opportunity, with their son, to learn to make the transition to the valuable relationship of 'adult friends' and explore each other's personalities in maturity, as they can so easily do with their married daughters. So it is up to you to see that this does not happen, by creating circumstances in which they can continue to develop their relationship – which his mother has every right to expect to be an on-going one, even in her old age. Too many women have been brain-washed for centuriesin to accepting the old saying: 'A son's a son till he gets him a wife, but a daughter's a daughter all her life.' If you consider yourself to be in any way progressive, and really want to play your part in demolishing the old legend of natural antagonism between mother-in-law and daughter-in-law, replacing it with the hope of friendship, then this is your chance.

Unless you have married a man who is unusually attached to his mother (which is another matter altogether), it will be unlikely to occur to your husband that he needs to do anything more to make his mother happy than to be a kind and dutiful son, who has given her sanctuary in his own home in her later years; but if he is a man of feeling, it will not be difficult to persuade him of her need for his company: her need to be taken out for a run in the car with him alone sometimes, to be kissed when he kisses you when he gets home in the evening, and occasionally to be brought a bunch of flowers instead of you. All are such small things, but they can be surprisingly effective in stopping the rot of jealousy from setting in and spoiling family life, and can make her much more contented and secure.

If, on the other hand you are married to a man who, on the surface at least, appears to be more attentive to his mother's needs than to yours, try not to become upset and regard her as a threat or a rival, and avoid jumping to the conclusion that your marriage is a failure and that you are unloved. Look for the reasons for his behaviour. There can be a great variety of these;

one of the most common is the death, absence, or emotional withdrawal of his father during the formative years of his childhood, which made him draw closer to his mother than he would otherwise have done. Bide your time. It may be that one strand of his personality has not yet matured, and even if it never does, that does not mean that he does not love you. Ride along with it as philosophically as you can, and try not to take your own hurt feelings or sense of irritation out on your mother-in-law, as this will only lead to unhappiness for you all.

You cannot expect her to agree wholeheartedly with everything connected with the way you run your home and raise your family, but you must not tolerate any interference in matters that are your concern – just as you must resist the temptation to try to tell her how she should run any part of her life. If she is wise, she will soon get the message, and think to herself 'Oh well, so long as they're happy, that's all that matters' – an attitude that has been the saving grace of many mother-in-law/daughter-in-law relationships.

If you are unlucky enough to find yourself living with someone who seems to you to be an 'impossible' mother-in-law, it does no harm first to take a good look at yourself and your handling of her, just in case you happen to be one of the original 'impossible' daughters-in-law! You may realise that neither of these labels could apply, and that there are just some bad faults on both sides that need putting right, through frank discussion, backed by a genuine desire to make the relationship work. You should never attempt to dominate her simply because she is living in your home, for when you invited her to come to live with you it became her home too – the only home she has now, and she must be allowed to remain her own woman. On the other hand, if she is someone who has been used to dominating those around her, you should quietly refuse to be included in her 'managing' tactics. Realising that it is far too late in her life to expect her to do more than make an effort to modify this trait in her character, you should see if you can direct it away from the home. This can sometimes be done very successfully by helping her to channel her energy and abilities into some local club or voluntary service organisation where her talent for management can be put to good use, as well as meeting her own need to be a little bit of a 'bossy-boots'. For what may be 'bossiness' in the home can turn out to be a valuable contribution of efficiency and 'drive' in a different setting, working with a team of strangers, where the usual social restraints keep it under reasonable control.

All in all, you will find that your chances of happiness together under the same roof will depend very largely upon your ability to respect and accept her individuality, to see that she gets her share of family affection, to make it possible for her to keep usefully occupied (within her limitations) in the home, and to engage as far as she can in all the outside interests she has always enjoyed.

When it comes to the mother-in-law/son-in-law relationship, this is often a little less complicated, in spite of all those mother-in-law jokes that depict it as a continuous battle between a slightly hen-pecked, but still spirited little man, and his wife's fierce, ugly, overweight mother. The truth is that most women want to be fond and proud of their son-in-law, and most of them are. They naturally find it much easier to take to an in-law of the opposite sex. If he treats her from the beginning like a woman, elderly perhaps, but still entitled to every courtesy and consideration and some of his undivided attention, and if she treats him with affection and interest, voicing her pride in his achievements, and turning to him for advice on various matters, their relationship is usually off to a good start. If we feel that someone has a high opinion of us we tend to want to live up to it, but few of us bother to make much effort with anyone we know who gives us a low rating, and this is very much the case between mothers-in-law and sons-in-law.

When there is failure to establish this good relationship there can be many reasons for it, which the wife, who loves them both, and is the best person to act as intermediary, should try to understand. In some cases, a mother-in-law may openly draw unfavourable comparisons between her son-in-law and her husband (who may be deceased and perhaps over-idealised in her memory). She expects her son-in-law to be just the same kind of husband and father, with all the same values and priorities, and finds it difficult to accept him as a man with a different set of strengths and weaknesses, however happy he makes her daughter, and this may need to be pointed out to her.

Sometimes problems arise from the fact that his relationship with his own mother has been unsatisfactory, and he is faced with the hard task of learning from scratch how to relate successfully to a woman of the older generation who has joined his household. She exacerbates all his old anxieties and feelings of ambivalence towards 'mothers', and because he cannot cope, he defends himself by ignoring her as far as possible. She, in her turn, interprets this as some kind of hatred of her. She begins to feel like an unwanted post-menopausal monster in his home. His apparent rejection of her seems like the rejection of all mankind. It cuts the ground from under her, and depresses her, at a time when she is fully aware that she is no longer sexually desirable, but is trying to build a new and satisfying image as an elegant, wise, elderly woman who is still interesting as a person.

These, and many other problems, have to be worked through patiently with the help of the wife, and fortunately they can often be resolved successfully. This is a relationship that always carries more seeds of hope in it than many others that break down (or never get started on the right foot). Sometimes a family crisis such as the wife's admission to hospital for an operation, or confinement, when mother-in-law comes to the rescue and willingly takes over the housekeeping, will draw them together, and help them to value each other as people for the first time; but more often it is a gradual process, the slow demolition of long-held prejudices.

An elderly person's relationship with his or her grandchildren can be one of the most rewarding experiences of their lives, and the old and the young usually find that they can share a rather special private world together. When Granny (or Grandpa) comes to live with the family in old age, it will be to everyone's advantage to encourage the close bond between them and the children, since it always contributes much to their enjoyment of life, and consequently to the happiness of the whole household.

For grandparents, a grandchild is a continuing dividend from their original investment of love, as well as a stake in the future: a part of them that will be living on, long after they are gone. They know the grandchildren will grow up with a mixture of character traits collected from way back, on both sides of the family, but they like to think that something of theirs, some good trait or talent, will be packed somewhere in their grandchildren's psychological 'baggage' when they set out on their journey into adult life.

Living with grandchildren gives them something to look forward to, as well as things to look back upon. Through them, they can re-live so much of the enchantment of their own and their children's childhood: the magic of Christmas, the first visit to a pantomime, birthday parties, the triumph of returning from country walks with bundles of limp bluebells, the discovery of all the pleasures of sea and sand, story books, make-believe, and a whole world of dreams. Children are like a fresh breeze in the stale corridors of old age, and the elderly have a great deal to give them too: a tender and strengthening relationship, the memory of which they will cherish all their lives. So we should never begrudge them any time spent together.

Some parents worry that their children will become spoiled if they have a rather indulgent granny or grandpa living with them (sometimes because they secretly, and often unfairly, blame their parents for the faults in their own personalities), but in fact very little damage is ever done in this way. Children are not harmed in the long term by too much loving. They soon learn to adapt to the realities of life as they grow older. They are far more likely to be adversely affected by having too little love and affection shown to them, and by being exposed to harsh discipline and examples of selfish behaviour in the adults around them. Most of us, looking back, can remember our own grandparents spoiling us a bit – to the consternation of our parents – but we seem to have survived it pretty well, and so will our children, provided their grandparents understand that they must give loyal support to the standards we have set for their upbringing and not attempt to interfere with our authority as parents. This is a situation in which one can afford to be quite flexible, though, and turn a blind eye occasionally, with no fear of any dire consequences in our children's development – realising how difficult it is for an old person *not* to spoil someone who loves them, wrinkles and all, and thinks they are the greatest thing since ice-cream!

As the children grow into adolescence, it can be irritating and even a bit hurtful to find that they may sometimes want to turn to their grandparent with their troubles or confidences rather than to us, but this is a perfectly normal part of growing up in some young people. They want someone to listen – just listen so that they can try to sort out their problem by stating it. They are not interested in either advice or criticism at that stage, which they know that we may be tempted, for their own good, to offer them. Anyway, they need us to rebel against in their teens, and our turn will come with them later, as they mature.

Occasionally, if a child is going through some phase of emotional disturbance that expresses itself in insolent behaviour, the grandparent may become the easiest target for cruel or unpleasant remarks, and we must cry halt to this without delay, for if they have not learned respect for the elderly by the time they leave home, heaven help them, and us, and their future in-laws! For most young people though, its a case of 'It's so nice to have a Gran around the house' – as many people who have been brought up in such circumstances will confirm.

Life with father (or father-in-law)
Much that has been said so far about caring for the elderly in your own home applies equally to people of both sexes although, since women live longer than men, it is more likely to be your mother who will need your help. On the rarer occasions when a father or father-in-law is left alone in old age and becomes part of a younger household, provided he is not mentally impaired he will usually tend to fit in a little more easily. At least there will be none of the problems of the 'two-women-and-one-kitchen' type to deal with, nor is he liable to be critical if there is dust on the furniture, so long as there is a good meal on the table. He will have his own kind of adjustments to make, though, which you will need to help him with. If he has lost his wife, he will want time to grieve and some 'mothering' from you if you are his daughter or daughter-in-law, so that he feels confident enough in your capacity for sympathy and understanding to be able to talk

freely about his loss and even to weep if he wants to, without embarrassment.

Even if he has retired from his work for some time before he comes to live with you, he may still be suffering from 'role loss'. Unless he developed interests and hobbies outside his job before he left it he can feel very lost, and feel that he has nothing to do but read the papers and go for rather lonely strolls. His loneliness in your home may be more intense too in some ways than that of an elderly woman similarly placed, for she can find more pleasure and interest in day-to-day family events, the comings and goings of neighbours which she can watch from the window and the conversation of your women friends who drop in for coffee, even if she is not actively involved in all that is going on herself. Whereas he may feel like a fish out of water and simply 'in the way' in the domestic scene.

If in his own home he was used to having the last word on everything and all his opinions accepted without question, he may find great difficulty in acknowledging the right of his son or son-in-law to be one of the main decision-makers as head of the household he now shares with you both, and if he is not allowed any voice at all in matters that concern you all this, of course, will distress him still further. This, plus the loss of authority he enjoyed in his job before his retirement, could be an anxiety-provoking threat to his image of himself and his manhood and make him very difficult to live with. In his determination never to allow anyone to write him off merely as an old fool, and behind the times in his ideas and views on life, he may overcompensate by trying to assert himself in every possible way; attempting to outshine his son or son-in-law, not only within the family circle but also in the presence of visiting friends (which in some ways he may be able to do, on account of his longer experience of business matters and life generally). If this kind of problem arises, unless your husband has the maturity that enables him to understand what is happening and cope with it with patience and good humour, it may cause jealousy, animosity and considerable disruption in the home.

Your task of trying to help them to adjust and become more tolerant of each other's shortcomings and appreciative of each other's strengths will not be an easy one. If there is conflict and competition it will be like trying to turn a horse-race into a pleasant jog-trot, but there are several positive steps you can take. Without expecting the two men of different generations to become 'bosom pals', which in most cases is an unrealistic hope, you should quietly prepare the ground for the building of a friendly acceptance of each other by trying to see both their points of view and discussing it with them individually, remembering that you are not only wife and daughter (or daughter-in-law) to them, but in a sense a mother-figure too, for whose approval and admiration they will be competing; and your fair-minded approach to their differences can contribute a great deal to their final settlement. When there is any sign that the dust of battle is dying down you might try to interest them in sharing some joint endeavour connected with the home or garden, such as redecorating a room or building a rockery, although they will need to enjoy other activities, of course, with friends of their own age.

If in spite of any problems there have been, your husband is willing to help him also to find interest and fulfilment outside the home, it may help if he introduces him to his own friends' fathers down at the 'local' or the golf club. And some of your older friends and neighbours could be encouraged to invite him to join their bowls, chess, bridge or darts clubs, or to do some voluntary service in the community. Such suggestions are more likely to be taken up by him if they come from an outsider than directly from you or your husband, for he may be highly resistant to any hint of your trying to organise his life for him.

Finding some special contribution he can make towards the comfort and smooth running of the home may do much for his self-esteem, and asking him to be responsible for one particular part of the garden, in which he can specialise if he wishes in growing his favourite flowers or some vegetables may also be a wise move.

But perhaps the greatest morale-booster of all for the healthy and active retired man is a paid part-time job of some kind. This opens up a whole new world of interest for him right away from the home, where he will almost certainly make new friends and regain some of his previous 'worker' status and feeling of usefulness.

His ability to settle down well in your home will of course depend on so many things: his personality, yours and your husband's, his state of physical and mental health, his adaptability to change and his previous home life. If he was waited on hand and foot by his wife you will have to make it clear to him from the start that he cannot expect this of you, although you will enjoy caring for him in a general way and making him comfortable and welcome. Be prepared to be flexible, remembering that all elderly people tend to swing somewhat between their need for dependence and independence according to the changes that take place in their health, emotions and circumstances. A firm approach may be needed sometimes, but at others they may need mothering and indulging a little to help them to cope with all the ups and downs of old age.

Elderly men, when they become depressed, tend more quickly than women to neglect their dress and personal hygiene and appearance – sometimes failing to shave each day, clinging to the same grubby old sweater, and living in worn-out bedroom slippers. Apart from the fact that this can be a social embarrassment for the family, it is also evidence of their loss of pride and purpose in life, and their depressed state of mind (in the absence of mental impairment). If you are faced with such a situation with an elderly father or father-in-law and he seems to be getting worse in spite of everything you are doing to try to help him, it would be wise to try to arrange for him to be seen by the family doctor as he may be urgently in need of treatment for his depression.

Just as the best hope of making an elderly woman relatively happy in your home lies in treating her as a woman, not an 'old' woman, an elderly man should always be treated as a man, never as an 'old' man. These are the labels that hurt and deprive them of their special identity as 'people'. They may be wrinkled, white-haired, bald or arthritic, but any one of them will tell you that, inside, they feel and think just as they did when they were thirty; it is to the person who lives inside the person we see that we must speak, and to whom we would often do well to listen.

Life with an emotionally disturbed parent

If you have the care and responsibility of a slightly brain-damaged parent, or one who is neurotic, demanding and possessive, or even openly aggressive towards you, you will know what a very distressing experience this is, and what pressures it can bring. These are discussed in Chapter 9. You will, no doubt, have tried with the help of your doctor to establish the real cause of her behaviour, but this may still leave you bearing the strain of her emotional disturbance, if her condition is untreatable. In-patient hospital care is the only answer in some severe dementias.

Most of us feel that the very thought that we could ever be driven to the use of really violent words, let alone actions, in our dealings with an old person is a shocking one. But the possibility of the expression of aggressive feelings under great provocation is inherent in any situation of intolerable stress and should be mentioned here, if only to assure those who may sometimes feel very close to losing their patience completely that they are by no means alone in this; that negative feelings are nothing to be ashamed of and that there are ways of preventing them from ever being translated into actions.

Some of the ways of dealing with stress generally are examined in Chapter 10, but many normally kind and tolerant people become so worn out by their parent's unreasonable demands and hostile attitudes that they find themselves becoming not only exasperated and short-tempered, but fearful that they will lose control of themselves; and some of them do. When this happens they, as well as their parent, are in urgent need of help – help which should have been sought and given long before this crisis point was reached, where they are beginning to move into the tragic area society now calls 'granny-bashing'.

Assaults on frail and defenceless elderly women are on the increase, and many of them take place within the family circle where one would expect old people to receive maximum protection from harm of any kind.

The term 'granny-bashing' is an interesting one and of fairly recent origin, although the act itself has always existed to some extent. There is a kind of trendy obscenity about it, bordering on the sinister, of which perhaps we need to be aware; it is becoming increasingly popular amongst the sick element in society as part of the jargon they use to try to reduce horrific acts of cruelty and cowardice to the level of harmless fair-ground games, concerned only with cardboard figures of fun, who feel no pain or humiliation when they are used as targets. Most people are beginning to feel that there are now too many faintly humorous terms in popular use to describe acts of violence, like smiles on the face of evil – cover-up words for 'grievous bodily harm'. 'Granny-bashing' is now well established on the list, along with 'mugging' and 'football hooliganism' – all of which can result in grave and crippling injuries to its victims. Some of us, no doubt, simply use these light-weight terms (for what we know can be appalling physical assaults) as we use laughter, as a defence against our fears; but when we are considering the whole question of 'granny-bashing' we need to be sure that we get the true picture of it clear in our minds, which can be an old person with a black eye, bruised body, cracked ribs, a dislocated shoulder or broken arms or legs, living in a state of constant fear of further violence from which she has no way of escaping. Behind her, in the shadows of her sad existence, stands either a mentally disturbed relative (possibly an aggressive psychopath) or one who is basically normal but emotionally exhausted, whose control has broken down completely under great stress, and who needs skilled help to deal with the pattern and habit of violence that has him or her in its grip.

There are many causes for assaults on the elderly. Some are so deep and complicated that they need to be left to the psychiatrists, psychologists and sociologists to explain, but it may be useful here to examine some of the more obvious ones, and some of the ways of coping with the situation in various circumstances.

If a very difficult and demanding old person is living in a household where one member of the family is mentally ill and whose tolerance of anyone who creates problems for him or her is very low, then she may not only be shouted at, but physically assaulted as well from time to time. In these extreme and unpromising circumstances, often the only solution is for other family members who may be aware of her plight, but unable always to be there to protect her, to contact her doctor and the local authority social services department in an effort to get her removed speedily to some place of safety, such as an elderly person's home. In this kind of situation, where the key factor is the mental illness of her persecutor, it is almost always useless to hope that frequent visiting of the home by outsiders, and an increase in friendly interest and support for the family, are going to change things. Delay may only expose her to further violence, with everyone becoming so engrossed in trying to sort out the problem by discussing it that the immediate protection she needs comes too late for her. As one experienced social worker used to say to her students, 'When it come to "baby-battering" or "granny-bashing" the first thing you do is to make sure that you stop the thumping. *Then* you can start talking.'

It is not only the mentally ill who assault old people. Alcoholism and drug abuse are other major causes of 'granny-bashing'. A man – or a woman – who can just about tolerate the presence of a very difficult elderly parent in the home when sober may lose control and become quite violent towards her after having too much to drink; and of course he or she may have started to drink heavily in the first place to try to ease the strain of caring for her, so that the whole thing becomes a vicious circle. Tranquillisers, which are often prescribed for relatives under stress may also, if used too heavily, lead not just to the relaxed state of mind for which they were intended, but to a condition in which the brakes come off the emotions, making the user more liable to outbursts of temper, in which he may hit the elderly person. Those who make such attacks are usually full of guilt and remorse afterwards, but often they have caused damage to their parent and to themselves emotionally that is very hard to repair.

Then there is the gradual decline of some exhausted relatives into the habit of allowing what starts out as a protest or reprimand to a difficult parent to become the occasional slap on the hand. Once this begins, if they manage to dispose of the feelings of guilt connected with it, it can soon progress to the 'push' and the 'punch' as their parent's behaviour deteriorates. And of course if they have any memories of excessive physical punishment from their parent in their childhood, this may tip the scales still further, for those who are treated violently as children often find it much easier to use violence towards others in later life when they are under pressure.

If you ever feel that you are at risk of losing control when you are caring for an elderly parent whose behaviour seems to be pushing you to the brink of despair, there are several things you can do. First, try to realise that it would be abnormal if you did not experience volcanic feelings in such a situation. Do not blame yourself for these feelings; accept them, and begin to deal with them in a very positive way. Seek help immediately from someone you can trust completely with your confidences and who will have the knowledge and the skill to understand your problem and advise you. Your family doctor or a social worker from your local social services department would be good people to turn to, and they will see that you get the long-term support you need. Your parent may need hospital treatment, or you may need a holiday right away from the cause of your stress, followed by regular interviews with the social worker, to whom you can let off the steam that you fear is constantly threatening to blow the top off your relationship with your parent. Do not be tempted to tell too many friends or neighbours of your anxiety that you may one day lose control, for unless they have had the same experience themselves they may not understand; you may be misjudged and later regret it. Try to select one close, sensible, and uncritical friend in whom you can confide from time to time, as well as your doctor and social worker, and with the right support from all concerned it is most likely that you will find that you will develop new strengths and strategies that will enable you to cope with your problem.

If you are bringing an elderly parent to live with you, you may not encounter any of the more serious problems mentioned in this chapter; but you will know that both you and they will have many adjustments to make. A household containing two, or maybe three generations, can be a battlefield in which people destroy each other, or a garden in which they grow together –

Bringing an elderly parent to live with you

hell or harmony: the choice is ours. Shooting of course is easy, but digging, planting, weeding and waiting for relationships to flower require patience and hard work. Those who have made a success of it tell us that it is an experience they would not have missed for anything.

7
Illness in the elderly

Since illness of mind or body can affect both function and behaviour in people of every age, it is particularly important that those who are trying to care for the elderly intelligently and well should have a basic knowledge of the types of illness to which they may be especially prone. It is equally important to maintain an optimistic attitude, to try to guard against dwelling in too gloomy a fashion upon the inevitable gradual deterioration in strength that old age brings to everyone, and to remember that in some people it can be a very slow process indeed, and that old age itself is not an 'illness'. It is, however, essential to understand that no marked deterioration in the health of an elderly person should ever be written off as 'just old age'. It should always be taken seriously and properly investigated medically.

If old people are ill, they are ill because some disease is present, not simply because they are old. Sometimes the kindness and respect we all want to show to the elderly in our care can all too quickly become undermined, and even turn to irritation and contempt, if we are ignorant of the presence of a physical or mental disease which may be the cause of some kind of 'difficult' behaviour. Those who should be the first to urge elderly persons to seek medical advice when they develop symptoms of illness are sometimes the last to do so. Not because they do not care, but because their mother or father has always seemed to them to be so strong and invincible. After all, they were the towers of strength they ran to with their troubles as children. That they should finally grow old and a little 'frail' seems understandable, but that they could ever become really ill – overtaken by a serious and disabling illness – that seems unthinkable. Surely it must be 'all in the mind'! If only they would cheer up a bit, try to get out more, and take a keener interest in life, those many and mysterious aches and pains would soon disappear. . . . And so we have a situation in which thousands of elderly people are walking around with quite serious but treatable illnesses, suffering chest pains or shortness of breath, frequency of urine or inflamed joints, and are being told by their relatives not to worry about it because it is 'just your age' instead of being urged to go for a complete health check. The feeling that someone we love who has always played a strong and protective role in our lives, must be almost indestructible, and the desire to reassure her – and ourselves – that all is well, are by no means unusual reactions to the appearance of symptoms of failing health in our elderly parents. But they must be encouraged to seek advice in the early stages of their illness and so save much pain and regret later on.

A misunderstanding of the symptoms of a very real illness can even result in some elderly people suffering a form of mental cruelty at the hands of their relatives, who, without realising it, slip gradually into the habit of granny-baiting. This can begin with mild teasing, which the younger children soon pick up from their parents. It can be very hurtful to an old person, and unless the existence of basic affection acts as a brake on it, and the adults recognise that they have no right to take advantage of the older person's weaker position, it can develop into verbal bullying. An old lady, for instance, who is nagged for being too 'fussy' over her food because she quietly declines to eat anything fried, may not be trying to be awkward – she may have a stomach ulcer. Or the one who gets teased by her family for her loss of hair, gruffness of voice and habit of wearing several cardigans at once indoors may have an undiagnosed thyroid deficiency. Such examples are legion.

Some of the saddest cases of all are those elderly people living alone whose relatives withdraw from them, frightened, mystified or angered by some trying change in their normal personality and behaviour, which they interpret as rejection, but which may simply be the result of a deep depression or some other illness which might respond well to medical treatment and good family support.

The pattern of illness in old age is rather different from that of younger people. In youth, illnesses usually come singly, with a fairly clear-cut set of symptoms, leading to the diagnosis of the disease, followed in most cases by a satisfactory recovery after treatment. But when old people are ill they often show a great variety of symptoms, which are the result of the co-existence of more than one type of disease. When this happens it can seem to those caring for them that they are complaining of something different almost every day. You can begin to feel at your wits' end to know how to help them. At this stage it is easy to become exasperated too with your parent's doctor, whom she may criticise secretly, or openly, for seeming to be incompetent or uncaring if he does not come up quickly with a diagnosis and plan of treatment, or if he is cautious about submitting an old person to a battery of impressive and complicated tests and investigations, such as are shown in medical programmes on television. Her anxiety is wholly understandable, but what she may not realise is that in treating the elderly, the doctor needs not only to be a skilled diagnostician, but also a kind of medical version of the circus juggler, trying to keep a dozen plates spinning on sticks at the same time. He has to keep his trained eye on the many symptoms that are the spin-offs of several co-existent diseases and then make the difficult decisions about priorities.

For example, it could happen that Mrs A may be suffering from: arteriosclerosis, osteo-arthritis of the hips, and a slow growing internal cancer; Mr B from an enlarged prostate gland, a hiatus hernia, and emphysema; Mrs C from a heart condition, diabetes, and diverticulitis. It is quite possible for a doctor to be faced with such a difficult combination of diseases in any one elderly patient, and anybody knowing even a little about these various conditions would appreciate the problems they pose in diagnosis and treatment, either active or palliative. The doctor often finds himself on the horns of a dilemma which would not exist if he were treating a younger person for a single illness.

We need to keep an open mind at all times when we are looking after the elderly and to be careful not to judge the reaction of older people by our own or that of other members of the family, or to expect their illnesses to follow a similar course. The elderly, for instance, may be less dramatically, but more seriously, affected by infections than the young, for they have less resistance, and their vital organs, such as the heart and lungs, often cannot cope with the extra strains they have to bear. Even a mild attack of influenza, which the younger members of the household may be able to shrug off quickly after a week in bed, may be lethal to an old person, with her lower resistance and the reduced efficiency of the lungs and defence mechanisms, and although she may not show any severe symptoms sudden collapse is not uncommon.

On the other hand, some diseases which can rage speedily and destructively through the youthful body, like various forms of cancer, sometimes take a much slower course in the elderly, and do not necessarily shorten their normal life-span, or prove to be the final cause of their death. In fact, some old people with cancers that are not producing any very painful or distressing symptoms are fortunate enough to die in their sleep from heart failure quite unconnected with the malignancy.

Some illnesses in the elderly are what the doctors call 'silent' – showing few or no symptoms – and it is possible for them to be suffering from illnesses as serious as pneumonia or kidney infections and many others, while experiencing nothing more in the early stages than a feeling of general malaise. The 'silent' coronary is another example. A heart attack that could be acutely painful in a younger person may, in the elderly, show up merely as a rapid pulse, slight breathlessness, pallor and sweating, following a few days of feeling excessively tired and 'played out', with perhaps some loss of appetite. This is sometimes dismissed by both the elderly person and the relatives as being nothing more than some 'little upset' due to a slight extra strain or exertion. It should be remembered, though, that if a normally active old person suddenly shows signs of weariness and apathy, and expresses a desire to remain in bed day after day, it is always possible that this is nature's warning of the approach of heart failure or the existence of an acute infection, and she should be seen by the doctor. Cancer – another 'silent' disease in some elderly people – cannot be ruled out if there is considerable weight loss, nor can the possibility of 'silent' tuberculosis in those with chronic bronchitis which they have 'learned to live with'.

A fall is a very important pointer sometimes in the health of an elderly person. All falls should be brought to the attention of the doctor, for it has often been known for an old person to have a fracture of the femur which has gone undiscovered for some time, particularly if the fall is due to a stroke and there is clouding of consciousness or mental confusion. It may also be caused by a giddy spell while getting up in the night to go to the lavatory or to use the commode. An elderly person can easily slip on a stair or a badly placed rug, and sustain a cracked or fractured bone without knowing it until she shows some weakness in the limb and is examined and X-rayed. Unless the doctor has been called at once, any weakness may be regarded by her and her relatives as nothing more than the shock of the fall, and appropriate treatment is delayed. For every one old person who makes an inordinate fuss about the slightest mishap, there are hundreds who hate to be a bother to those around them; so we always need to be extra vigilant on their behalf in times of illness or if they have an accident.

Hypochondriasis in the elderly
If someone has been over-concerned about their health all her life and inclined to be hypochondriacal, worrying constantly about every slight fluctuation in her normal sense of well-being, interpreting each minor ailment as a herald of malignancy, then it is likely that her pessimistic attitude towards her health will become worse, rather than better, in old age, and we have to accept it as patiently as we can. Some elderly people, however, who rarely worried about their health in youth and middle age, become hypochondriacal as they grow older, and very absorbed with their bodily functions – particularly their bowels. In fairness it has to be remembered that the elderly *do* have more aches and pains than the young, and more time to think about them. Many suffer from constipation if they do not, or cannot eat enough roughage, and the internal muscles are less efficient. Many old people find a good daily bowel movement very reassuring. They feel that if their waste-disposal unit is functioning properly it is an indication that probably all is well with the rest of their body.

Some increase in concern over the health is perfectly understandable, but those who are seriously hypochondriacal are much more difficult to help. They are often restless and agitated. Their drawers are full of patent medicines of all kinds, as well as those actually prescribed for them. They make their various symptoms the main topic of every conversation and go to their doctor and relatives and friends constantly for reassurance, which they reject. They demand X-rays and numerous investigations which, even if they are granted, fail to allay their fears. Sometimes they become so disturbed that there is a delusional quality about their complaints. They may believe, for example, that a relative is making them feel ill by poisoning their food. The symptoms of hypochondriasis can be very difficult to live with and also a great trial to relatives, for the elderly person may be tortured by irrational fears and be totally unable to control the expression of them. Also – most important of all – we need to recognise that hypochondriasis may spring from two main causes which are very much within the realms of reality: a true depressive illness, or an underlying 'silent' physical disease, both of which may be amenable to treatment. So the elderly person who keeps 'crying wolf' should never be ignored. There is always a chance that the 'wolf' really does exist, though not necessarily in that part of their body with which they seem to be obsessed. Even if their complaints are proved to be without foundation, the fact that they are distressed enough to continue to make them is in itself a symptom that requires sympathetic handling and careful investigation.

Mild hypochrondiasis is sometimes the first symptom of a depressive or anxiety state in the elderly. The often more dramatic symptoms of brain damage or deterioration are usually brought to the notice of the doctor by relatives much sooner, particularly if there is a shared household and the home-life is being disrupted by odd or anti-social behaviour. Old people can sometimes become very depressed and anxious and yet only show it by being apathetic, withdrawn or rather irritable, and although it is true that the last years of life do bring certain sorrows to many of them, depression should never be regarded as an inevitable part of ageing and much can be done to relieve it.

8
Physical illnesses

Although it is valuable to be armed with a little knowledge of the illnesses common in old age you should never attempt to diagnose such illnesses in anyone who is in your care. If you feel worried about them, you should always seek the doctor's advice; accept his opinion, and act upon all his recommendations. Nor should you allow yourself to become too anxious and absorbed in the matter of 'symptoms', for this will tend to make you overprotective and tense, and lead to the creation of apprehension in your elderly parent. You should aim for the middle way: that of quiet concern and observation of her well-being as she grows older, bearing in mind that some old people are fortunate enough to enjoy reasonably good health all their lives, and that your parent may well be one of them.

Many excellent and easily understood books have been written by experts on the diseases of old age, and it is not intended here to do more than try to present some simple information on those illnesses most frequently met with in the elderly, information that may reduce anxiety and increase understanding and efficiency when the need for action arises in the face of some serious health problem.

Circulatory disorders

Heart disease is one of the major causes of illness and death in the elderly, although those who suffer from it in its various forms can often live for many years with their symptoms well controlled provided it is properly diagnosed and treated, and provided sufferers are prepared to adopt a reasonably disciplined life-style recommended by their doctor. This will usually include weight-control, regular exercise and the avoidance, as far as possible, of stressful situations.

The heart is a pump, manned mainly by valves and a system of arteries which carry the blood away from it to the various organs of the body, and veins which bring it back again. The symptoms of heart disease arise from its failure to pump with enough force to maintain this essential function of circulation correctly. Congestion occurs at some point along the line, in one or other of the body's organs, resulting in their deterioration. The affected organs are unable to produce their usual performance as part of the general orchestration of the body, because of deficient blood supply, and a number of different symptoms can be seen as a result. These may appear in some part of the body apparently distant and unconnected with the heart itself, and may wear many different disguises, such as swollen ankles, headache, drowsiness, indigestion, flatulence, nausea, breathlessness, cough, depression, loss of appetite, insomnia and changes in normal behaviour and judgement. Not surprisingly they are very difficult for elderly people or those caring for them to identify, particularly as some of them can also be symptoms of other illnesses which may be much less serious and nothing whatever to do with heart disease. The golden rule is, if in any doubt – persuade your elderly parent to see a doctor.

Many people think of heart trouble only in terms of pains in the chest, breathlessness, a racing pulse and blueness of the lips, and while all these can be a part of the general picture in some cases, they are by no means the whole. It is possible for a 'heart' patient to have a long list of distressing symptoms or, on the other hand, to appear to be fairly well, just a little tired, yet suffering from a 'silent' heart condition which may finally cause sudden collapse. So it will be sensible precaution to encourage your elderly parent to have a routine general check-up at regular intervals – every year at least, without raising the level of anxiety about health matters in any way.

Apart from those symptoms of heart disease which have already been mentioned, some of the most serious ones which would indicate that medical advice should be sought without delay are: a marked increase in feelings of tiredness and lethargy, breathlessness, chest or arm pains, extreme pallor or blueness; a very slow or a very rapid pulse, a temperature above or below normal, vomiting, diminished urine, dropsy (oedema) of the feet, ankles and legs, shivering, delirium, fainting and collapse into unconsciousness. You may never be faced with having to deal with sudden heart failure in your elderly parent, but it is important that you should know exactly what to do until the doctor arrives, should such an emergency arise. First aid procedures for this are described in Chapter 13.

Coronary heart disease
Hardly a day passes when we do not read in the papers or hear on the radio that some well-known person, usually in the middle or older age-groups, has suffered a 'coronary'. Sometimes this type of attack results in death within minutes, hours, or days, but often the patient makes a good recovery after a few weeks of rest and treatment, and can resume a normal life-style unless it consists of exceptionally hard and strenuous physical work.

As we grow older, there is a gradual build-up of deposits of fat in the lining of the large blood vessels that pump the blood around the body. Sometimes these vessels become so narrow that the blood supply to the heart is reduced, which may cause the pain known as angina, in the chest and (usually) the left arm. In some cases there is a complete shut-off, when the heart is temporarily or permanently deprived of blood. If this is permanent, of course, the patient dies, but if it is only temporary the heart muscle suffers some damage and the patient is seriously ill for a time, but survives.

The most obvious symptoms of a coronary include severe chest pains, pallor, sweating, coldness and general distress, followed by collapse. But it is also possible for an attack to take place with little or no pain – only feelings of extreme weakness and lethargy and perhaps a slight dimming of consciousness. These attacks should be taken just as seriously as the more dramatic ones. If your parent suffers an attack of this kind, take the appropriate first aid measures; do not attempt to move her from one room to another or to get her upstairs to bed. Just allow her to rest in whatever position she finds to be most comfortable,

Physical illnesses

make sure that she is warm (but not hot) and that the room is well ventilated, and get the doctor as quickly as possible while trying not to convey your own feelings of extreme anxiety to your parent.

Some 'mild' coronaries can be treated by complete rest at home, but moderately severe, or severe ones are often treated in the intensive care unit of a general hospital, where a patient's condition can be monitored and closely observed day and night, and where resuscitation equipment is readily available. After the danger period of the first few days is past, she may be moved to a medical ward, where she is gradually mobilised and often sent home again within a week or two, if suitable care and support is available during her convalescence. If, however, you and your elderly parent live in a remote part of the countryside many miles away from the nearest hospital with an intensive care unit, and when she suffers a coronary heart attack it is considered inadvisable to try to move her, do not for one moment assume that this is tantamount to a death sentence. Statistics have shown that the difference in the survival rate of patients treated skilfully at home and those treated in intensive care units is not as great as many people imagine, and in fact some patients of an anxious temperament may make a speedier recovery in their home surroundings. You can in any case leave all the decisions regarding your parent's treatment safely in the hands of the doctor.

As they return to their normal routine of life, coronary patients are usually advised to keep their weight down, give up smoking, cut down on alcohol, strong tea and strong coffee and on their consumption of dairy products such as butter, cream and cheeses with a high level of cholesterol, and limit their eating of eggs to once a week instead of once a day. They are also usually told to take regular exercise, walk up to three miles a day (if this does not exhaust them and is suitable to their age and general physical condition), and live life at a slightly slower pace, avoiding whenever possibly any emotionally stressful situations such as arguments and high degrees of excitement. Thus they are encouraged to regard themselves as fit in the general sense, but accepting the fact that some damage has been caused to the heart muscle by their attack, which means that they can continue to live their lives normally within any limits that this may impose upon them – which may be very small indeed.

The encouragement of the right attitude to health in people who have suffered a coronary is most important, for it is naturally easy for them to feel very apprehensive about how their heart is going to behave in the future. You can do much in a quiet way to help your parent through these anxieties, to avoid the development of a 'cardiac neurosis', but you will also need to remember that she has passed through a rather special experience. She has looked death in the eye and survived, and as anyone who has done this knows, life is never quite the same again. It may, in fact, be better – with time itself being more precious – but never the same. Also, she will usually be well aware that she now has one vital organ in her body which is particularly vulnerable, and however sensible and philosophical she is about this, the knowledge is something she will carry with her for the rest of her life, knowing she may be at risk again at any time from another attack. She may not discuss this possibility, and neither of you should dwell upon it, but it may give her a greater feeling of security if you make it clear to her just once, that you have trained yourself fully in all the correct first aid methods of resuscitation should a further state of emergency arise; although your attitude towards her future health prospects should be one of optimism and confidence.

Most coronary patients follow their doctor's instructions regarding diet and exercise faithfully for the first six months or so after recovery from their heart attack, and many continue to do so, realising the importance of not putting any extra strain on the damaged organ. But there are some who, when the memory of all the pain and distress they have suffered begins to fade a little, and they are feeling fairly fit again, gradually return to eating habits which lead to their gaining weight, neglect their daily exercise, take up smoking once more, and slowly drift back into the high-risk area for another heart attack. If your elderly parent is inclined to throw caution to the wind in this way, although she is entitled to make her own decisions about her health, you should do all in your power to persuade her to live her life in accordance with her doctor's recommendations.

Physical illnesses

Consider too what reasons there may be for her rejection of what she knows to be sensible preventive measures. She may be suffering from depression, feeling that her life is not worth preserving, comforting herself with nicotine, alcohol and overeating, and in need of medical help (or simply more family interest and affection). Or, in your anxiety to carry out the doctor's orders to the letter after her heart attack, you may unwittingly have set up too strict a regime of dieting and exercise for her, making her feel tense and dominated, and this may be her way of protesting. If you think this is a possibility, you should try to encourage a gradual return to a reasonable but more flexible routine, making sure that her diet is correct, but as varied and interesting as possible, and not without the occasional 'treat' of a cream cake or a glass of light wine – whatever she most enjoys, which will do no harm at all if it is really *is* occasional. Offer to accompany her sometimes on her daily walks, too, if you feel she would like this, and ask her to pick up a library book for you, or some light-weight item of shopping, from time to time, to give her some reason for going out, for merely 'walking for health' can be a very boring business.

Try not to be over-protective, and if she is still young enough, and well enough, to take a full or part-time paid or voluntary job, and the doctor agrees, this will probably do more for her morale than anything else. Even if you fear inwardly that the work may entail too much strain, remember that it is the quality of life and not its length that is most important.

It will be wise for your parent to have a regular check-up at whatever intervals the doctor suggests, and with reasonable care, he or she may live an active and contented life for many years following a coronary.

Disorders of the peripheral blood vessels

If your elderly parent complains of cramp in the legs after exercise, which improves with rest, you should suggest a visit to the doctor. Cramp may be of little significance, but it is sometimes caused by a reduction of the blood supply to the limbs due to a narrowing of the blood vessels. If this narrowing exists it may be very slight and give no cause for alarm, but it is a condition that needs to be watched, especially if the toes become red and the nails begin to crack. If this happens, you should arrange for him or her to be seen again by the doctor without delay. Any sign of the toes turning blue may be an indication of the onset of gangrene, which requires immediate attention.

Stroke

'Stroke' is a strange word, with so many different definitions – including 'a blow' and 'a hand passed lightly over'. But for those who experience it as an illness, it can be the temporary or permanent end to the active way of life they have always known, and for some, a major disaster.

Medically, it usually describes the form of brain damage called cerebral haemorrhage, which can indeed occur like the force of a blow, causing havoc and sometimes death – or, when its touch is lighter, causing only minor symptoms of passing weakness in one side of the body. At its worst it is by no means a gentle illness, for a major stroke can sometimes cause complete loss of speech, sight, and mobility, confusion, double incontinence, bedsores, urinary and bronchial infections, painful contractions of the limbs, and feelings of frustration and deep depression. These are possibilities to be faced, but this depressing description certainly does not apply in every case. Many patients make a good recovery, with only a few residual effects, so if your parent is struck down in this way, there is always room for optimism.

There can be several causes of 'stroke', all of which create a disturbance of blood supply to the brain. If the stroke is on the right side of the brain the left side of the body will be affected, and vice versa, the most obvious signs being weakness or paralysis of the limbs. If the left side is paralysed there will often be speech difficulties as well, but these usually begin to improve after a few days.

Some people suffer a series of small strokes, which can sometimes be nursed at home if the doctor agrees and the level of care is adequate. More severe attacks usually require admission to hospital (see Chapter 13) for the prevention or treatment of serious and painful complications. In a good hospital ward, so much can be done to make the patient more comfortable, and the attention of specially trained medical, nursing and auxiliary staff can increase the chances of a successful recovery, particularly from the point of view of regaining mobility.

The outlook for a deeply unconscious patient who remains in this condition for several days or weeks is not favourable, although like everything else in the progress of illness, there are always exceptions, and the situation should not be regarded as hopeless. For those who either never lose consciousness after a stroke, or who recover it in a matter of hours, even if the mind is still clouded, the prospects are good.

If your elderly parent suffers a stroke, your first visit to her in hospital may fill you with despair, for she may be paralysed, speechless and confused. It will be distressing for you to feel so completely out of touch with her, and at this early stage in the illness it may seem that all is lost, but this may not be so. Try to keep calm and speak to her normally, reassure her that everything is under control, and that you will be visiting frequently and keeping in close touch with those who are treating her. Most important of all, sit beside her, hold her hand, stroke her forehead occasionally, and remember to kiss her affectionately when you arrive and depart. It may be impossible to know how much of what you say gets through to her, but if she is conscious, she will be aware of your love and support, even though she may not be able to communicate. It may seem absurd to think that you might need to remind yourself to touch and kiss your sick parent when visiting her in hospital; but sons and daughters who see their mother or father for the first time after a stroke are often so shocked, that they are almost afraid to speak to him or her after the first few words of greeting, and tend just to talk to each other across the bed in hushed tones, place their gifts of flowers on the locker and leave without having given their parent what they really need, which is some demonstration of their affection at a personal level.

To begin with you may feel very pessimistic about the outcome of the illness, but the change that can take place in a stroke patient during the first four to six weeks can often be very encouraging. By then, your parent may be eating normally, have overcome any urinary or bronchial infections, regained control of bowels and bladder and be responding to physiotherapy and speech therapy. And even if there are still some difficulties in concentrating and communication, and he or she has to rely on a walking aid to move around the ward, it will be clear that the first steps have been taken on the long road back.

A stroke is one of the most depressing and frustrating illnesses anyone can suffer from. Although you should urge your parent to co-operate fully in all the efforts that are being made to strengthen her muscles and her general performance by physiotherapy, occupational therapy and speech therapy as well if necessary, you should remember that there may be a period of deep depression during which there is no motivation. It will be useless to scold and chide her like a child for 'not trying' – much better to concentrate on expressions of pleasure and praise for each small achievement. She will have to be helped to persevere and to do just as much as possible while her depression is recognised and treated. Once this begins to lift, she will show signs of reaching out for life again and looking to the future.

As soon as you are told that your parent is likely to survive the stroke and ultimately return home, you should start to make plans for this by discussions with the doctor, ward sister, physiotherapist, occupational therapist, speech therapist and the hospital social worker, so that you can be put in touch with workers in your local health and social services to arrange for the installation of any aids or adaptations in the home before discharge, and work out a programme for rehabilitation. You may need to be very determined in this matter, to make sure that your parent gets all the help that is available, for if she has been making good progress in hospital and then comes home to sit all day in a chair with nothing to do or to stimulate her interest, ground may quickly be lost.

Owing to the problems of staff shortages you cannot expect frequent visits from physiotherapists and others, but you can indicate your desire for your parent to be seen by them as often as possible, and you can learn from them how to help her with the correct exercises to increase mobility and how to provide suitable occupational therapy to combat the feeling of uselessness and improve manual dexterity. If there are speech problems it

Physical illnesses

will also be very important for you and other relatives and friends to talk with her patiently and *often*, as she will need practise in this, as in everything else, to help her back to normality. In some areas there are stroke rehabilitation teams made up of experienced volunteers (who have nursed their own relatives through a stroke) who will visit patients in their homes and concentrate particularly upon helping them with their speech difficulties. You could enquire about this from your parent's doctor, district nurse or health visitor.

This period of rehabilitation may be a very trying one for you as well as for your parent, for you will need to show a great deal of constructive sympathy over many months, but improvement may continue to take place even after a year or more has passed. Then when the doctor indicates that he thinks the stage of maximum possible recovery may have been reached, the object must be to help your parent to accept any residual limitations in her mental or physical powers.

Some, but not all, stroke patients undergo certain personality changes, becoming childishly irritable and rather egocentric. This is something for which they cannot be blamed, but if your parent is affected in this way, you may need to be reasonably firm if he or she becomes so demanding and erratic that your own life, and that of the household is being disrupted. But occasionally changes in behaviour are due not to brain damage but to depression and frustration and an improvement then takes place as the patient's physical condition improves.

The first six months are the vital ones following a stroke, and your parent should be encouraged to continue with all the prescribed exercises. During the first year you should also help her patiently to re-learn the simple routines of daily living connected with washing, dressing, going to the lavatory and eating her meals, all of which may be painfully difficult at first, but which can be made much easier by the use of some of the specially designed clothing and aids described in Chapter 12. Your aim should be to help her to become as independent as possible, but the amount of headway made will depend not merely on her willingness to co-operate and persevere, but also upon her age and the severity of her disabilities. She must be gently led, never driven, and you should consult the doctor about how much can be attempted. In some areas stroke patients attend Stroke Rehabilitation Centres for physiotherapy, occupational therapy, speech therapy and group therapy, but these services are not yet available in all parts of the country, nor are they suitable for every patient, and some are so brain-damaged that little progress can be expected.

If you are caring at home for an elderly parent who is recovering from a stroke, all the various methods of helping her that have been shown to you by the physiotherapist and others will be of great value and should be followed faithfully, but by far the most important thing that you can do is to provide a *reason* for wanting to get better and return to as normal a life as possible; and this reason will be that she still feels loved and needed, and is encouraged to have a continuing, useful role to play.

Blood pressure

With very few exceptions, there is always an increase in blood pressure with age. Many people worry unnecessarily about it, as it can vary considerably in quite healthy old people. If your parent's blood pressure is usually high, the doctor will no doubt recommend sensible weight control. Drug treatment is kept to a minimum now and is reserved only for those with abnormally high or low blood pressure, and particularly those who have heart disease or who have recently had a heart attack.

Varicose veins and leg ulcers

Many elderly people have varicose veins which cause little or no trouble, while others suffer from aching and swollen legs; sometimes too, the skin over the veins becomes irritated and breaks down into an ulcer. In some cases a vein may rupture and bleed profusely and this requires immediate medical attention.

If your elderly parent has painful varicose veins you should suggest a visit to the doctor, but if they are giving no trouble, help her to keep her weight down, to avoid standing for long periods, or becoming constipated, and encourage her to take daily walking exercise which will improve the circulation.

Physical illnesses

Foot troubles

Foot troubles are very common in the elderly. Some are caused by poor circulation, arthritis, diabetes, the wearing of badly designed shoes, or the constant wearing of slippers around the house which do not give the foot good support.

If your parent is having any pain, discomfort or loss of sensation in the feet you should suggest first a visit to the doctor rather than going straight to a chiropodist. If it is only chiropody that is required, and not some attention also to the general health, the doctor may be able to arrange this under the National Health Service, although your parent may choose to go to a chiropodist privately if he or she wishes to do so.

Diseases of the lungs

BRONCHITIS

Persistent cough, phlegm, wheezing and breathlessness can all be symptoms of chronic bronchitis. If your parent has such symptoms she should see the doctor, because if she is found to have bronchitis he will want to do everything possible to control and alleviate it, as it is a progressive illness, though one which rarely actually begins in old age. Usually it overtakes those in middle age who are prone to attacks of coughing and expectoration in cold damp weather, which become worse as they grow older, and it may develop into a serious illness. Antibiotics and other drugs are often given to reduce the infection and irritation, and if your parent smokes she will undoubtedly be told to give it up completely and advised to keep her weight down, so you will need to watch her diet if you are doing the cooking.

If a severe attack develops you should call the doctor at once as hospital treatment may be necessary. Help your parent to avoid colds and infections as far as possible and to stay away from crowded places if there is an influenza epidemic.

Breathing exercises (which are best taught by a trained physiotherapist) can also be extremely helpful, and your parent's doctor may be able to arrange for this if he thinks fit.

CHRONIC EMPHYSEMA

This is a condition that often goes hand in hand with chronic bronchitis, which may precede it. It needs expert diagnosis and treatment, as in its worst form it can result in cardiac failure. The air cells of the lungs become dilated so that there is loss of elasticity and partial obstruction. The blood fails to pass through the lungs normally, so that the right side of the heart is affected as well as the venous system generally. In the early stages, breathlessness is only marked after exertion, but later it becomes more continuous. The treatment is broadly similar to that given for bronchitis, and if your parent suffers from this condition you should make every effort to protect her from colds or influenza, or anything that may throw extra strain onto the damaged respiratory system, and so onto the heart. It may be difficult sometimes to discourage members of the family, or friends, from visiting and coming into contact with your parent if they are suffering from a heavy cold, but you should try to do so. You should not treat her as an invalid, or ruin her social life, during the winter months, but simply take reasonable precautions.

TUBERCULOSIS

In our grandparent's day, pulmonary tuberculosis was often a killer disease. It claimed the lives of thousands of people every year, in every walk of life, but since the discovery of antibiotics and the improvement in living conditions it has, to a large extent, been brought under control. However, these advances in treatment have been so remarkable and dramatic that we are often inclined to forget that tuberculosis still exists and that it is by no means confined to the young. Elderly people can contract it, although it is not so easy to recognise in them, as it is so often a part of the general picture of ill-health.

Elderly men are more at risk than women, although both sexes can develop it. Sometimes those with chronic bronchitis or those who have had abdominal surgery for a stomach complaint are found to have it, and any elderly person who develops a persistent cough with yellow phlegm or blood and who loses weight, looks very pale, or has an unexplained rise in temperature should be

Physical illnesses

examined by the doctor. A chest X-ray and a specialist opinion will then usually be arranged.

If your elderly parent is found to have tuberculosis, it is most likely that she will be treated by drug therapy for as long as is necessary to rid her completely of the disease. The doctor will explain how important it is to take the drugs regularly until he tells her that she may stop. As some old people are forgetful, or decide not to be bothered with drugs any more if they are feeling better in themselves, you will need to keep a very strict check on this to make sure that these important drugs are taken regularly and at the right time and in the right dosage, for if this is not done, the results can be very serious. Some of these drugs have side-effects which include stomach upsets and nausea, and although you should not tell your parent to anticipate these, if they occur you should report it to the doctor at once, as he may be able to help.

You should make sure that your parent has a nourishing diet, plenty of fresh air and the amount of rest each day that is recommended by the doctor.

Diseases and disorders of the alimentary tract

Since the alimentary tract starts at the mouth and ends at the anus, it is not surprising that many problems can arise along the course of its long and winding route, particularly when it is as well worn as it is in old age. In fact it is remarkable how efficiently the alimentary tract often manages for threescore years and ten (and sometimes much longer) to digest food, absorb its nourishment and then dispose of its waste products. In those elderly people who do have trouble in this area the main complaints (apart from any malignant disease) are:

MOUTH ULCERS

These are often due to ill-fitting dentures, but they can sometimes be the side-effects of necessary drugs that have been prescribed for some other condition. In some cases they are due to shingles or a poor diet. If your parent complains of a painful mouth and this does not clear up within a few days, encourage him or her to see the doctor as this should be investigated. If it is neglected there could be a tendency to begin to rely only on soft foods which may be low in nutritional value and ulceration will then be slow to heal.

INDIGESTION, ULCERS, AND HIATUS HERNIA

Many elderly people suffer from indigestion in some form from time to time, but persistent attacks should never be written off as being merely one of the trials of an ageing stomach. There may be a gastric or duodenal ulcer causing the pain, or a condition known as hiatus hernia, which is fairly common in the elderly when the muscles are weaker. A small part of the stomach breaks through the diaphragm into the chest area next to the oesophagus. This can cause a variety of unpleasant symptoms including heartburn, wind, a feeling of fullness and discomfort after meals, regurgitation of stomach acid into the throat and mouth, and chest pains that can sometimes be so severe that they may be initially mistaken for angina or a coronary thrombosis. Sometimes, also, internal bleeding takes place very slowly, which causes anaemia. Surgical treatment is rarely recommended for this condition in the elderly, but their symptoms can be eased considerably. If this is diagnosed in your elderly parent it will be likely that the doctor will advise weight reduction if necessary, and the avoidance of stooping, smoking, alcohol and heavy meals. Nourishing but easily digested foods of a bland nature may be recommended. They will also be told never to lie down flat after a meal, and to sleep in a semi-upright position, with four or five well-arranged pillows to give comfortable support; also to avoid tight clothing, tight foundation garments and long-line brassieres if they tend to constrict the diaphragm at all. Many of these measures are taken to prevent the gastric juices flooding up from the stomach into the oesophagus, and the various drugs that are prescribed also to relieve pain and discomfort and deal with any anaemia which may be present can be very successful.

CONSTIPATION AND DIARRHOEA

Constipation is a cause of great anxiety to many elderly people, who often regard it as a sign that something is amiss, and sometimes they are right; but often it is just due to weakening muscles,

Physical illnesses

a soft diet lacking in adequate amounts of fresh fruit, vegetables and roughage, and, if they are disabled in some way, their inability to take enough exercise. In many cases a slight alteration in their food (under medical supervision) – substituting wholemeal bread for white bread and natural bran (which can be bought in the palatable form of All-Bran including malt and sugar) with milk for their daily breakfast cereal – is all that is needed to keep them 'regular'. We may tend to smile at the way our elderly parents sometimes worry out loud over the fact that they do not have a satisfactory evacuation every day, or at least every other day, but this is not quite so foolish as it sounds. They are correct in supposing that a regular bowel movement is important in old age, for constipation leads to straining and to taking strong laxatives. The result of this can be physically stressful evacuation, probably involving much fluid loss and exhaustion, which can be very bad for those suffering from certain diseases, especially those of the heart.

Constipation of any duration can certainly be harmful if your elderly parent lacks mobility. If the bowels are not moved regularly, the motions can soon become hard and impacted, a condition that can cause discomfort and occasionally a form of diarrhoea too, which is actually a leakage of bowel mucus, but does nothing to relieve the constipation itself. Other complications can set in as well, such as bladder obstruction. If this happens to your parent, do not attempt to administer strong purgatives or to give an enema. If an elderly person is severely constipated, medical advice should be sought, and the doctor will decide on the best course of action, bearing in mind your parent's general health and condition.

Obstruction of the bowel sometimes occurs in old people, particularly if they are bedridden for a while. This can often be prevented by a sensible diet with adequate fluid intake, gentle laxatives which the doctor will prescribe to keep the faeces soft but not loose, and glycerin suppositories when necessary. Other causes (apart from growths in the bowel) may include strangulated hernia when the patient has pain and sickness and requires urgent medical attention. Another condition, common in old age and called diverticulitis, occurs when small bulges develop in the wall of the large bowel. These sometimes become inflamed and infected, giving pain low down on the left side of the abdomen and alternating attacks of constipation and diarrhoea. Diverticulitis can usually be controlled by rest, diet and antibiotics, and surgery is only suggested if there are more serious complications.

Other causes of diarrhoea can be tainted food, or food that is not prepared in hygienic conditions – and an elderly person living alone, whose eyesight or memory is failing, may let her standards of cleanliness in the kitchen slip a little without realising it. Eating too much fruit at one time can also bring on a sharp and exhausting attack of diarrhoea in an elderly person, and if this happens to your parent, give plenty of fluids to avoid dehydration and inform the doctor if it continues. If he or she suddenly develops incontinence of faeces, make sure that the doctor is told, as this can be caused not only by impacted motions in constipation with the resulting 'leakage' from the rectum, but by growths, infection, or as part of a 'stroke' illness, and can frequently be relieved.

PILES

Piles (or haemorrhoids as they are sometimes called) are usually regarded as something of little consequence by those who have never had them, but these varicose veins in the rectum can be exceedingly uncomfortable, and they are often found in the elderly. They cause a sense of fullness in the rectum and sometimes pain and bleeding. They are often the result of habitual constipation and straining, which can usually be relieved by a sensible diet of a high fibre content, with wholemeal bread, bran and a couple of items of fruit each day if the doctor approves. In particularly troublesome cases they can be treated by injection or surgery, and should in any case be investigated to detect any pre-malignant condition.

Diseases and disorders of the genito-urinary organs

URAEMIA

In normal health the kidneys eliminate the waste products of the chemical 'routine' of the body by extracting them from the blood and disposing of them through the urine. Anything that interferes with this important process causes the condition known as uraemia. Amongst the many precipitating factors are heart disease, blocking of the urinary tract, enlarged prostate gland, diabetes, dehydration from diarrhoea or vomiting and internal bleeding. Any of these may respond well to treatment, but if the uraemia is caused by chronic kidney failure the outlook is often poor.

As there is, anyway, a gradual deterioration in the kidney function in old people, this is not an uncommon illness, but it is not easy to diagnose unless the patient is in hospital with all the facilities for tests and constant observation by trained staff. Its symptoms – headache, thirst, loss of appetite, drowsiness, confusion and sometimes twitchings or convulsions – are those of many other diseases too, but if your elderly parent has some or all of these symptoms you should seek medical advice for him or her without delay and give strong support to any suggestion the doctor may make concerning admission to hospital.

KIDNEY DISEASE AND URINARY TRACT INFECTIONS
There are many types of kidney disease and it has numerous causes, which can include kidney stones, tumours, diabetes, and diseases of the prostate gland or of the nervous system. It may manifest itself in backache, general weakness, anaemia, loss of weight, frequency or retention, the passing of blood or pus in the urine and a rise in temperature, and any of these symptoms in your parent should be reported to the doctor at once.

ABNORMALITIES OF URINE
Any very marked change in the colour, odour, or amount of urine passed should be mentioned to your parent's doctor, as it may be a sign of disease or infection of the kidneys, bladder or urinary tract. Blood in the urine can be due to a variety of conditions, including: cystitis, enlargement of the prostate gland, tubercular kidney, leukaemia, or a benign or malignant growth in the bladder. It should be remembered, though, that certain kinds of food, drink and drugs can affect the colour, odour and quantity of the urine passed. If your elderly parent mentions any

of these changes to you, you should be as reassuring as possible, for there may be a very simple reason for it (for example, a helping of asparagus at lunchtime can give the urine passed later in the day an offensive smell); but bear in mind that any unexplained abnormality in the urine should be medically investigated.

RETENTION OF URINE

Retention of urine in the bladder can be caused by over-distension, loss of tone – after abdominal operations – hysteria, uraemia, prostate gland enlargement, impacted faeces, lying for long periods flat in bed, stroke, disease of the spinal cord and various gynaecological conditions which affect the bladder. If your elderly parent becomes at all confused, he or she may not realise that the bladder has not been emptied for some time. Any restlessness or pain and discomfort in the lower part of the abdomen, may be due to this, so keep a careful check to see that there is a regular and normal output of urine. Otherwise, if the bladder becomes distended, overflow incontinence may occur – a situation which should never be allowed to arise, as the bladder loses its tone and there may be some difficulty in establishing control again. Nor should retention be allowed to continue for more than ten hours under any circumstances, and you should inform the doctor of the problem well before this limit is reached, so that the appropriate measures can be taken to relieve it and investigate its cause.

INCONTINENCE OF URINE

Incontinence is one of the giants amongst the many big problems of geriatric care, although tremendous advances in its treatment have been made in recent years. But as you will know if you are caring for an elderly parent who has complete loss of bladder control, incontinence bludgeons and humiliates its victims and has the power to do more than almost anything else to lower the morale and resolve of those who are caring for them at home. Those who have willingly fetched and carried, and cleaned and comforted an elderly parent for a long period can sometimes, when suddenly faced with wet beds, mountains of washing, a

Physical illnesses

constant smell of urine and an agitated and depressed parent, be reduced to a state of mental and physical exhaustion within a matter of weeks. And small wonder, for after a while they begin to feel that their parent's uncontrollable flow of urine is turning into a Niagara of disaster for both of them. Fortunately there are many ways of easing the problem, some of which are considered in Chapter 11, although it still remains a very formidable one.

Brain damage is one of the commonest causes of incontinence in elderly people. There are three levels of command in the central nervous system which control the bladder: two centres in the brain, and one in the lower part of the spinal cord which works by reflex action. In a healthy person these three co-operate well: the two centres in the brain acting as 'head office' and always in control of the lower centre which at their bidding does the work of emptying the bladder. If the two centres in the brain become damaged, the lower one in the spinal cord is left uncontrolled to function on its own. The bladder itself then starts to work only by reflex action, and empties involuntarily as soon as it fills with a small amount of urine. This is a situation which often occurs when the patient has had a stroke. In the absence of very severe mental confusion, infection and poor general health, there is always hope that with good nursing and medical attention bladder control may be regained, but if there is much brain damage in an old and severely weakened patient the outlook is not promising, and incontinence will continue.

There are many other causes of incontinence. These include muscle weakness; enlarged prostate gland; various conditions in women, such as a prolapsed uterus, growths in the uterus and growths and infections in the urinary tract; damage or disease of the spinal cord; emotional shock; diabetes; an overloaded bowel; and the effects of certain drugs given to sedate agitated patients, or to increase the output of urine in heart disease. Such lists of possibilities can sometimes in themselves be depressing to contemplate, but the new drugs, techniques and special equipment that have now been developed have much to offer to the incontinent patient both in and out of hospital. If you are caring for a parent with this problem at home, you can look to your local nursing and social services for a good deal of help and advice on its management, while your parent's doctor is arranging for the investigation of its cause and decisions are being made concerning treatment. Once you are properly organised and equipped to deal with it you will be surprised how much less anxious and defeated you will feel, and the difference this will make to your parent's comfort and peace of mind, although of course it will always be hard work.

PROSTATE GLAND ENLARGEMENT

The prostate gland sometimes becomes enlarged in elderly men, causing difficulty in passing urine. It often begins with a tendency to frequency; sometimes there is sudden incontinence of urine or there may be equally sudden painful retention which needs immediate attention. The enlargement is usually benign, but there can be malignancy in some cases. It is usually dealt with surgically, but if there is inoperable malignancy drug treatment is used and can provide some improvement and relief. If you are caring for your elderly father or father-in-law at home and he seems to be suffering from frequency, try to persuade him to see his doctor rather than allowing it to be dismissed as 'just old age'. It may be due to some slight infection, but if he has to enter hospital for treatment of enlarged prostate remember, when he returns home, that on the whole older men are much more reticent than older women about discussing operations, particularly those of an intimate nature. What to the younger generation may seem to be a perfectly normal topic of conversation may, to an elderly man, be a considerable embarrassment.

CYSTITIS

Many elderly people develop cystitis, which is an infection of the bladder. It can be caused by germs from the blood stream; an obstruction somewhere in the urinary tract which causes the urine to stagnate; prostate enlargement; catheterisation; diseases of the nervous system, such as a stroke which has weakened or destroyed bladder control; or prolonged bed-rest. Its symptoms are frequency, with burning pain on passing water and pain in the lower part of the abdomen: often the urine has an offensive smell and may be cloudy or contain blood, and there may be a rise in temperature. If your elderly parent has these symptoms she should see the doctor at once, and if cystitis is diagnosed he will prescribe an antibiotic and advise a high fluid intake. There will then almost certainly be an improvement in a day or two, but it will be absolutely vital for you to see that your parent takes the full course of the drug prescribed to combat the infection and does not stop the tablets as soon as the pain and other symptoms cease.

In elderly people, unless there are frequent attacks or complications, often no physical investigations are undertaken. Specimens of urine are however tested during and at the end of treatment.

If your elderly parent is disabled and unable to get into a bath, and has no shower, he or she may merely wash the genital area daily with a 'flannel'. This should be strongly discouraged, as it creates a risk of introducing faecal matter from the anus into the urethra, which travels up and sets up infection in the bladder. The flannel itself can become full of harmful bacteria even if it is rinsed through thoroughly after use. If there is no way at all of improving the washing facilities, washing and drying with disposable gauze or cotton wool should be suggested.

PYELITIS

Pyelitis is a kidney infection with somewhat similar causes and symptoms to those of cystitis, but the symptoms come on suddenly, with pain usually on only one side of the abdomen and a high fever. This disease also responds well to treatment by antibiotics.

GYNAECOLOGICAL ILLNESSES

The types of gynaecological illnesses suffered by elderly women (apart from malignancies) are often associated with internal muscles that were weakened at childbirth, although childless women can, and do, have similar problems sometimes. The uterus may become prolapsed – dropping down into the vagina, causing backache and a dragging feeling in the abdomen, and sometimes incontinence of urine, which occurs with the slightest strain, such as a cough or sneeze, or laughter. In some women there may be weakness and displacement of the bladder, with possible infection, and again incontinence, but if it is confirmed that the incontinence is not due to any brain damage, and that it is caused by one of these forms of muscular weakness, treatment by an insertion of a ring, by physiotherapy, or by a surgical 'repair' operation can yield excellent results, even in quite elderly women.

The need for a hysterectomy (the surgical removal of the womb, the fallopian tubes and one or both ovaries if necessary) is undertaken usually to cure the symptoms of fibroids or cysts, which in many cases are non-malignant. It is done more often in middle age, but sometimes has to be recommended for elderly women, too, particularly if there is any suspicion of a pre-malignant condition. It is almost always a highly successful surgical procedure, and not to be feared, although if your elderly mother needs to have this done she may have vivid memories of the stories told to her by other women, thirty or forty years ago. The techniques of surgery and anaesthesia were then very different, and the operation often entailed spending a month in hospital and suffering various complications which were not so easily dealt with. If she is very anxious about it, reassure her and try to find some sensible friend who has had the operation herself to have a chat with her. Postoperatively, things are rather painful and uncomfortable for a few days, as after all abdominal operations, but recovery is usually rapid and in many cases hospitalisation lasts only from about eight to fourteen days and there are no unpleasant side-effects. You will need to be sure, however that she gets the amount of rest recommended by her doctor when she returns home. Although most women are pleased to be rid of a painful uterus, some of them, including the elderly, mourn a little for its loss, and have to be assured that its removal will not make them less feminine. These feelings usually pass quite quickly, though.

Diseases of the eyes

CATARACT
Cataract is one of the most common forms of eye trouble in the elderly. The lens of the eye becomes opaque, and as soon as the

Physical illnesses

patient reaches the stage of finding great difficulty in reading or writing, an operation can be performed to remove the lens, after which they have to wear spectacles. But as most elderly people will, by then, have been wearing them for some time, this is no hardship, and the operation is usually very successful in restoring vision.

GLAUCOMA
The symptoms of glaucoma can be blurring of vision in one or both eyes – sometimes only for a few minutes – pain, redness, vomiting or seeing haloes of colour around lights. This is a serious condition which can lead to blindness if it is not investigated and treated speedily by an ophthalmic surgeon. The treatment may take the form of drops in the eye and taking certain drugs, or surgery to the eye.

There are of course many other diseases of the eyes to which elderly people are prone, some of which are connected with circulatory disorders, and partial blindness can be caused by small cerebral haemorrhages in diabetes. The important thing to remember is to encourage your elderly parent to have his or her eyes tested annually and to see the doctor immediately if there is any sudden loss of vision, pain or inflammation, so that serious damage can be prevented. If you go with her to choose new spectacle frames and new lenses are needed it is worth bearing in mind that plastic lenses are much lighter than glass and therefore make the spectacles more comfortable, particularly for elderly people, whose facial skin is thinner and more liable to develop little pressure sores sometimes if they have to wear spectacles constantly. But plastic scratches easily unless the spectacles are handled and put down very carefully, and glass will stand up to much rougher treatment if your parent is inclined to be forgetful about such small matters.

If your parent has partial or complete loss of sight, he or she can be visited by a social worker from the local authority social services department to discuss the provision of the many aids and services available to those who are disabled in this way, such as home adaptations if necessary, 'talking books' (books recorded on tape and provided with a small tape recorder) and cheap bus, rail and air travel in some parts of the country. Large print books may be obtained through the public library. You should also write to the Royal National Institute for the Blind, 224 Great Portland Street, London, W.1 for information on all the help and advice they can give.

Your parent may understandably become deeply depressed if sight is lost, and will go through a period of mourning for it, in which you will need to give a great deal of sympathetic support as well as encouragement to her to become as independent as possible. Then, when she is beginning to adapt to what may well seem an almost intolerable situation if she lived a normal active life before her sight failed, you should encourage her in any social contacts or interests which may appeal to her and help her to try to face life again, since it can still offer some happiness and fulfilment. But remember that most severely disabled people prefer quiet acknowledgement of their courage to being told how well they are 'adjusting'. Real personal tragedy is never helped by jargon.

Hypothermia

In elderly people, the mechanisms in the body that help it to react to and compensate for changes in temperature are usually impaired, particularly if they have had any illness causing disturbance of the normal circulation of blood to the brain, such as heart disease, a stroke, or infection. Also, tranquillising drugs may to some extent detach them mentally from the external discomforts of a cold atmosphere.

If your elderly parent is living alone, it is possible that he or she may be at some risk; for hypothermia has caused the deaths of thousands of old people. If she is handicapped and not fully mobile following a stroke, crippled with arthritis, or slightly confused and unable to organise adequate warmth in the home and wear suitable clothing in cold weather, you will no doubt be considering what action you can take to provide the care that is needed, either in her home or in yours, as has been discussed in Chapters 3 and 6. In the meantime, it is important for you to know something about the effects of hypothermia.

Physical illnesses

People suffering from hypothermia look very pale and feel cold all over to the touch, even the abdomen, which would normally be warm under their clothing. Their breathing will be slow and their limbs stiff. If you visit, and find your parent in this condition, quick action should be taken to obtain medical assistance, as she may need to be admitted to hospital as an emergency. While waiting for the arrival of the doctor, wrap her lightly in warm blankets and concentrate on raising the temperature of the room to about 75°F., not forgetting to keep it properly ventilated at the same time. Do not use any direct heat in the form of hot water bottles or electric blankets, as this could be fatal. The other measures that will need to be taken must be left to the doctor and subsequently to the staff of the hospital to which she will be swiftly removed, and you will of course be invited to accompany her in the ambulance.

If your parent is living in cold and unsuitable conditions but is taking some time to make up her mind about which kind of help you can offer would be most acceptable, all you can do is to try to improve matters as much as possible in every way. One good preventive measure will be to buy her a single-sized quilted nylon zipped sleeping bag filled with 38-oz. Terylene. This will help to keep her warm and protected from draughts when she is sitting in an armchair. (This, however, should not be given to any elderly person who is confused or forgetful as it could cause a fall if she gets up suddenly and tries to walk without unzipping it.)

Anaemia

If your elderly parent is extremely pale and complains of tiredness you should suggest a visit to the doctor, as these can be the first and most obvious signs of anaemia, although they can of course also be symptoms of other illnesses.

The causes of anaemia are many, and can be as simple as an inadequate diet or bleeding piles, and as serious as a malignant disease such as leukaemia. Old age itself does not cause anaemia, which is always due either to one or to several co-existent conditions. Once the diagnosis has been established by a blood test, investigations can then proceed to discover the reason for it and decisions can be made about treatment.

Diabetes
Diabetes is a disorder in which the pancreas, a gland behind the stomach, fails in its normal function to produce the insulin needed to burn up the glucose in the body's tissues. The muscles then are no longer able to use the glucose as a fuel, so that it collects in the blood and passes into the urine. Due to this malfunctioning of the pancreas, poisonous substances accumulate in the blood. This in turn poisons the nervous system, which can cause the patient to go into a coma. The main symptoms are excessive thirst, an increase in the amount of urine passed, and often, but not always, loss of weight. Muscular wasting may also occur and soreness of the genitals in women.

In mild diabetes, which most often develops in the elderly, a carefully planned diet, recommended by the doctor, which avoids most of the carbohydrates, is frequently sufficient, without the use of insulin. If this method fails, it is followed by anti-diabetic drugs given by mouth. Only a few elderly diabetics require injections of insulin, and if they do they will usually only have to have them once a day. Doctors aim to keep the treatment of the elderly diabetic as simple as possible, with a few clear instructions for them to follow in the matter of diet and medication, as these are more likely to be remembered and adhered to than any complicated programme.

Diabetes is a serious disorder at any age and if your elderly parent suffers from it you should make sure that a regular check is kept on his or her progress. This will be done through a simple urine test and an examination by the doctor. You should also be always prepared to deal with the onset of a diabetic coma (see Chapter 13), for this is a complication that can be fatal. It occurs if the blood sugar falls too low, or if insulin is given too long before a meal or in too large a dose. It can also happen if there has been some departure from the prescribed diet, or if the patient has an infection. Diabetic coma in elderly people is more likely to come on slowly, sometimes over a few days, so it is not very likely that you will be placed in the position of having to take life-saving measures, but it is very important to inform the doctor at once.

Other complications of diabetes in old people can include serious disturbances of vision caused by small blood clots which shut off part of the brain, with the result of partially blocking the vision, so that the patient may only be able to see out of the lower part of the eye. Cataract can also occur. There may be extreme irritability and tiredness, wounds take longer to heal, and the patient may suffer from kidney disease and septic conditions of the feet. In severe cases, as the illness progresses it can also cause cerebral haemorrhages and thrombosis which can in turn cause dementia. The outlook is usually by no means as gloomy as this, however. With proper care and medical attention many diabetics can live a normal life, as modern treatment methods do much to control the condition. Success in maintaining health in this, as in many other disorders, often depends upon the acceptance of it, and on constant vigilance, so that any complications which do arise may be dealt with before they get out of hand.

Diseases of the gall bladder

Diseases and inflammation of the gall bladder can create various types of discomfort in the abdomen, such as indigestion, biliousness, and sickness, and an inability to digest food with a high fat content. Sometimes the bile forms 'stones' which are very painful when muscles of the bile passages contract as the gall bladder tries to expel them into the duodenum. If they cause obstruction, jaundice may result, but jaundice itself, although serious, may be painless. In the young and middle-aged removal of the gall bladder is usually undertaken, but in the older age groups it is not often recommended unless there is jaundice or repeated bouts of pain, as this particular surgical procedure is not so well tolerated by the ageing body. This is a matter of judgement by the patient's doctor and surgeon, and their decision should be accepted with confidence.

Disease of the thyroid gland

The thyroid gland, in the front base of the neck, produces an important hormone. If it is under-active and produces too little, the patient can seem slow in thought and movement. He or she tends to feel the cold badly, the facial appearance becomes thickened, the skin coarser and the voice hoarse, with an occasional 'break' in it. The hair also becomes thinner. If the gland is over-active, producing too much hormone, the patient loses weight and becomes rather 'jumpy', agitated and over-energetic. There may also be swelling of the ankles and breathlessness, and he or she may complain of feeling hot in normal temperatures.

It can be seen from these symptoms that the diagnosis of thyroid disease in the elderly is not easy, because so many of them could be mistaken for some of the normal signs of ageing. But if this diagnosis is established in your elderly parent it can be treated successfully with drugs, which have transformed the lives of many very sick and unhappy people by removing their feelings of uneasiness and lethargy, or reducing their agitation and over-activity.

Parkinson's disease

There are several types of Parkinson's disease. Those most common in the elderly are paralysis agitans, and arteriosclerotic Parkinsonism, which are caused by brain damage and deterioration.

The symptoms are slowness of movement, stiffness and rigidity of the body and a peculiar gait, in which the patient bends forward slightly and tends to shuffle rather than walk, taking small, uncertain steps and sometimes tottering forward, as if about to fall. There is loss of expression in the face, which becomes mask-like in appearance. Tremor, a 'pill-rolling' movement of the fingers and some loss of control of the saliva, mastication and swallowing may occur, and the disease, which is a very depressing one, is progressive. But modern drugs can now do much to relieve the symptoms. If your parent develops Parkinson's disease, she may be painfully aware of her steady decline and an increasing inability to attend properly to personal hygiene. The tendency to drop food, and spill drink, due to the tremor in the hands, may also cause distress. She will therefore need help with bathing, and should be encouraged to wear easily washed drip-dry clothing. Remember also that she must *never* be hurried. Apart from this, your main aim should be to try to keep your parent mobile by helping her to persevere with the prescribed exercises, free from infections, and as contented as possible, and to install every aid in the home which may make life easier (see Chapter 12).

Rheumatism

There are many forms of rheumatism, but the main ones are rheumatoid arthritis and osteo-arthritis.

RHEUMATOID ARTHRITIS

This is an acute form of rheumatic disease, producing pain, inflammation and fluid in the joints, and often leading to deformity. Although it tends usually to occur between the ages of twenty and forty, it can also arise in the older age groups, and mainly in women. The joints of the hands and feet are the first to suffer, swelling slowly, first giving 'twinges' and then a dull ache, and other joints in the body then follow suit. There is some muscle wasting, and sometimes sweating and a rise in temperature. Anaemia and eye troubles can be some of the complications, apart from the very miserable pain and disablement it brings to many people.

In severe cases where there is actual fever, an initial period of bed-rest and treatment in hospital may be advised for splinting of the limbs to prevent deformity, and other measures requiring skilled attention and close observation may be indicated. But many patients are able, with help, to remain in their own homes and attend hospital as out-patients.

The disease may take several years to burn itself out, and the main object of treatment is to improve the general health, and to keep the joints functioning as well as possible. This is done in a variety of ways. Drugs are used to reduce pain and to control anaemia if it is present, and also to deal as far as possible with the inflammation; physiotherapy plays an important part too, with the application of heat, short-wave diathermy, and exercises both in and out of water. Weight reduction is advised when necessary, but some patients who are under par and underweight have to be built up physically with a good diet. In suitable patients, surgery is sometimes undertaken to correct deformities (particularly of the hands) and this can be very successful.

Occupational therapy, when it is available, is one of the great aids to rehabilitation, as it provides the patient with an incentive to exercise the stiffened joints and wasted muscles in the course of purposeful and creative work within her limitations. The company of others in a working group also helps with the depression these sufferers naturally feel because of their pain and the changes in their physical appearance and mobility. Any one of these 'pills' alone is hard enough for most people to swallow, so if you are caring for an elderly parent with this illness you need to remember that you are dealing with a woman who is in almost constant pain that is only relieved by analgesics, whose limbs may be so twisted and swollen that her 'body image' of her own femininity (which is important at any age) is becoming destroyed, and whose desire to remain independent and still able to contribute something to life is frustrated by sheer weakness. She is carrying a very heavy burden and needs all the help and encouragement you can give her, as well as sympathetic understanding of her inevitable mood-swings.

Even the consultant caring for your parent may not be able to predict exactly how long the disease may last, for there may be many remissions and 'flare-ups'. Your task will be to make life as comfortable as you can for her and to find out from the doctor and physiotherapist exactly how to do this by exercises, adaptations to the home, and the installation of various aids, for even when the disease is no longer 'active' your parent may be left with deformities and disability (see Chapter 12).

OSTEO-ARTHRITIS

Osteo-arthritis is the chronic form of rheumatism so many elderly people suffer from, and unlike rheumatoid arthritis there are no marked changes in the patient's general health. Any complicated piece of machinery that depends to some extent on 'joints' for its successful functioning will tend, in time, to wear out more quickly in those joints than anywhere else, and the human body is no exception. In ageing there is a thinning and wearing out of the cartilage around our joints, particularly those of the hips, knees, and spine, which have a lifetime of weight-bearing. For some people this will only mean a slight stiffness and the odd ache or pain now and then, but for others, in whom the deterioration is greater, it can mean much pain and disability, which leads sometimes to depression and social isolation. What often makes it worse is that osteo-arthritis, which creates so much misery for the sufferer, often attracts little sympathy from those who may yet have to experience it, for there is little to show. It is not a dramatic illness. It is more a painful slowing down, which the patient is often expected to accept as the price for living on into old age.

The reason some people's joints suffer more in old age than others' is still debatable and research is being done on this, but doctors agree that there are a number of factors that contribute to the condition. The most important is being overweight. But joints can also become worn by faulty posture, or by working for years in a situation that throws particular stress on certain parts of the body. Accidents and falls which damage joints can also make them more vulnerable to wear and tear. The joints affected often 'creak' and become enlarged around the edges, and pain is felt following exercise. More rarely, one particular joint becomes inflamed and fills with fluid; this always merits immediate medical attention. But normally the two main problems are pain and stiffness. In many elderly people these are moderate, but in some they can be severe. The pain is a long dull ache, from which they feel they never escape, and occasionally it becomes sharp and acute if certain nerves in the area come under pressure. Sometimes it eases up for a while, but they feel under constant threat of its inevitable return. In its worst forms it can make life quite wretched for them especially if it also brings loss of mobility with it, for then they feel literally trapped in their pain, and naturally view the future with some misgivings.

Fortunately there are now many treatments that can help them. The first and simplest measure is weight reduction if necessary. Patients are put on to a medically approved reducing diet, and this alone can do much to ease the pain and stiffness in the load-bearing joints. It is of vital importance, however, that they eat the right kinds of food that supply the correct amounts of proteins, fats, minerals and vitamins. There is little point in relieving an elderly persons of some of their osteo-arthritic pain at the expense of their general health, or leaving them unprotected from the many illnesses to which they are prone if there is a dietary deficiency.

Pain can be eased by a variety of drugs, the front-runner amongst them being still the simple soluble aspirin (always preceded by a drink of milk, unless for some reason this is not allowed in the diet). As some people are unable to take aspirin even in small quantities without gastric upset they must be taken only under medical supervision, particularly if they are to be taken daily for long periods, when internal bleeding and other side-effects may occur. There are other valuable drugs the doctor can prescribe if aspirin is contra-indicated.

Stiffness of the joints and muscle wasting can be greatly improved by various kinds of physiotherapy including heat treatments, massage and a programme of exercises, which must, if they are to be effective, be done regularly – at least twice a day, at home as well as in the hospital's physiotherapy department. These exercises will consist mainly of putting the stiff joint through the full range of movements of which it is capable and then making a little extra effort in spite of the discomfort which may be felt, to extend the range; also tightening and then relaxing muscles in order to strengthen them gradually. It is very important however, if your elderly parent suffers from osteo-arthritis, that the programme of exercises should be taught to her by a trained physiotherapist (who will be glad to explain them to you as well if necessary), since the exercises must be appropriate for her age and condition. Too much, or the wrong type of exercise, can be damaging. Serious harm may be done to the joints (and in some cases the general health also) by a courageous old person and an enthusiastic relative who decide to work out an exercise programme of their own which has not been recommended by the doctor and physiotherapist. Again, the possibility of improvement in mobility and general well-being may be lost completely by those who do not bother to persevere with exercises they have been taught.

Physical illnesses

Surgery is sometimes recommended for the knees, and joint replacement for the hips if the pain and disability become severe. These operations are usually very successful, and the hip replacement operation is now often undertaken in people over seventy if their general condition is good. But such patients are carefully selected for this major operation, which requires a reasonable degree of physical and emotional stamina as well as a willingness to co-operate in physiotherapy afterwards, and they must be strongly motivated towards a return to normal life again. But if your elderly parent undergoes this type of surgery successfully, do not be surprised if, however pleased she is to be free of pain and more mobile, depression sets in for a while afterwards, for although the time spent in hospital may only be a few weeks, it will have been a very exhausting experience, and good care and understanding will be needed during the convalescent period while she is recovering emotionally and gaining confidence in the stability of her new joint.

Most elderly people are keen to remain as independent as possible and one of the greatest contributions you can make to the happiness of your elderly parent if he or she is disabled by rheumatic disease, or any other disorder, is to see that the home is properly adapted and equipped with the many aids needed for daily living (see Chapters 3 and 12).

The Arthritis and Rheumatism Council has produced a very useful booklet: *Your Home and Your Rheumatism*, which is a catalogue of hints on how to do many household chores without putting undue strain on damaged joints, and information on the installation of a number of simple gadgets to make life easier and less painful for the handicapped. It is obtainable from the Arthritis and Rheumatism Council, 8-10 Charing Cross Road, London WC2H oHN.

FROZEN SHOULDER

Frozen shoulder is an extremely painful condition encountered by many elderly people suffering from osteo-arthritis, and also by some who do not have it. It can be caused also by a fracture or a blow, or by strained and damaged tendons, and it can follow a stroke, a heart attack and several other conditions. However, all the patient will be in the mood to think about when he or she is seized by such acute shoulder pain will be what relief the doctor can offer, and how quickly. The immediate assumption of most people is that they must have dislocated the shoulder, since the pain is so intense. Although this is a possibility it is very rare, and they usually find to their dismay that there is no quick solution to the problem. If this happens to your elderly parent, he or she may have to have X-rays, blood tests and an examination by an orthopaedic surgeon before the diagnosis is confirmed and treatment commenced. This will usually be a matter of resting the arm for part of each day in a sling at first when the pain is acute, taking pain-killing drugs, perhaps having an injection into the shoulder joint, and then physiotherapy – heat treatment, and a very gradually increasing range of gentle exercises which must also be done regularly at home according to whatever instructions are given. Occasionally manipulation under anaesthetic is recommended, but more often the shoulder is allowed to recover in its own time. The pain and restriction of movement may take many months to clear up, but with very rare exceptions recovery is complete in eighteen months to two years, provided the exercises are not neglected. Frozen shoulder is more painful to bear in the long term than many fractures, and the loss of sleep due to the difficulty of getting into a comfortable position in bed is an additional problem. Your parent is bound to complain frequently about the pain, because it can be so severe and continuous that it wears most people down. You should try to bear with this, within reason, as it will be a relief for her to discuss it, and constantly reassure her that it is a self-limiting condition, which in time will be just a bad memory, although this is always hard for anyone to believe in the acute phase.

OSTEO-ARTHRITIS OF THE SPINE AND OTHER ALLIED SPINAL CONDITIONS

When man first managed to stand and walk on two feet instead of four, he unknowingly made a down-payment on trouble for himself and his children, on one of the most important parts of his anatomy – his spine. For, at once, it was put under compression strain, topped by the weight of his head, and weighed down

Physical illnesses

as well by the heavy bones in his arms. The young spine, with strong muscular support and healthy cartilage, copes with this upright posture remarkably well, unless it becomes damaged by accident, strain or disease. But after about the first thirty years of life it often starts to complain at the demands made upon it. In middle age it sometimes produces symptoms of wear and tear, and in later life pains in the back and neck are very common and account for much disability in the elderly.

After loneliness, probably one of the greatest threats to their happiness and reasonable enjoyment of life is the painful and disabling effects of the rheumatic diseases, and the spine is very high on the list of problem areas in the body in later life. Yet many people know very little about it, or how it works, except that it contains the spinal cord which it protects.

The spine is a column of strong bones of varying sizes: a beautifully designed collection of small joints that give the body its wide range of movements. These bones, the vertebrae, have small shock-absorbing 'cushions' between them called discs, which have strong covers but soft centres. These joints, like others in the body, can become osteo-arthritic, stiff and painful, but often the cause of 'rheumatic' back or neck pain is the slipping (prolapsing) of one or more of the discs. This means that through injury, strain, faulty posture or deterioration with age, a small tear or crack appears in the tough cartilage 'cushion' cover, and some of its soft contents, or a piece of the cartilage cover itself, protrudes. If its direction is away from the spinal cord and its nerves, it is often painless (although the whole disc is now at risk), but if it protrudes into the most sensitive part of the spinal cord and 'nips' the nerve roots it can cause anything from moderate to very intense pain. This will be felt (according to the position in the spine of the slipped disc) in the head, neck and arms, the upper back, the lower back or in the legs, these conditions being known respectively as torticollis, fibrositis, lumbago and sciatica.

Numbness of the hands and feet sometimes occurs also. The rarer complications are frequency or retention of urine, and some degree of paralysis of the limbs; but these are symptoms very few disc sufferers ever have to face.

If your elderly parent develops back pain and a diagnosis is made of 'slipped disc' (or prolapsed intervertebral disc as it is sometimes called) the doctor will prescribe treatment directed towards encouraging the protrusion to reduce itself spontaneously by taking the weight off the spine – resting flat with just one pillow on a very firm bed. If your parent's bed is soft it will be essential to put a fairly thick wooden board between the mattress and the bed-base to give the whole body firm support. If you have nothing else, even an old door would do until you can get a local carpenter to make a bed-board. This should then be used permanently unless the doctor recommends any particular type of orthopaedic bed (but if you buy one of these, take *his* advice on the make to choose rather than relying on the claims of advertisers). In most cases three to four weeks in bed relieves the really intense pain which makes any movement almost impossible to contemplate, and relief may begin to be felt during the first week. Your doctor may also prescribe pain-killing drugs, tranquillisers of the sort that will promote relaxation of the muscles that are in spasm, as well as reducing the feelings of panic and despair which often accompany pain of such severity, and possibly temporary night sedation to get him or her over the worst period. But you should of course leave the matter of medication entirely in his hands. During this period of bed-rest it will be very important for your parent to be under strict medical supervision; for prolonged immobility of this kind carries with it certain risks to the elderly, such as kidney failure, pneumonia and other conditions, so it is vital to see that the various systems of the body are functioning properly in spite of inactivity.

If this conservative treatment fails, so that your parent continues in great pain with no signs of improvement, and the disc protrusion is causing other serious complications, an operation known as laminectomy may be advised, to remove the damaged disc. This is not always successful, and in an older person, surgery would be a last resort. Other forms of treatment are used in suitable cases, under the direction of an orthopaedic surgeon, such as manipulation and the stretching of the spine by traction, and various forms of physiotherapy. If the damaged disc is in the neck, a temporary plastic collar support is sometimes recom-

Physical illnesses

mended, and a surgical corset with shaped rigid steels at the back for those with a slipped lumbar disc.

When your parent recovers he or she should be shown how to protect the back from further attacks, which are very likely to occur when patients become overtired, or bend or lift in the wrong way. The doctor may decide to arrange for her to see a physiotherapist at the local hospital for instruction in simple exercises, if her condition permits, to strengthen the back and stomach muscles so that they form a natural 'corset' to support the spine. Disc patients must also be shown how to correct bad posture, how to stand, sit, and rise from a chair correctly, and how to bend, push and lift when they have to, without putting too much strain on to their now weakened spine. Above all, they are advised to avoid becoming overweight, as this will aggravate and perpetuate the condition and may precipitate further attacks.

Apart from making sure that your parent has a firm bed, you should see that he or she has a fairly high easy chair with a comfortable but very firm seat (which can be achieved by putting a pastry board under the seat cushion). It must also have good lumbar support and, if necessary, a high-density foam orthopaedic back cushion to keep the right curve in the spine (see Chapter 12). It should have a high back which gives support to the whole length of the spine, and padded arms on which the arms can rest to relieve the spine of their weight. Many disc sufferers find that the Parker Knoll High-back wing armchair is very comfortable, particularly if a strong piece of board is fitted under the seat cushion (See Chapter 12).

A disc sufferer will always find it safer and easier to take a shower than to have a bath, but if this is not possible the bath should have a seat in it with a back support. A removable raised lavatory seat will also be a considerable help when the back is painful; so will a 'back-wash' hair rinser, a 'helping hand' gadget with which to pick up light articles from the floor without bending, and many other aids which are described in Chapter 12. If your parent often has to travel by car or taxi, two square inflatable Li-Lo cushions which will give firm support to the back and buttocks (which many car seats do not give) will be a very good 'buy' (from most Milletts Stores) and they can be folded and easily carried when not in use in a large handbag or a lightweight nylon shopping bag. You should remind him or her too, that travelling in the front seat of a car where there is usually more leg room will be most comfortable.

Many elderly people sit for several hours each evening watching television, and if your parent does this, you should encourage him or her to get up and walk about for at least five minutes each hour, as sitting puts a good deal of compression strain on the spine. When he or she is going on holiday a reminder should be given that ordinary deck-chairs are 'back-breakers' for disc sufferers, who should always choose to sit on hard seats or upright chairs. You should also make sure beforehand that the hotel to which he or she is going can provide a bed-board for the bed (as many now can).

If your parent feels a disc attack starting, you should advise her to rest flat on the bed *at once* rather than trying to struggle on in the hope that the pain will pass, as rest taken early in an attack can often reduce its severity.

Although slipped disc and arthritis are responsible for a high proportion of spinal pain in the elderly, there are, of course, many other conditions, such as thinning and reduction in the bones known as osteoporosis, which sometimes causes backache. Osteoporosis responds well to drug therapy, a high protein diet and a spinal support corset.

Cancer

Cancer is a word that strikes fear into the hearts of most people, and not unnaturally so, since most of us have had a relative or friend who has died of it. But although any symptoms which suggest that an elderly parent in our care has the disease should be carefully and speedily investigated, there is some small consolation to be found in the fact that malignant disease in the elderly sometimes progresses very slowly over a period of years, without causing much distress or incapacity. Many cancer specialists no longer recommended massive and inevitable painful surgical procedures to remove growths, since these sometimes give little trouble to an old person, who may well finally die of something quite different.

Physical illnesses

If cancer is suspected, the important thing to do is to encourage your elderly parent to see his or her doctor without delay, and if it is diagnosed as such, to trust him and his specialist colleagues to make the right decisions regarding treatment in the light of her age, needs, and severity of symptoms.

Cancer is not infectious or contagious, so you have no need to worry on this score if your parent has the disease. Nor is it always incurable; many people are cured of it every year.

The warning signs which may be early symptoms of cancer (but which may only be symptoms of some much less serious disease) are: bleeding from the bowel, bladder or vagina; any unusual change in bowel habits; continual attacks of indigestion with loss of appetite; difficulty in swallowing; a cough or hoarseness which lasts for more than a month; a sore anywhere on the body (but particularly on the face or in the mouth) which does not heal in a few weeks; bleeding from a wart or mole or a change in its size or colour; discharge or bleeding from the nipple; a lump in the breast or anywhere else in the body; or enlarged glands in the neck, groin, or under the arm.

The question of whether your elderly parent, or any adult person, should be told if they have cancer is one to which there can be no answer that would be applicable in every case. The decision must depend upon the opinion of the doctor, your knowledge of your parent's personality, and above all your understanding of what his or her wishes would be in the matter, which is something you both may have discussed in general terms before the onset of the illness. But it must be remembered that it is always extremely difficult to be quite certain of how much anyone wants to be told of the nature of very serious illness when the time comes, whatever she may have said about it when she was in good health. The fact that people have a right to be told the truth about themselves is undeniable, but so is their right to expect those who love them to shield them from it if they prefer only to half-guess at it.

If your parent has always reacted to very anxiety-provoking situations in life with reasonable optimism, and if the disease is in its early stages with a good prognosis, the doctor may decide anyway that it will be in his or her best interests to be told of the diagnosis, for in such circumstances evasion may create much more worry than a full statement of the true facts and may hinder his or her ability to co-operate in treatment. But if the outlook is poor and no cure is possible the doctor will probably wish to discuss it with you first. If so, although you may feel that the responsibility for the decision is now yours, he will no doubt explain to you that it is in fact one that, in time, your parent will make. Your responsibility will be to try to discover (more by listening and observation than by probing) just how much he or she wants to know about the illness and its possible outcome (see Chapter 14).

If we find that we have to be the bearer of bad news in any situation in life we have, somehow, to wait for the moment which we know to be the right one and deliver the message as gently and gradually as possible, so that the truth can 'dawn' rather than be heard as a thunder-clap. Accepting the fact that there can be no 'good' moment to tell someone that she is going to die, we can still try to soften the blow slightly for her by telling her that her recovery now seems unlikely unless some new treatment is found in time to control her disease. This will be no betrayal of trust and will still leave her with that slender straw of hope to hold on to that exists at the heart of every major disaster, and that we destroy at our peril.

If in spite of an obvious rapid decline in health, your parent persists (for his, or her, own sake, or for yours) in denying the reality of the seriousness of the condition, you should try to go along with this. But if by constant direct questioning he or she makes it clear that there is a definite desire to hear the truth actually spoken (which may have been known inwardly for some time) then you should speak it – or ask the doctor to do so, and then be willing to share the burden of it openly.

There are many ways of facing the prospect of death (our own or that of someone we love) with courage, and all of them are right if they are the choice of the one who is going to die. Sometimes people who are very close share the knowledge of the approaching death of one of them and support each other through all its trials without ever discussing it; just as sometimes two people can know without doubt that love exists between

Physical illnesses

them but may have reasons for never declaring it. Others find mutual help and consolation in being able to speak freely about death with no pretence – comforting each other and trying to make sensible plans for the future of the one who will survive. And many people speak of this experience as having been a very important and constructive period in their life and relationship with another person, in which they drew even closer as they worked together towards a final acceptance of the inevitable.

HOME CARE OF CANCER
With modern methods of treatment and pain control many cancer patients only have to be cared for in bed during the last few weeks of life, when the disease has sapped their strength and produced the type of bodily malfunctions which need constant skilled nursing. So you should encourage your parent to try to live a normal life for as long as possible and help him or her to keep occupied. This will not be easy, for anyone suffering from serious illness often feels very depressed and unwell generally, but if your parent can be persuaded to maintain special interests and friendships this will help you both.

It is not always wise in the early stages of the illness to tell neighbours and acquaintances of its exact nature, for although it is such a common disease and nothing whatever to feel ashamed of, some people are so terrified of it that they find that their own inner fears become unbearable in the presence of one who has it. Others, without meaning to do so, tend to 'write off' those who are terminally ill and lose interest in them, while some are simply overcome by embarrassment, feeling that they should express sympathy, but afraid of saying the wrong thing. In this way many cancer sufferers are surprised and deeply wounded by the fact that some of the people they used to meet and talk to every day tend to withdraw and avoid them if they know what they are suffering from, and this can make them feel like social outcasts. It is much better at first to confine the knowledge to close friends and relatives if possible, but this will have to be handled with great tact so far as your parent is concerned or your efforts could misfire and make matters even worse.

If your parent has undergone hospital treatment – radiotherapy, drug therapy or surgery – he or she will need a good deal of support, for all these treatments are unpleasant and exhausting, though they may result in curing the disease, or at least effecting a remission or the alleviation of painful symptoms.

If it has been necessary for an operation to be performed to make a temporary or permanent opening in the abdomen or neck for the functioning of the digestive system, bowels, bladder or throat, the management of this, and the use and cleansing of the necessary appliances will be taught to your parent (and to you also if she has difficulty in coping with it) before discharge from hospital. And if your parent has had radiotherapy or drug therapy the doctor will give clear instructions regarding the care of the skin, and the highly nutritious diet which will be required. He may also prescribe extra vitamins, and iron to combat any anaemia which may be present. You should mention your need for various kinds of help in the home before your parent returns from hospital, as he will be able to arrange this. If necessary a district nurse will visit regularly, and if you and your parent wish, a social worker from the local social services department will give support and advice on any financial problems or special needs. If your parent requires day or night nursing, or both, this can also be arranged through the local domiciliary services. The Marie Curie Memorial Foundation Day and Night Nursing Service, the British Red Cross Society and the St John Ambulance Brigade can also provide home nursing aids and equipment.

THE CANCER SERVICES OF THE MARIE CURIE MEMORIAL FOUNDATION

Although there are many excellent services and organisations which exist to help cancer sufferers, this independent voluntary association, the Marie Curie Memorial Foundation, 124, Sloane Street, London SW1X 9BP, telephone 01-730 9157 (Scottish Office: 21, Rutland Street, Edinburgh EH1 2AH, telephone 031-229 8332), has during the past twenty-seven years pioneered the only comprehensive cancer service in the world. Normally it is capable of answering promptly and effectively every genuine call for help. It works in full co-operation with general practitioners, district nurses and hospitals. Besides offering a 'Day and

Physical illnesses

Night Nursing Scheme' and an 'Area Welfare Grant Scheme' (which gives help 'in kind' to necessitous cancer patients immediately the need is apparent, without any administrative delay) it also has eleven residential homes in Hampstead (London), Tiverton (Devonshire), Glasgow, Newcastle-upon-Tyne, Liverpool, Penarth (South Glamorgan), Caterham (Surrey), Ilkley (West Yorkshire), Belfast, Solihull (West Midlands) and Edinburgh. These provide extensive nursing care by fully trained nursing staff, and a visiting Medical Officer. They also care for patients requiring convalescence, those whose relatives need a rest from heavy nursing duties, and those who have to travel long distances as out-patients for radiotherapy at hospital. The Homes are open to all cancer patients, who are invited to contribute towards their maintenance, but financial hardship in no way affects a patient's admission or subsequent care. Priority in admission is decided solely on medical and social grounds.

If you think that your parent could benefit from a period in one of these Homes (which in some cases care for patients until they die) you should, if he or she agrees, discuss it with the general practitioner or the Medical Social Worker at the hospital where treatment is being given. Application forms and further information can be obtained from: The Homes Officer, Marie Curie Memorial Foundation, 138 Sloane Street, London SW1X (not from the Head Office address). Sixteen information leaflets on the subject of cancer and its prevention and care are also available from the Marie Curie Memorial Foundation Education and Welfare Department at the same address, and anyone caring for a relative with this disease would find these very helpful.

If your parent's cancer proves to be incurable you will naturally hope that it will be possible for him or her to die peacefully at home. As you can see, there are many services now available that may enable this to happen. But if your health or circumstances make this impossible, then both of you will be happier if care is given during those last months or weeks in a Home where pain can be controlled and symptoms eased by those who are experts in the field of terminal care – where you can visit them frequently in a homely atmosphere to give all the love and support that is needed right to the end.

9
Mental illness and impairment

One of the most harrowing experiences life can bring is that of caring for an elderly parent at home if he or she has become seriously disabled mentally with the type of illness or brain damage which produces distressing symptoms such as severe memory loss, delusions of persecution, restless agitation and the kind of aggressive behaviour that places him or her totally beyond the reach of reason.

Those who have been through this with a parent, however well-balanced they are themselves, usually describe the horror of it in terms that leave us in no doubt at all about its nightmare quality. Some of them recall the acute anxiety which sometimes turned to fear for their parent's safety as well as their own and other members of the household, the hammering of their nerves by their parent's unreasonable demands, repetitious talk and inability to hold a normal conversation, the emotional stress and sheer physical tiredness that reduced them to a state of utter exhaustion, and the sorrow of losing contact with someone they loved. They remember too their feelings of guilt connected with their occasional, understandable loss of patience, and the final decision they had to make when they were no longer able to cope with their parent at home, and had to allow those professionally qualified to deal with serious mental illness to relieve them of the burden of caring, in circumstances so intolerable that they were themselves being driven to the brink of a breakdown.

Some too have painful memories of the long battles they had to fight to get help in the home, and later the hospital treatment their parent so urgently needed from an under-staffed, over-worked and under-financed National Health Service, with its shortage of beds for psycho-geriatric patients. Their feelings of anger and resentment at the failure of the State and the community to give them the support to which they were entitled are of course quite justifiable. In many instances they had had to struggle for long periods against impossible odds, sometimes suffering as much, if not more than their sick parent, and their sense of disappointment at not being able to care for her at home until her death contributed more than they may have realised at the time to the intensity of their feelings of distress about the situation generally. The truth is that although most doctors, nurses and social workers would like to be able to produce help speedily for the elderly who are severely impaired mentally and in need of hospital treatment, the resources available to them in an increasingly ageing population are now so stretched that the caring relative sometimes finds herself and her request for help passed from one service to another for many months before action is taken. She may have to bring her plight and that of her parent constantly to the notice of the doctor and the local authority social workers to make sure that they are aware of the impossibility of her continuing to care for her parent at home. In fairness to them it must be stated that most of them act as quickly as they can to facilitate the admission of a mentally ill old person to hospital, but they cannot manufacture vacancies where none exist, and the whole situation is fraught with enormous difficulties which need to be dealt with by a massive injection of more money, more staff, and more accommodation for psycho-geriatric patients everywhere.

If you are struggling with a situation of this kind at present and trying to get hospital care for a very disturbed, tyrannical or completely unmanageable parent, you will no doubt be feeling desperate for some practical help in your endeavours. There are no easy answers, but it is hoped that some of the information and advice in this chapter may be of help to you.

If on the other hand you are caring for a parent who is showing no sign of mental impairment, it is very important that you should not allow yourself to live in constant dread of her ultimately developing some form of mental illness, for the number of old people who become mentally disabled is very small. Most escape it completely. Only a few show significant mental changes from the age of about sixty-five, and of those few an even smaller percentage become violently aggressive and a danger to themselves or others. Some suffer loss of memory, others have harmless delusions or hallucinations which may worry them (or, more rarely, may even please them) but do not necessarily lead to anti-social behaviour, and others suffer from anxiety or depression. But it is the hostile, over-active and disruptive dementias that we hear most about, and although their symptoms cause untold suffering to those who are caring for them until they are admitted to hospital, it should not be forgotten that many of the mentally impaired elderly whose illnesses take a gentler form *are* being cared for quite adequately at home with the help of modern drug therapy, psychiatric out-patient treatment and sometimes psychiatric Day Hospital support, even though their relatives are always under strain, and it is never easy.

So in considering, as we must do here, some of the worst types of mental illness and brain damage suffered by a small minority of the elderly, try not to dwell upon the possibility of such disasters overtaking your own parent, or you will spend your time looking anxiously for the appearance of 'mental' symptoms in her and misinterpreting every slight eccentricity, forgetting that, as the psychiatrist Dr K. Bergman pointed out in his excellent book, *The Aged – Their Understanding and Care* (Wolfe Publishing Ltd, 1972) the elderly are usually just 'themselves only more so'. Elderly people who show very slight changes in their ability to concentrate and think quickly, or whose memory for recent events is not as sharp as it used to be, should never be assumed to be beginning to fail seriously in their mental powers, and history has taught us that many people produce the best work of their whole lives in their later years. For most of us, some slowing down of the mind is as inevitable as the slowing down of the body in old age, and the fact that your mother may no longer want to be bothered with complicated knitting patterns or make her own dresses, as she may have done expertly all her life, is not a sinister sign of mental decay.

Real mental illness or impairment – that is, disorders of either the emotions or the intellect – is something quite different, and its symptoms are fairly easily recognised by the general practitioner, consultant physician, or psychiatrist. These illnesses often

Mental illness and impairment

exist with (and sometimes are even caused by) a physical illness, and if this can be dealt with recovery, for some, is by no means rare. Clear cases of incurable brain damage are another matter, and there are tests and X-rays which can confirm the diagnosis of these conditions, but there are surprisingly few other forms of mental impairment in the elderly that doctors can confidently pronounce without doubt to be permanently and totally irreversible. This encouraging fact should always be borne in mind, and if your parent begins to show signs of mental disturbance of any kind, you should ensure that she is seen by her doctor as early as possible in her illness. You may be tempted to put this off in case your fears about her mental condition are confirmed, since the reality would be so hard to accept. In wanting to protect your parent, and the family, from what you may wrongly regard as the stigma of mental illness, you may be reluctant to admit that there is anything seriously wrong with her at all. The thought that the doctor may suggest her admission to hospital for observation and assessment may also worry you unnecessarily, but if you delay in seeking medical aid valuable time can be lost, particularly if your parent's mental condition has a physical cause which requires urgent treatment.

As the aim of this book is to give general advice to those who are caring for elderly parents, it would be inappropriate and confusing to attempt to describe all the many different causes, effects and treatments of mental illness and impairment in old people. This is something that should only be done by a qualified medical practitioner. If, however you wish to go into the subject more deeply, your local public library will be able to provide you with books by medical and psychiatric specialists in this field, and your parent's own general practitioner should be the first person to whom you should turn for the diagnosis and treatment of any mental disturbance he or she may develop.

There are a number of different mental disorders elderly people may suffer from, but the main ones about which you should be informed are:

Confusion
A confusional state can affect an elderly person in many different

ways. He or she may not be aware of what year, month, day or time it is. Memory may be affected. There may be difficulties in recognising even close relatives, and everything is 'muddled'. If the onset is sudden – which it often is – and an old person who seemed fairly well one day becomes very confused within a matter of hours, the cause may be a physical one which will respond to the appropriate treatment, provided medical advice is sought quickly. There may be a urinary or chest infection, an undiagnosed or improperly handled diabetic condition, or retention of urine or faeces. There could have been a slight stroke or a 'silent' heart attack. Even the possibility of a brain tumour cannot be ruled out. Other causes can be the drinking of too much alcohol, an adverse drug reaction, or a drug overdose. Occasionally the 'trigger' can be severe emotional shock, such as a bereavement or a sudden change of surroundings to an unfamiliar environment.

If the onset is slow the outlook is not so promising, as there may have been a mild state of dementia (see below) beginning before the actual confusional state arose. On the whole, though, if the patient's condition is diagnosed and treated early enough, there is more room for optimism in this situation than in many other disorders of old age. If you ever find yourself faced with this problem with your parent, you should call the doctor immediately and ask him to visit. He will probably want your parent to be examined by a consultant psychiatrist or geriatrician (which can be done under the National Health Service) either at home, or at hospital. If he thinks it is necessary, in-patient hospital treatment may be advised. If he decides that it would be better for your parent to be treated at home, you should make it very clear what facilities (or lack of them) you have for giving constant care and attention and if you feel that it will be impossible for you to cope, say so. If, on the other hand, the consultant is of the opinion that the confusional state is going to be only a temporary disturbance, and that good sleep at night, and quiet days can be achieved for your parent by drug therapy, you may feel that you can manage for the time being, provided you are assured that regular medical, nursing and social work support is going to be available to you. You should not be afraid to discuss your feelings, your fears, and your limitations with the doctor, and any consultant he may call in, right from the start, and to explain quietly but firmly what your expectations are with regard to help with your parent.

Organic dementia

If you are caring at home for a parent with incurable and progressive brain damage, or visiting him or her in hospital, you should be aware of several things which often happen to relatives in this situation, as it will help you to understand your feelings and reactions as you go through this painful experience. Like everyone faced with a major problem, you will naturally, at first be looking and hoping for a solution, and perhaps expecting that with all the advances that have been made in medical science, even if the experts cannot cure the illness, they can at least render it manageable. As it becomes clear that this is not easily done, feelings of anger may take over, some of which you will know are unreasonable but may not be able to help having. Anger against your parent, as the cause of your acute anxiety and disrupted life, anger against yourself for being unable to protect him or her from the ravages of the illness and the possibility of the need for permanent hospital care, and anger perhaps towards everyone connected with the treatment situation; for whether they are neglectful, or faithful, in their duty towards your parent, you may feel a need to blame someone for the disaster, and they will be the obvious candidates. (This last reaction is one which is well known and understood in the medical and nursing professions.)

Only when you reach the stage of accepting that there *are* no solutions to the problems of irreversible brain damage, and only very minor ways of easing the great strain on relatives until (if there is gross deterioration) the patient is finally hospitalised will you be able to concentrate effectively on helping your parent and yourself through the various phases of his or her inevitable decline.

There are two main types of organic dementia: *arteriosclerotic*, associated with arteriosclerosis – the hardening of the arteries, which in some cases causes brain damage through poor blood supply to that part – and *senile*, where there is a gradual loss of brain cells. But it should be remembered that most elderly people escape these disorders completely.

ARTERIOSCLEROTIC DEMENTIA
Not everyone suffering from arteriosclerosis will inevitably end up with arteriosclerotic dementia; but if your parent has a serious heart condition, due to the narrowing and hardening of the arteries in the body generally, or a very high blood pressure, or has suffered one or more strokes, it is possible that he or she may be at risk. Some of the early signs of the development of this type of dementia, such as lethargy, lack of initiative, emotional instability, irritability and some memory loss can, of course, be symptoms of many other illnesses too, as can a sudden attack of confusion, so do not assume immediately that your parent is beginning to dement. Ask the doctor to visit and act upon his advice and that given by any consultant he may call in. They may wish to arrange for certain tests and examinations, not only in order to establish a psychiatric diagnosis, but to check on your parent's general condition. If it is decided that she is suffering from arteriosclerotic dementia they will probably be reluctant to suggest admission to hospital if the disease is in its early stages and if you agree that you can cope with the situation at home, as, quite apart from the bed shortage, such patients are happier in a familiar environment. But as previously stated, your own health and circumstances should be fully discussed when these decisions are being made.

You will no doubt find the change in your parent's personality sad and bewildering, and if she remains at home it will be a considerable strain unless you have very good support from your family, friends, and the local nursing and social services, so that you do not have to spend every hour of the day with her. It may be possible for your doctor to arrange for daily transport to a Psychiatric Day Centre on weekdays, where some patients in the early stages of dementia can be cared for very well. If slight signs of restlessness by day and sleep disturbance develop, so that you find you are having to deal with the need for vigilance and broken nights, it is possible, in some cases, for drugs to be prescribed of

Mental illness and impairment

sufficient strength to control this, and you should seek the doctor's advice immediately. Fortunately for them, and for their relatives, many elderly people who suffer from arteriosclerotic dementia, and other forms of organic dementia, die from a heart attack, a stroke, or some other disease before the illness progresses to the stage at which behaviour may become aggressive or even violent. At that stage delusions of persecution and hallucinations, coupled with complete disorientation, slovenliness and restless wandering, call for constant care and observation that relatives cannot possibly give. But if your parent develops arteriosclerotic dementia, and it becomes advanced, while making an effort to remember that her behaviour is due to a brain-damaged condition, trying to prevent her from becoming bed-ridden, humouring her as far as possible, and making no attempt to appeal to a reason which no longer exists, you should concentrate all your efforts on her admission to hospital before you become ill yourself with mental and physical exhaustion. You will, no doubt have feelings of ambivalence at the prospect of this – longing to be free of the burden of anxiety, but deeply distressed that the nature of the illness makes it impossible for you to continue to provide adequate care at home; but you will realise that unless you are wealthy and can pay very high fees for private residential care, or have a large house, part of which can be suitably *and* securely adapted for the exclusive use of your parent and day and night nurses, there is no other answer.

SENILE DEMENTIA

This form of progressive mental impairment produces symptoms somewhat similar to those of arteriosclerotic dementia. In its early stages the most obvious sympton is failure of memory for recent events. The memory for events of past years is usually still intact, and the patient tends to tell stories of past happenings in her life over and over again. There is usually a steady slow decline in mental ability and in the performance of simple tasks, and some disintegration of the normal personality, but it is rare for this type of dementia to start before the age of about seventy.

Sometimes a personal or family crisis, a bad fall or an infection can precipitate a sudden state of agitation and confusion, when there is restlessness, and wandering out of doors alone and getting lost. Less advanced cases of senile dementia, when the patient is vague and forgetful but has not developed any anti-social habits, can sometimes be looked after at home if there is a strong family network near at hand to share the responsibility, and very good support from the local medical, nursing and social services, but the strain on the caring relative is great.

If your parent is suffering from this illness, he or she will normally have been seen at regular intervals by the doctor once the diagnosis was established, but as the illness advances you may find yourself faced with the development of symptoms which you cannot handle. These may (though not always) include noisy, abusive, threatening behaviour, delusions of persecution, hallucinations and illusions, restlessness at night, agitation during the day, sexual indiscretions, the hoarding of rubbish, incontinence of urine and faeces, loss of interest in personal hygiene and complete disorientation. As problems of this nature begin to arise it will obviously no longer be possible for you to provide care at home. When you give the doctor a clear account of the bizarre symptoms you are having to try to cope with, he will probably suggest that your parent should be admitted to hospital, and make every effort to arrange this without delay. But if it seems that your parent may have to wait for an indefinite period for a bed, and your situation is desperate, make sure that the doctor understands this, and if necessary remind him of the fact by frequent telephone calls to the surgery. Contact the local authority social services department also (if you are not already receiving regular visits from a social worker who is involved in your problem) and ask for a visit from a social worker, to give you some emotional support in the numerous crises you will be facing in the home. Both you and the social worker will know that what you need is not just emotional support (although this may help) but the admission of your parent to hospital. The involvement of the social services department may help you to achieve this, for if the staff are constantly being asked to call to see you when you are at your wits' end, they will report this to your parent's doctor, and their view of the deteriorating situation in which you are trapped will add weight to his efforts to find

Mental illness and impairment

your parent an immediate vacancy. In any case, you will find that frequent cries for help at this time will bring much better results than trying to keep a stiff upper lip. It is never pleasant to feel that one is pestering an already overworked service, but if you do not press hard when no move is being made it may be assumed that your need is not really urgent, and that your silence is evidence that you are still managing to cope fairly well. You should of course be reasonable in your attitude towards the considerable difficulty your parent's doctor may experience in getting her into hospital, but you will also have every right to expect that he will see that her case is treated as an emergency if it is one.

Do not imagine that there are always problems and battles to be fought when a patient with advanced dementia needs to be admitted to hospital urgently. This is not so, but if you ever have to face this situation make sure, when you are drawing the doctor's attention to your plight, that he is aware that you are 'not waving, but drowning'.

Delusions, hallucinations and illusions

If your parent is dementing, your lack of basic knowledge of some of the very strange and upsetting symptoms may add to your burden of fear and anxiety. Delusions, hallucinations and illusions can be particularly distressing to witness and to live with.

DELUSIONS
Delusions are false beliefs which cannot be altered by any appeal to reason. They are found to exist in many different types of mental illness and impairment but in dementias suffered by the elderly they are most likely to take the form of delusions of persecution, which are often connected with the failure of the memory. For example: they may mislay some article of clothing, money, cheque book, or private papers and become convinced that those who are caring for them, often with great devotion, have stolen them, or that they, or some mysterious outside force or organisation, are plotting their ruin and downfall. Some believe that people they pass in the street are whispering about them, or that their neighbours are setting out deliberately to annoy

them. If, for instance, a child's ball or the cat next door finds its way into their garden, they may think that this has been planned to upset them. There are others who believe that their house has been broken into or that they have been sexually assaulted, or they may begin to accuse a faithful elderly marriage partner of adultery. A conviction may exist that they have suddenly been plunged into a state of dire poverty, or a bizarre type of physical illness (for example, that a snake is inhabiting the bowels), or they may have delusions of grandeur in which they believe themselves to be rich, powerful or famous. Some may imagine that their home has been bugged, or that live wires are being run through the floors of the house by the Electricity Board. They can, in fact be tortured by any kind of false belief, and in turn torture those around them with their suspicions, wild accusations, threats and (more rarely) acts of violence.

The type and severity of delusions vary of course with the nature of the illness and the personality of the patient. It is possible for people of any age to develop them, whether their mental illness is organic or functional, and not all elderly people who begin to show signs of paranoid tendencies with delusions are necessarily suffering from one of the dementias. A few may have had the seeds of this illness much earlier in life, being 'touchy' and suspicious of other people in their places of work and personal relationships. This becomes worse, and the whole picture more florid, in old age when the circumstances of their lives seem more threatening and mental control is less.

Others may develop this 'paraphrenia', as it is sometimes called, after a severe infection of the chest, bladder or other organ, and it is not uncommon for it to start after a bad attack of influenza. It can also be precipitated by certain drugs, and poor sight and hearing may be contributory factors. The removal of what appears to be causing their distress – the curing of some infection, or the departure of a hated neighbour – does not necessarily restore their mental equilibrium, but treatment with drugs, and other forms of therapy if they are depressed (as is often the case), can be successful in many instances.

If you are caring for a parent who is suffering from delusions characteristic of this group of illnesses, and it has been recommended that for the time being she should remain at home and receive hospital treatment on an out-patient basis, or if she is awaiting admission to hospital, you will no doubt be having a very trying time. There will be nothing you can do to dispel her delusions and you will have to learn the wisdom of accepting them up to a point to avoid confrontations, but you should not decide to agree to go all the way with her false beliefs just for the sake of peace and quiet. If you do, you and the whole household will soon find yourselves being drawn into your parent's world of unreality and caught up in an unhealthy web of lies and pretence. On the other hand, frequent and vehement denials of a person's paranoid beliefs usually make matters worse and bring out aggression. A quiet, low-key attitude is the most satisfactory one, and you should try to hold fast to truth yourself, while accepting that your parent's 'truth' is in fact part of the illness from which she is suffering.

It is also worth bearing in mind that not all 'touchy', suspicious or even slightly paranoid elderly people who complain of anti-social behaviour by their neighbours, who report the theft of a purse, or acts of cruelty or neglect from those paid to attend them, must always be assumed to be merely expressing a delusion of persecution. This may be so in many cases if the elderly person is known to be mentally ill, and good nursing staff and others are often wrongfully accused of unkindness when they are doing everything in their power for their patient in what is an extremely stressful occupation; but if your parent, living alone or in hospital makes allegations which you feel may possibly be true you should always make a tactful but very careful check on them. It is far easier of course to dismiss a complaint with 'Mother (or father) is just imagining things again', but unpleasant and sadistic people do occasionally put in an appearance in the lives of old people, just as they do sometimes in the lives of the young, and they are entitled to be protected from them if they are found to exist in reality. The possibility is always a long shot, but one which should not be overlooked.

A good example of such a situation is the case of the old lady who was informally admitted, depressed and agitated, to a psychiatric hospital. She complained that she could no longer stand the 'black moss' that was spreading all over the walls of the rooms in her council flat, which, she said, in spite of their many promises, the council were not dealing with. This was initially thought to be a paraphrenic delusion of persecution, but after a few days of observation, interviews and tests the psychiatrist felt there was some doubt about the original diagnosis, and that although she was certainly depressed and anxious she did not 'present' as someone suffering from paraphrenia. With the patient's permission, he asked the hospital social worker to go to view her home, and when the flat was inspected the old lady's so-called 'delusion' was found to be a plain statement of fact. Although her use of the words 'black moss' had been a little misleading, it had been the only way she could think of describing it, and large areas of the walls and ceilings in every room were covered by a dark fungus – the result of a severe condensation problem.

HALLUCINATIONS AND ILLUSIONS

Hallucinations, which are often interwoven with delusions in many types of mental illness, both organic and functional, are false sensory perceptions; for example, a patient who 'sees' a non-existent tiger snarling at the bedside.

Illusions are real perceptions which are falsified and based on misinterpretations of external stimuli. For example, it could be said that Heathcliff in Emily Brontë's *Wuthering Heights* was suffering from an auditory illusion when he mistook the sound of the wind on the moors for the voice of his dead beloved, Cathy.

If your parent is suffering from a mental illness, she may have hallucinations or illusions of sight, sound, smell, taste or touch. The most common are the auditory hallucinations, in which the patient hears voices which may seem to be threatening, abusing, or informing her of the evil intent of those around her. The delusions of persecution which sometimes follow can lead on to aggressive behaviour.

Visual hallucinations, which often occur in toxic confusional states and other illnesses, can sometimes be very frightening. The patient may 'see' things like a pack of savage wolves, fearful monsters, burning bodies, or knives pointed at the throat.

Mental illness and impairment

Sometimes too a particular ornament or pattern on the curtains may be 'seen' as an animal or some strange little creature with a human face who fills them with fear. According however to the consultant psychiatrist Dr Ian Martin, who wrote an article 'A haunting malady' in the magazine *New Society* in May 1975, some very lonely people coming from all levels of society, with a wide range of intelligence and insight – people of temperate habits, with no past history or present signs of major mental illness – occasionally describe 'seeing' and 'hearing' various kinds of small, benign and comforting 'visitors' in their homes, often in the form of friendly and entertaining children or animals. He suggests that these particular phenomena, which would normally be referred to as hallucinations, may primarily be a rare sign of loneliness. This is obviously a debatable point of view, and he makes it clear that the situation requires more study than has so far been possible with the limited material available, but it serves to show how careful relatives should be not to jump to hasty conclusions if an elderly mentally stable parent, living alone, mentions any strange feelings or occurrences, particularly those which comfort rather than disturb them. He or she *may* need to see a psychiatrist, but the need may simply be for more family support and interest to reduce feelings of isolation. The bereaved who are not mentally ill, but suffer strong feelings of deprivation, often experience hallucinations or illusions and tell those they can trust with their confidences that they sometimes see, hear, and talk with their deceased partner, which is a great consolation to them. This is discussed very fully in Colin Murray Parkes's book *Bereavement*. He points out that studies of grief in adult life show that, in the newly bereaved widow, the perceptual element is very strong, and it is not surprising that 'searching' and 'finding' go together.

If you are caring for an elderly parent who suffers from hallucinations or illusions which distress her and those around her, you should have a word with her doctor about it; but if they are not of an upsetting nature, you should wait and see what, if anything, develops from this, meanwhile making sure that she is receiving all the love and support she needs. Sometimes, given this support, the lonely and deprived find in time that they no longer need their 'visitors' – rather like lonely childen whose imaginary 'friends' often disappear when they start to go to play-groups or nursery school.

Even if your parent is suffering from delusions and hallucinations which are part of a serious mental illness, it is by no means impossible for these to be eased considerably by drug therapy and other forms of treatment. The doctor will take the appropriate steps to see that this or, if necessary, in-patient hospital treatment is provided.

If your parent does have to go into hospital, you may find it very helpful to talk through the feelings of guilt and anxiety which are so naturally felt by relatives in this situation with the hospital social worker or senior nursing staff. It will be valuable, too, for those who are caring for your parent to be told of his or her previous personality and achievements so that they may have a glimpse beneath the sad mask of the mental illness.

Depression and anxiety states
People of every age experience feelings of depression and anxiety from time to time – often connected with disappointment, boredom, loneliness, lack of love, or fears about their health or their future, and in normal health most people manage to take these in their stride. But sometimes the needle gets stuck in some particular groove of depression, and what should have been a passing feeling becomes a true depressive illness.

The elderly, some of whom have plenty to be depressed about anyway, are a particularly vulnerable group where this illness is concerned. Not only can it hit them 'out of the blue' with few warning signs – just as it can a younger person – but it is also often tied in with one of the many disabling illnesses of old age, such as a stroke, or crippling arthritis.

Depression is not easy to diagnose in old people. Many of them have been brought up to believe that they must always control the expression of feelings of pessimism and defeat, and they dread the thought of being labelled as old miseries. Unfortunately these are often the ones who long to reach out for the phone, and ring their doctor, or the Samaritans, when they feel at the end of their tether, but reach out for an overdose of sleeping tablets

Mental illness and impairment

instead, for the highest rate of suicides in our society is in the upper age groups.

Some of the elderly suffer from depression for no immediately obvious reason, but others have all the ingredients for a depressive or anxiety state forced upon them by their circumstances. Life seems to deal them one shattering blow after another in the space of just a few years, and for some of them the theme of old age is grief, a long sorrow unrelieved by the element of hope that exists for the young. They may lose a husband or wife; they may grieve too for the loss of their health or a previous role of parent or worker, to which they gave themselves so completely that they now have difficulty in establishing their own identity, having lost the knack of functioning happily in the world just as themselves. They often feel like strangers in the community, which no longer seems to need them in the ways in which they wish to be needed. There can be grief also for the gradual loss of some of their mental and physical skills; and if there is even a mild degree of real impairment, plus an awareness that the tide of their normal capabilities is beginning to turn, this can cause tension, agitation and anxiety as well. Added to all this, the elderly person may be grieving for the loss of mobility, sight or hearing, and be wondering just how much more life is going to take away from them before they reach the stage of 'sans everything'.

This picture of depression and anxiety in old age remains in many cases hazy and difficult to make out, like a photographic negative. There are shadowy outlines: the signs of general slowing up, insomnia, loss of concentration, withdrawal from previous interests and social contacts, poor appetite, sometimes hypochondriasis, agitation, a feeling of impending disaster or self-reproach. If someone notices and cares enough to see that help is given, the diagnosis can be established, the cause investigated, and the condition treated. The results of treatment are usually very good. In many cases drug therapy is all that is needed if the elderly patient is receiving good support from family and friends but there are several other forms of treatment used, including psychotherapy, group therapy, occupational therapy and others for suitable patients.

If your elderly parent develops some of these symptoms of

depression and anxiety and there is no sign of improvement in the course of a few weeks in spite of all your efforts to ease any feelings of loneliness she may have, to ensure that she feels loved and to try to bring as much interest into her life as possible, it is useless to attempt to jolly her along, or to suggest, even in the kindest way, that she should try to pull herself together. In a true depressive illness the patient has no emotional strength left to do this. She will need medical advice, and treatment, with your support while she is undergoing this, and your help in planning a way of life when she has recovered that will give her the social contacts and interests which may have been lacking previously. A discussion with the doctor, hospital psychiatrist and social worker involved in the treatment should be useful to you in this connection.

Alcoholism

Alcoholism is on the increase in people of all ages in our society, and the elderly are no exception, although they tend to drink in more solitary situations. Those who drink to excess do so for the same reasons as members of the younger generation – because it is a kind of anaesthetic to ease the pain of living, available across the counter, without prescription. It gives them a 'lift' of comfort, courage and temporary well-being, and boosts their confidence, but too much of it, for too long, can also bring them mental impairment by permanently damaging the central nervous system.

Elderly men who are able to go to a pub and drink in the company of friends are not quite so vulnerable, but the lonely widow, living a solitary life, who previously never felt the need for the consolation of the bottle, or the ex-career woman who has retired can often be at risk. Sometimes the 'slide' starts when a well-meaning friend advises them at a time of crisis, such as bereavement, to 'take a couple of glasses of tonic wine each day to build yourself up' – and the 'tonic' may turn into an addiction.

Women who become heavy drinkers usually feel a far greater sense of guilt about it than men do and they receive more condemnation from society. Provided a man is not violent or abusive in drink, he is often regarded by his friends and neighbours as just 'a bit of a lad', but a woman alcoholic knows that when her secret is discovered she will be treated with contempt and receive little help or compassion from many of the people she knows. This leads women drinkers to go to great lengths to conceal their addiction by drinking alone, and doing their heaviest drinking at times in the day when they are fairly sure they will have no callers. They will also tend to keep just one bottle of sherry in their drinks cupboard or trolley to offer to visitors, their other bottles (often of something much stronger), being hidden in their wardrobe, in their bedroom, where even visiting sons or daughters are unlikely to discover them. Women drinkers often suck strong peppermints to mask the smell of alcohol in the breath, and make excuses to cut a telephone conversation short if a relative or friend rings them during or after a drinking session, when they know that their speech may be slurred and their reactions slowed up or they may be uncharacteristically maudlin and voluble. All these are small points to look for if your elderly parent is living alone and you suspect that she is drinking too much. If this is so, clearly you have no right to interfere in her life just because she is old, but you naturally feel both a desire and a duty to do everything you can to help her. This can best be done by bringing the problem out into the open between the two of you, so that it can be discussed with sympathy, understanding, and acceptance of her difficulties. The root of them may be loneliness; if this can be eased, many alcoholics have a good chance of breaking the habit. Contact with Alcoholics Anonymous (whose number may be found in the telephone book) can also be a help in some cases, but most important of all, your parent should be encouraged to consult her general practitioner; not only because he may be able to suggest a form of treatment that she could not find elsewhere, but because, if he is already prescribing certain drugs for any physical illness, it is vital that he should know about the drink problem.

Accepting changes in the personality and behaviour of elderly parents

Everyone's personality and behaviour changes to some extent as they mature, but those who have not yet had to face the problems of old age sometimes find it difficult to understand the changes taking place in their elderly parents. White hair, wrinkles, and slowness of movement are changes we all expect, but alterations in response and reaction in those we have loved for so long are not quite so easy, and can be very disturbing. For years we may have felt little need to look to our parents for support, but the memory of the strength they represented to us in our youth remains. However independent and self-confident we become, it is a comforting thought that they are always there to go home to (if only in the emotional sense) if life plays us false. If they begin to change in old age, becoming more self-absorbed and slightly detached from us, it can be a strange and bewildering experience. We see the 'tree' we played and sheltered under as children beginning to wither, and all safeties and certainties are brought into question. We then have to face the truth that in time everything changes.

Our first reaction, although we may not realise it, may be one of anger and resentment, a feeling of being in some way let down by them. How could they do this to us? *We* are doing all we can for *them*, and all we ask is simply that they should continue to be themselves – the people we have always known. Why are they being so different, and sometimes so difficult? We forget how difficult we ourselves may have been for *them* to handle in the past, at times of change in our own lives. Getting to know just a little about the changes and mental impairment that can be the result of even very slight brain damage or deterioration in the elderly can soon supply us with some of the answers, and help us to accept what is happening with no weakening of the relationship.

If there is a total change in the personality, with the development of aggressive behaviour, this of course is much harder. It comes as a tremendous shock, and the ability to accept it will depend very largely upon our parent's personality prior to the mental illness, which, if it was warm and loving, can still be remembered with gratitude. Some caring children faced with this situation find that it is only after their parent's death that they can start to come to terms with it, after a period of grieving which really began as soon as they realised that their parent was 'lost' to them emotionally in the mists of serious mental impairment.

Mental illness and impairment

As the body grows weaker with advancing years, the personality traits which make up the individual usually grow stronger, and in some cases become exaggerated. Attitudes harden, just as arteries do. The father who had qualities of leadership, who was always a man of strong opinions, but controlled his slightly aggressive nature well in his younger days, so that he was an interesting companion and an asset to any group, may, in old age, gradually lose his capacity for reasoning or listening with attention to another person's point of view. He may become impatient and hostile to those who do not agree with him, and a social bore – avoided because he turns every conversation into a monologue, running the 'train' of his thoughts over and over the same old tracks. The mother who was a gentle, rather shy, but well-adjusted woman may, in later years, become increasingly hesitant, lacking in self-confidence and withdrawn in company. Both of them have walls of loneliness and social isolation thrown up around them through no fault of their own. Similarly someone who was an efficient, conscientious career woman, a bit of a perfectionist but an interesting and popular person, may, when she grows old, develop an exaggeration of the very traits that brought her happiness and success in her field, becoming over-meticulous, obsessional, and so demanding of perfection in others, that she is socially quite unacceptable to all except a few who really love and understand her.

In some cases of mental illness or impairment, the elderly tend to regress and develop irritating and distasteful habits. Examples of these can be neglect of their personal hygiene and dress, the greedy gobbling of food, sniffing, nose-picking, teeth-clicking, munching movements of the lips, burping and breaking wind in the presence of others, indecent exposure, open masturbation, and inappropriate sexual overtures to adults and children; and of course the big problem of incontinence may arise. If your elderly parent is showing these signs, some of his or her problems may be physical, due for instance to ill-fitting dentures, indigestion, weak internal muscles and stiff arthritic joints which make it very difficult to bathe regularly and care for their clothing. Others may be due to mental impairment, but the result is the same, and you will be under considerable strain while you are caring for your parent at home. 'Second childhood' seems to have arrived, a childhood that lacks the benefit of the allowances that society is prepared to make for true childhood; and lacks also the hope of gradual graceful development, of learning how to control its own mind and body, and relating with increasing ease to the demands of the adult world.

In these circumstances, the question to which you will be wanting an answer is 'How do I cope with this?' The only answers anyone can give you will, unfortunately, seem miserably inadequate, simply because there are no easy solutions to problems of this kind. All you can do is to arrange for your parent first of all to have a thorough physical check-up by her general practitioner (and any consultants in mental and physical health to whom she may be referred), and to see what steps can be taken to treat any underlying illness and the trying symptoms that are evident. Make sure that her dentures fit well, and that her spectacles (and hearing aid if one is used) are correct. Encourage her to wear easily washed clothing in drip-dry fabrics, and try to establish regular routines at set times in the day for bathing, hand-washing and going to the lavatory. If there is only very slight incontinence, a visit to the lavatory every two hours will often avoid accidents. Unless there is gross mental impairment, many old people who are naturally creatures of habit, respond well to set routines, as children do, as it gives them a feeling of security. Much can be done by kindly habit-training, provided the old person is always treated with respect and not humiliated in any way. If however your parent has deteriorated, developing the kind of habits which are totally unacceptable, and is aggressive and impossible to live with, you should not hesitate to discuss the question of admission to hospital with the general practitioner, who will probably also ask a local authority social worker to visit you if you agree to this.

Admission to hospital under the Mental Health Act, 1959
If hospital treatment for mental disorder becomes necessary for your parent it will be arranged on medical recommendation under one of the sections of the Mental Health Act, 1959 (a copy of which is available in the reference sections of all the larger

public libraries). The sections most likely to apply will be:

SECTION 5,
under which the patient will be admitted informally, just as she would be to a general ward of a hospital, with her full consent, on medical advice.

SECTION 29,
under which the patient may be admitted as an emergency for observation for up to seventy-two hours on the basis of one medical recommendation.

SECTION 25,
under which the patient may be admitted compulsorily for a period of up to twenty-eight days for observation on the basis of two medical recommendations.

There are other sections of the Mental Health Act which may be used, and in Scotland the Mental Health (Scotland) Act, 1960, applies, but in many cases it is possible for patients to be admitted informally, and you should trust the judgement of your parent's doctor in this matter. He, in consultation with his psychiatric colleagues and possibly trained social workers from the local authority Social Services Department (with whom he may have put you in touch in the earlier stages of your parent's illness) will make the best possible recommendations or decisions for her. The point has already been made in this chapter of how important it will be for you to make it clear that you can no longer deal with the situation at home, and you should be sure to emphasise this.

Not all elderly people who enter psychiatric hospitals for treatment are admitted with brain damage, which may necessitate permanent in-patient care. Many, who are treated successfully for other types of mental disorder, make a good recovery and return home again. But if your parent is suffering from an advanced form of one of the dementias and needs indefinite care, you should be prepared to find that visiting her in hospital may be a distressing experience. Even in the most efficiently run psycho-geriatric wards, where every attempt is made to keep the patients as clean and comfortable as possible, the problems connected with incontinence are often obvious, and the sight of some of the most severely disturbed patients can be quite a shock. Try to remember, though, that your parent, who is also mentally ill, may not be as keenly aware of his or her fellow patients or surroundings as you are. And however hard it may be, and whatever reception or reaction you get from your parent, *visit regularly*; for your faithfulness in this will be of the utmost importance to your parent, to the staff on the ward, and not least to yourself.

10
Coping with stress

If you are caring for an elderly parent who is disabled, bereaved, depressed, suffering from loneliness in her own home, or failing to settle down contentedly in yours, or if you are living alone with her and feeling anxious, isolated and unsupported, then apart from the unhappiness she may be experiencing you will probably be suffering too from the effects of excessive stress and wondering how you are going to cope with it. If so, try not to feel too discouraged, for there are a number of ways in which you can ease your feelings of strain and tension.

There comes a time in every difficult and demanding undertaking when, however sure a person is that their original commitment was right, the problems it presents may bring them to the verge of exhaustion in which they feel they have reached the end of their tether. It is this 'tether-end' type of stress which is the real enemy of peace of mind, for it is only when stress becomes heavy and prolonged that it turns into a potentially destructive force that can be damaging to both mind and body. Normal stress is a necessary part of life. It is, in broad terms, a response to stimulus of any kind, pleasant or unpleasant, and the natural result of the daily and hourly demands made upon us all to adjust to new experiences and changing conditions. Heat, cold, hunger, thirst, pain, exercise, sexual activity, learning new skills, moving into an unfamiliar environment and meeting challenges and frustrations in our work, play and interpersonal relationships: these are some of the stressors we all encounter. We adapt very well to them under normal conditions, but in some circumstances, when the need for adaptation becomes excessive, so does the stress and it is then that the trouble starts.

It would be misleading to infer that stress is a simple subject, or that it can be examined in any depth in the space of a few pages. Doctors and scientists throughout the world have been studying it for many years and are still not in complete agreement as to its cause and effect; but at least they are now able to provide some very useful signposts for those who want to prevent it from ever reaching panic-point in their lives.

Your ability to endure a considerable amount of stress before becoming strained, tense, and even physically ill depends very much upon your personality-type and inheritance, so do not add to your troubles by blaming yourself for lack of moral courage if you are being dragged down by a situation which you think others might ride more successfully.

If, in spite of your difficulties in caring for an elderly parent, you have the advantages of a warm comfortable home and no serious financial worries, you may sometimes take yourself to task for not spending more time 'counting your blessings', even though your cup may not exactly be overflowing with them. No doubt you remind yourself how many people there are in the world who are worse off than you are, some of them not even knowing where their next meal is coming from. You may feel a sense of guilt about sailing too close to the wind of self-pity when your circumstances make you feel depressed, deprived, or frustrated. 'Counting your blessings', useful though it may be as an occasional emotional exercise, is a non-starter if you are suffering from 'tether-end' stress. It is far better to begin by 'counting your stressors', for by recognising *them* you can begin to decide how to mitigate the damaging effect they are having on you.

What constitutes excessive stress for one person may be manageable stress for another, but the main stressors connected with caring for an elderly parent under adverse circumstances are much the same for most people. By now you are probably making your own mental list, which is quite likely to include at least a few of the following: loneliness, financial worries, lack of time and opportunity to maintain outside interests and friendships, boredom, a possessive or domineering parent, clashes of opinions and attitudes, conflict between the elderly parent and other members of the family, deafness in a parent who is unable to use a hearing aid, ill-health or severe menopausal symptoms in the caring relative, long-term anxiety over the parent's health, loss of any previous rewarding feedback of companionship, shared humour and affection if the elderly parent becomes brain-damaged. Added to these are loss of sleep and exhaustion, with no 'breaks' or holidays away from the treadmill of a seven-day working week, in which the caring relative is under constant time-pressure stress in order to maintain the set routine that is often necessary for an old person's mental and physical well-being. And lastly, the greatest stressor of all: fear. Fear of the possibility that the elderly parent's terminal illness, when it comes may be protracted, painful and distressing for her; fear of not being able to cope with this adequately without help and moral support, which may not be readily available; and, finally, fear of the inevitable experience of bereavement, the parting from a parent, who, although she may have had to lean heavily for some time on the care-giver, may still be deeply loved and needed by her.

Practical ways of coping with some of these stress factors have been discussed in earlier chapters, but just as there is no pill for every ill, so there is no solution to every problem. When certain stressors can neither be eliminated nor manipulated, the only way to deal with them is to deal with your own response to their unpleasant stimulus so that they are no longer able to cause you so much distress.

Primitive man's reaction to excessive stress was 'fight or flight', but our complicated modern society makes it difficult to do either of these things under stress. Our alerted bodies are flooded with adrenalin, noradrenalin and hormones that make us ready for aggression or escape, but most often circumstances – or our own conscience – render this impossible. We may have to pay a high price for the suppression of these instincts in terms of headaches, digestive troubles, bowel and bladder disturbances, raised blood-pressure, anxiety, muscular spasm and many other discomforts.

There is another way open to us, though, if 'fight' or 'flight' are inappropriate responses in our own particular situation: we can learn instead how to 'face it'. This is the third, very tough but workable option, called by the deceptively easy sounding name of 'adaptation'. Man's effort to adapt usually goes through three stages. The first is a state of alarm, in which we say to ourselves, 'This is difficult, I don't know whether I can cope with it.' The second is the stage of finding that we can adapt to a stressor, in which we say, 'I'm getting used to it. I'm managing to handle it successfully.' The third is the stage of exhaustion, when the stress has been heavy and prolonged and we say, 'I don't think I can stand this any longer.'

Obviously the trick is to learn how to extend the second stage, that of successful adaptation. You have to extend it long enough to enable you to stand by your elderly parent in her time of need, before complete exhaustion sets in, so we should look at some of the ways in which people try to achieve this.

High-risk methods of stress control

There are quick and easy ways of learning to do almost everything moderately well these days, and people have become millionaires overnight by selling us short cuts to desired goals. The end result is never totally satisfactory, but most of us are in a hurry and only too anxious to buy the method or the product if it goes even halfway towards meeting our need without involving us in too much hard work. It is possible for example, to produce a passable meal by learning how to use a tin-opener instead of learning how to cook. But when we are tempted to go for the quick and easy methods that are on offer for freedom from anxiety and tension we should be very wary indeed. The main ones are drink and drugs, and although they can both do much to control the unpleasant effects of excessive stress they provide no long-term answers and sometimes create even greater difficulties.

Alcohol, which is always safest when it is enjoyed in moderation in the company of others, should never be used merely as an aid to relaxation of tension. It is such an easy straw to clutch at if you feel 'strung up', lonely or depressed, but a bottle has no arms, it will never reach out to you. It always stands aloof, its heart a false promise; and if you find yourself saying at some point in every day, 'I *need* a drink', it may be that you are much more in need of the support of some good friends in your stress situation or even of skilled help with what may be the beginning of an alcoholic problem.

Tranquillising drugs and night sedatives can also be dangerously addictive unless they are taken for the right reasons under the strict supervision of your doctor. He may prescribe them for you for a limited period, but it is unwise to get into the habit of asking for a repeat prescription without consultation, so that he can assess your need to continue with them. If he feels that you should, you have no need to worry, but in most circumstances they should not be regarded as anything more than a valuable crutch in an emergency. If they are abused, they may become a way of constantly bypassing your problems instead of facing up to them.

Compulsive eating is another method used by some people to control their anxiety; but the misery they experience as they see themselves gradually growing to look like the cream buns they eat, and the health hazards to which their obesity exposes them, far outweigh the temporary comfort and relief from tension that constant nibbling gives them.

It should be borne in mind, though, that those who have fallen into these traps in their search for relief from what can sometimes seem like intolerable stress are in no way deserving of contempt, nor are they necessarily spineless individuals. They are simply over-stressed people who have lost their way somewhere along the line and they are suffering intensely, not only from strain, but often from painful loss of self-esteem as well. They need all the help and understanding they can get from family and friends to enable them to back-track to the point where they can begin to learn the correct method of dealing with their problems.

The adaptation method of stress control

If the stress that exists in your present circumstances is heavy enough to be putting you under constant strain you will no doubt feel quite desperate at times to find something to alleviate it. Fortunately there is a set of techniques you can learn that will help you, when you want to, to eschew the idea of 'fight or flight' in favour of standing your ground.

Their success does not depend upon the removal of your stressors, but on showing you how to live at peace with them in an extended period of the stage of adaptation, so that your reserves of emotional strength will last long enough for you to see your elderly parent through to the end, in the way you wish, before exhaustion has the chance to overwhelm you. No method of controlling stress can ever carry with it a hundred-per-cent guarantee, because people differ in their ability to persevere and benefit from the adoption of new ideas, but if you are at the end of your tether, you will probably feel that any plan that offers you a good chance of obtaining relief from the strain you are under, as this one does, is worth considering.

The method, which may sound incredibly simple, but is of proven value, consists of:

Positive thinking
Avoidance of stress-triggers
Diversion
Relaxation
A network of good relationships

At first glance this may look to you like a rather weak collection of ideas, but when you have examined each of them in detail, you may come to the conclusion that anyone who learns to handle them properly is going to be much better equipped to deal with their stress.

Positive thinking
Healthy mental attitudes can increase our ability to adapt to excessive stress in any difficult situation, so if you are feeling strained, worn down by anxiety, or frustrated by the heavy emotional demands of caring for an elderly parent, now is the time to check-up on your attitudes to your problems.

If you have counted your stressors, identified them, and decided to try to reduce the unpleasant effect they are having on you, begin by examining carefully the view you have of yourself in your present role, for much depends on this. What are your feelings about it? Are they negative or positive? Do you see yourself as a reluctant drudge or as a homemaker, taking a pride in a worthwhile job, and learning new and useful skills while you are doing so? Does the fact that you are caring for an elderly parent make you feel down-graded socially, or are you confident that you have exactly the same status and value in society as any other woman, married or single, whose career is either temporarily or permanently based in the home? Do you see yourself as sleep-walking your way through an unending nightmare of menial tasks and boring household duties, or do you see what you are doing as an important many-faceted job from which, if you aim for excellence, you can, in spite of the monotony of certain aspects of it, extract that feeling of satisfaction experienced by the expert in any field who knows he is turning in a good performance? Do you feel that you are simply doing your duty while life is passing you by, or do you feel that by caring for your parent you are casting a vote for love and loyalty, meeting the challenge with courage, and making a valuable contribution to the maintenance of family life, and so to the structure of society as a whole?

If your answers to these questions reveal your view of your present role to be a negative one, it is possible to change it if you want to. This will mean making a determined effort to break away from self-defeating attitudes in order to learn new ones, and recognising the value of the job you are doing and the rewards it can give you if you become more relaxed and open to them. A long stint of caring for an old person can easily create a kind of frigidity of the heart, a constant expectancy of shock, pain and disappointment. If your world has become a narrow negative place, you need to allow yourself to discover gradually the tremendous advantages of positive thinking. Positive thinking cannot be dismissed merely as the cheap jargon of amateur psychology, for it is acknowledged by the medical profession to be one of the best recipes for mental health, and some of them must wish that it were possible to prescribe it in tablet form for those who have difficulty in learning how to use it as an effective weapon against their excessive stress.

Now that you are beginning to examine your role, accept the fact that most of us do not spend our time on the stage of life in long-running successes. We are lucky if we land a star part once or twice in a lifetime. We are like members of a large repertory company in which we are constantly being given different roles. Occasionally we are allowed to play the lead: the adored child, the lover, wife, mother or successful careerist. Then there are times when we are handed what may seem to be a much less interesting part. When this happens, if we decide to play it for all it's worth, however far out of the limelight we may be, then we not only help to carry the 'play', but we can gain great personal satisfaction from knowing that we are performing well; and who knows what our next role may be, or how much it will benefit from the experience we have gained in this seemingly minor one?

Next, take a good look at how you feel about the words 'happiness' and 'time'. Unless you are thinking positively about these you are unlikely ever to be able to adapt to your stressors. Is happiness, for you, something you regard as your right? Do you believe it can only be found in the conventionally ideal package of good health, a successful career, marriage, children, a lovely home, holidays abroad, no financial worries and a full social life? Or do you think it can also exist in all kinds of odd and difficult situations, even in the hurricane of some of life's hardest experiences, by those who know that they are in the right place, doing the right thing at the right time?

And what are your thoughts about 'time'? Do you see it as an enemy or a friend? Is it a voice that spoils the present by constantly reminding you of lost joys, and so keeping you chained to the past? Or is it one that leads you to consider the possibility of fresh opportunities for fulfilment in the future, however dark the way ahead may seem? Do you think that time is for hoarding, or do you feel that it is better to spend it generously, with no regrets, in whatever situation you may find yourself? Is it something you worry about because you see it as finite, with an end called death? Or have you a wider concept of it, as being limitless, stretching behind and before you, with an eternal quality? Do you trust time's justice? Even if you firmly believe that the 'here and now' is all we shall ever have, are you capable of being philosophical about it and still glad that you are part of the game, even if life has been dealing you a poor hand recently? If so, then you will be defeating self-pity and thinking positively in your own way about 'time'.

These are big questions, perhaps some of the most important we ever have to ask ourselves when we are taking stock of our mental attitudes. As you encounter one problem after another in the care of your elderly parent, your aim should be gradually to try to establish an entirely new pattern of responses to them if you need to, based upon objectivity and optimism. Stand back from them a little and try calmly to imagine what practical advice you would give to a friend who sought your counsel in a similar situation, and then apply it to your own.

Identifying your stressors will have helped you to split up the heavy burden of your stress into smaller, more manageable 'parcels'. Then, as problems arise, if your life seems to be getting out of control, do not panic. Just sit down quietly and look at the problem from every angle. However bad it is, there is always some action that can be taken to improve matters. If you are determined to consider all the possibilities with optimism, you will be practising positive thinking, the first and most important defence against excessive stress.

Avoidance of stress triggers

Although it is vital to face up to your stressors with positive attitudes, it is equally important to learn how to avoid those situations which you know always trigger off feelings of great strain in you, provided that this can be done without detriment to the care of your parent. Obviously these are different for each individual, but it may be helpful to examine a few of the most common ones.

Since even the happiest of married couples get on each other's nerves sometimes, it is not surprising that those who are living with someone of a different generation, often in very stressful circumstances, should find some of her harmless habits, mannerisms, and predictable verbal responses very irritating. And what starts as an irritation can develop gradually into a sore in the relationship unless some way is found of dealing with it. Of course, it is usually the little things. That moment when a mother or mother-in-law with a very healthy appetite is asked at the dinner table if she will have a helping of a particular vegetable and she delicately and unfailingly replies, 'Well, just a taste please, dear', or when she is asked if she is ready for her 'elevenses' always answers, 'Yes please, dear. If you're sure it's not too much trouble.' Surely, some people would say, it should be easy enough to smile and not to worry about such harmless responses; and that is true, but not for the daughter who hears it every day and is already heavily stressed. For her it can be like sand in her shoes.

These are just two of the many examples which could be given, but the way in which one daughter-in-law coped with them is worth describing because it illustrates how such small things that begin to grate and cause a feeling of strain can be dealt with. Because she had many other more serious stressors in her life, her reaction to these minor ones was, not unnaturally along the lines of, 'If she says that just once more I feel I shall scream!' Then, on the advice of an understanding doctor she decided to use a technique of reversal. She formed the habit of phrasing some of her questions to her mother-in-law quite differently, so that the stress-trigger of the older woman's response was unable to operate. She did this by calmly, kindly, and without sarcasm taking the ball right out of her court. In the mornings she would ask, 'Would you like your elevenses now? It will be no trouble at all if you're ready for it.' Then at lunch time she would say, 'Can I help you to a little taste of –?' (whatever food she happened to be serving) and she would then give her the same size helping as she gave the rest of the family. She soon found that she could avoid other small stress-triggers too in this way, and because she was a caring person who was basically quite fond of her mother-in-law, it worked very well without causing offence. When asked how she would have felt if her mother-in-law had innocently defeated her little ploy, by repeating her question almost word for word by saying, 'Yes please, dear, just a little taste', she replied, 'You know, strangely enough, I don't think that would bother me at all, provided *I* had said it first.'

Those caring for the elderly need to remember, of course, that they too may have some very trying quirks of conversation or behaviour which may be creating excessive stress for the old person, but here we are mainly considering the strain that is suffered by the caring relative.

Perhaps one of the reasons why people of all temperaments get along so well with their dogs and cats is that they cannot communicate by word of mouth. If they could, they might be 'falling out' with them every day over something or other, for the things people *say* to each other usually far outweigh the things they actually *do* in terms of irritation. It is often the innocent remark or gem of wisdom that is constantly repeated to the point of tedium that is the cause of feelings of strain, but in some cases, when the stress-trigger takes the form of persistent criticism from an elderly parent or in-law which cannot be controlled by reasonable discussion, feelings of rage and injustice may frequently be engendered and then suppressed, which can be very harmful. The only solution to this lies in avoiding the stress-trigger, and since it is not possible simply to walk away for more than a limited time from an old person in your care, distancing yourself from its source is obviously not the answer. You may, however, find that you can gradually avoid experiencing the destructive emotions that spring from it if you can learn how to counter criticism with the one thing it cannot easily survive – a mixture of humour and mock-agreement with your critic. This is never easy at first, but it can be done, and it works. If, when criticism is levelled at you, you treat it consistently in a relaxed, light-hearted manner, appearing, at least, to refuse to take it seriously and even occasionally going so far as to agree with it in the, 'Yes, aren't I just the limit?' way, you will draw its sting before it gets to you. In time you will find that not only will its power to hurt you become less, but your limp reaction will make it such an unsatisfactory exercise from the elderly person's point of view that he or she may not bother to continue with it.

If there is much conflict in your relationship with your elderly parent, how you deal with it must naturally depend upon your personality and hers, as well as her age and mental condition. There can be no hard and fast rules. In some circumstances control is called for, but in others it can be better in the long run to lose your temper a little occasionally, provided you are capable of doing so without violence and that you can forgive each other afterwards when the air has been cleared. You should never let yourself be forced into a position in which you are being unconsciously blackmailed into silence and robbed of the right to state your own opinion on major issues simply by virtue of the fact of your parent's age or poor health. Long noisy verbal battles should be avoided as far as possible, though, for both your sakes. So it is sensible to avoid confrontations over minor matters which do not impinge seriously upon your life and sometimes to allow an elderly person to have the last word even when it seems unreasonable. This can give your parent a harmless, but necessary occasional feeling of power, and the assurance that he or she is by no means under anyone's thumb. There is much wisdom in the old saying, 'Say yes, it won't take you long'.

Another common stress-trigger for those caring for elderly parents is the indifference sometimes shown by other members of the family who do not take their fair share of the care and support the elderly person needs. Often this is made worse for the care-giver by the fact that when they do spare the time to visit their mother she is naturally so delighted to see them that she gives them the VIP treatment and expects the daughter at home to wait on them and provide meals. This can cause intense feelings of bitterness and strain in the one who is shouldering all the responsibility.

If this is one of your stressors, it is important to try to come to terms with it as soon as possible. Such feelings are understandable and very difficult to dismiss, but it will certainly be in your best interests to do so. The way to avoid the worst effects of them, after your quite justifiable anger has boiled over as it may do once or twice in confidence to a trusted friend, is to turn down the heat inside yourself and start to mop up the mess it will have made of your emotions before it stains your whole life with the ugliness of a permanent grievance. An acceptance of the fact that we all have our blind spots when it comes to the question of duty and priorities may sound like a comforting cliché, but it is as good a place as any to start. To hold the selfish attitude of your relatives in contempt is not unreasonable, but to hold *them* in contempt as people, as you will know if you think about it, is a judgement you should not be willing to make. You are 'family' and need to stick together somehow, even though you may all be at different stages of emotional maturity, and however badly any of you may behave in each other's eyes from time to time. It is not easy, but try to give them the benefit of the doubt. They may not fully realise just how selfish they are being at present in letting you carry, on your own, the heaviest end of what is a family problem.

Refuse to allow yourself the false pride of being unwilling to ask any favours of them. If they do not offer to invite your (and their) parent for regular holidays in their home, or to sit-in with her regularly to give you a break, put your point of view to them quietly, but without aggression, and see what response you get. This is far better than allowing your feelings of resentment to simmer and make you tense and miserable and finally bitter. If their reaction is unsatisfactory, do not let it cause a rift between you, and do not waste precious time afterwards on thinking angrily about them and their neglect, for such feelings are destructive and can quickly develop into a recurring motif in the pattern of your day, all to no avail. When the negative thoughts begin, switch them off at once, and deliberately avoid them by switching on the radio or thinking of something quite pleasant and entirely different. And finally, remember that if you have committed yourself willingly to caring for your elderly parent, a very important part of that care, and perhaps the last gift of love you can give her, is the preservation of good relationships within the family. So do not allow anyone to rob you of that privilege. Although life may be difficult at present, you are probably going to be the one who will emerge from it all in the end with peace of mind and few regrets. Try to be as generous and accepting in your attitude towards your relatives as you can; for in later life, they may well reach a stage in their emotional development (perhaps when their own children are grown up) when they come to realise how often they neglected their parent, how much they took for granted and how little they gave in return, and will suffer quite badly from feelings of guilt.

DEAFNESS
Deafness in an elderly parent who for some reason cannot use a hearing-aid can also become a major stress-trigger for the one who

is caring for her. It is one of the commonest handicaps of old age and sometimes imposes a severe strain on the relationship, however affectionate it may be. The elderly deaf often feel isolated, rather depressed, and in some cases even a little suspicious, wondering if they are being talked about or denied information and excluded from life going on around them. The patience of relatives can be stretched to the limit, especially if they are also becoming physically exhausted by other aspects of the caring situation. The result can sometimes be two very lonely people, struggling along together under heavy and prolonged stress, deprived of many of the pleasures of normal conversation that could have made their other problems far easier to bear. Some of the most important small currency of companionship is lost to them: the humorous remark (which can sound absurd if it has to be repeated), the casual comment, usually delivered in a low tone, words of sympathy and tenderness too, normally spoken softly in times of pain or distress – all these are denied to them, for it is not easy to give comfort in a loud voice, or to be comforted by someone who is having to shout in order to be heard. Consequently many such feelings remain unexpressed.

It is often difficult too to judge just how loudly to speak to a deaf person if your voice has to compete with other sounds in or outside the room, and her response may sometimes be a slightly irritable 'All right, don't shout', which can fill a weary daughter with despair if she is doing the best she can to adapt herself to her parent's handicap.

If you are living with a deaf parent and feeling the strain, there are several things you can do to avoid the strong stress-triggers connected with it. Some you may be doing already, but others may be new to you and worth trying.

Part of the sense of most conversation is conveyed not only by the sound of the voice but also by facial expression and lip and hand movements, so whenever possible position yourself where your face can be seen when you are speaking.

Try to avoid speaking just at the moment when he, or she is yawning or eating any crunchy type of food such as toast or celery, as you will then be unlikely to be heard.

Remember to adjust your voice when there are background

noises from the radio, television, traffic, or other people talking in the room.

The act of shouting is linked in the minds of most people with violence and quarrelling, so even if you need to speak loudly, never allow yourself to wear a 'shouting' facial expression. The forward thrust of the chin, the strained look and the carefully mouthed words can easily become a habit when speaking loudly to the deaf, and some of them feel under mild but continuous emotional assault from such approaches, or feel that they are being treated as though they are stupid. So speak clearly and loudly, but try to maintain a pleasant and relaxed expression. This will help you both.

You can avoid a good deal of strain too if you learn to use a simple 'trial run' method of starting a conversation with the deaf, which works like this: Having gained her attention, begin to speak in a tone which you think has a reasonably good chance of being heard, then, if it is not, stop, relax yourself physically (see notes on relaxation later in this chapter), take a deep breath – all of which will help to forestall any upsurge of impatience – and calmly repeat what you said, in a slightly louder voice which you are quite certain will be heard. You will then have eased your way gently into the conversation without making your parent feel shouted at. You may wonder if this 'trial run' method of communicating with the deaf could be irritating to them, but, on the contrary, most of them react to it very well, and appreciate the fact that someone is prepared to take the trouble to repeat themselves if necessary, with no sign of impatience, instead of opting for trying to save time initially by shouting – often rather too loudly. Sometimes, of course, you will be lucky and your parent will hear you the first time, but try to launch every conversation successfully, without the need to smash a bottle over its bows before it can get under way. This gentle approach takes only a few moments longer.

If you are sharing a home with a deaf parent who needs the volume of the radio or television turned up to a degree which you cannot tolerate without discomfort, or which may disturb the neighbours, the anxiety of trying constantly to make suitable adjustments without spoiling his or her entertainment can be a powerful stress-trigger. It can easily be avoided by buying two small, lightweight earpieces which fit into the ear rather like a hearing aid, and are plugged into the radio or connected to the television set (a different type being required for each). They are not expensive and last for several years with care, and further information about them can be obtained from any good radio or television shop. These may be a great boon to your elderly parent, and there is the added advantage that they enable a deaf person to listen to programmes you may not wish to hear, thus giving you the silence you may want for reading or writing letters.

Entertaining at home, if you have a deaf elderly parent living with you, can also be a stress-trigger for several reasons, but mainly because the deaf often feel left out of conversations. You will sense this, and the pleasure of the occasion will be spoiled for you too. So try to avoid this by reminding your friends and relatives of his or her deafness on their arrival, and asking them to speak up as much as possible.

You, of course, will be well aware of what your own particular stress-triggers are, and you will find that with a little careful thought and planning, you will be able to do much to avoid many of them.

Diversion

Diversion from one activity to another can, in some circumstances, do more to reduce feelings of strain, and to extend the period of adaptation to severe stress, than merely 'resting'; and it seems that the old saying, 'A change is as good as a rest', would, had the words, 'and sometimes even better' been added to it, have been even truer.

There are many ways of recharging your energy if a stressful situation is making you feel low. Various techniques of mental and physical relaxation can be of a great help, and these are to be examined later, but never underestimate the value of engaging in divertive activities. If you are caring for an elderly parent and suffering from strain you would be wise to check up on your arsenal of these, for without them you are going to find it increasingly difficult to combat exhaustion.

No doubt there are periods in the day when you rest from your work of caring. Everyone needs to make time simply to 'stand and stare' or to be quiet and alone with their thoughts for a while, but do you also have one or two divertive activities to which you can turn as well when you are heavily stressed? Activities which, because they challenge you with other stresses which are within the normal limits, are going to make a significant contribution to the reduction in your tension? Listening to music, watching television, or doing a crossword puzzle may all be immensely helpful in their different ways when you want to unwind, but sometimes the best type of diversion is an activity which brings with it rewards other than those of entertainment, which brings only temporary relief.

An enjoyable diversion which is also creative, socially useful, or one that is going to contribute towards the success of some plan you may have for the future, however distant, can be particularly valuable. This could be anything from gardening, painting, dressmaking, or some home improvement scheme, to learning to play a musical instrument or some other new skill, involvement in a neighbourhood or community project, reading, studying a subject of particular interest to you in depth, or even becoming a student of the Open University. Any of these, and many more may be worth considering.

Relaxation
It is important to learn how to relax when you are under prolonged stress, and this does not mean just putting your feet up and resting, for it is possible to be in a state of extreme tension even when you are lying down and completely still. It is more a matter of learning first how to feel and recognise what tension is in the main groups of muscles in the body and then how to let go and relax them – not merely when you are resting quietly on a couch or bed, but at any time, in any situation, especially those that are stress-triggers for you.

A certain amount of muscle tension is normal and necessary in order for the body to function properly, for it to be held in an upright position, and for the limbs to move at the command of the brain; but in those who are suffering from excessive stress the whole musculature is often under uncomfortable tension for long periods, in readiness for 'fight' or 'flight'. A tense muscle is constantly sending electrical impulses back to the brain (these are actually measurable) and when the brain is being continually bombarded in this way in an anxious person it begins to react, rather like an over-loaded telephone exchange, with reduced efficiency. This, of course, is a simplification of just one aspect of a very complicated process, but it serves well enough to illustrate the point.

Relaxation of the body leads to reduction in anxiety. You can prove for yourself that it is very difficult to feel tense and anxious if your muscles are relaxed; so it can be said that physical and mental relaxation complement one another. As the body relaxes, so the mind seems automatically to kick off its tight shoes of tension, relieved that the strain has been taken off it for a while.

Some people derive benefit from meditation, and there are local authorities now who run classes for this. Some hospitals run classes for physical relaxation, which is usually taught by a physiotherapist or some other member of the staff who has been specially trained for the purpose, and it is always a good idea to learn a new skill under the personal supervision of an expert. But if your home responsibilities or other factors make it impossible for you to join such a class, you can still teach yourself enough about relaxation in your own home for it to play a very useful part in your successful adaptation to the stresses in your life, once you are prepared to spend half an hour a day on it. This is not long for what you can confidently expect to be a helpful and pleasurable experience.

There are a number of different ways of learning the technique, and any public library can supply you with books on the subject, all of which are based upon learning the difference between tension and relaxation of the muscles and the trick of knowing how to train your body to obey you so that you can relax to order. Don't make heavy weather of it, though. Choose the way that will be the easiest and most comfortable for you (although they all call for a certain amount of application and self-discipline) and never allow yourself to become tense about relaxing, or it will not work. The following is an outline of one simple method you could use and adapt to your own needs if you find it is impossible to attend classes.

Begin by lying flat on your back on your bed, with one pillow under your head and another under your knees, in a warm, well-ventilated room. After lunch, when the house is quiet and your elderly parent is settled for an afternoon rest is a good time to choose. This first half-hour session will be the only one you cannot expect to enjoy, for with the exception of a ten-minute rest at the end, it must be spent on tensing each muscle group in the body in turn, holding it until it feels distinctly uncomfortable, and then letting it go, in order to learn to recognise what a really tense muscle feels like.

Start with your scalp. Tighten it, hold and let go. Then wrinkle your forehead, hold, and let go. Close your eyes very tightly, hold, and let go. Clench your jaws, hold, and let go. Clench your fists, tense your biceps, chest, trunk, back, buttocks, leg and feet muscles all in turn, holding and then letting go. Realise that the discomfort you feel is simply an exaggeration of the tension which exists all over your body when you are under strain and preparing yourself for 'fight' or 'flight'. Rest quietly for the last ten minutes.

The next day, and every day when you find it convenient to do so, spend half an hour in the same position on your bed, but now, provided you feel that you have learned what a tense muscle feels like, concentrate on relaxing. Some people, whose imagination will allow them to do so, find it helps to begin by 'thinking themselves' into some situation of great peace and beauty, such as lying on a grassy bank on a warm summer's day, looking up at a blue sky through the branches of a tree, floating down the river in a punt, or sunbathing on a quiet beach. If setting the scene for yourself in this way appeals to you, then it will get you off to a good start, but if not, don't worry, because it is in no way essential and you will be able to achieve relaxation just as well without it.

Your object now is to concentrate on each muscle group in turn, and relax it, until your whole body feels limp and heavy. Close your eyes very gently, make sure that your tongue is not touching the roof of your mouth and that your teeth are not clenched, and bend your elbows, resting your open hands at your side or on your hips, whichever is most comfortable for you. Then start, as you did yesterday with your scalp muscles, working slowly down your body, but this time, instead of first tensing your muscles, take a deep breath, concentrate on them just as they are, and as you breathe out, let them go, relax, and then relax more, breathing deeply until gradually you feel the tension draining out of them all over your body.

After you have done this daily for two weeks, start to try to achieve a similar state of relaxation sitting in a chair. Finally you should be ready to use the technique in any situation which makes you feel particularly tense. When it occurs, begin to breathe deeply, relax your jaw slightly, drop your shoulders, unclench your hands and relax every muscle in your body which is not required to be under tension to maintain its sitting or standing position at the moment of emotional threat.

Most people who are under stress find that it is very important, even when they have mastered the technique of relaxation, to continue with the half-hour sessions each day after lunch, as this breaks the continuous pattern of stress halfway through their waking hours, and reduces their anxiety considerably.

A network of good relationships

To anyone who is under great stress, the value of having a supportive network of good relationships, is inestimable. No one committing themselves to a difficult assignment should have to go it alone if it is possible to do so with the back-up of friends. No loner ever climbed Everest or landed on the moon. People in other stressful circumstances, prisoners of war, and concentration camp victims, have all testified too to the fact that it was those who had a good network of relationships within the camps even in those terrible conditions, who were best able to adapt to prolonged stress.

For all but the most exceptional people, survival under heavy stress depends not only upon their own courage, but also on the fact that they have a certain amount of help and encouragement from others who care about them: friends in whom they can confide, and who strengthen them and act as a safety-valve, accepting their negative feelings and anxieties. This of course sounds fine in theory, but what if you are caring for an elderly parent, you have no family or friends near at hand to help you, and your present way of life makes the maintenance of friendships seem almost impossible? The answer to this must of course be a positive one. You must, for your own sake, and in the long run for your parent's sake also, find a way of dealing with the 'impossible'. If you have allowed old friendships to lapse, consider trying to revive them, even if only through correspondence and the telephone at first. If you have not been in touch with friends for some time, you may have been imagining that life for them has been all smooth sailing, only to discover that they too have their troubles, need you as much as you need them, and are delighted to hear from you again. And do not be afraid either to make a determined effort to make as many new friends as possible. Hilaire Belloc wrote, 'There's nothing worth the wear of winning but laughter and the love of friends'. If you are short on these two vital ingredients of the balanced life, now is the time to go right out and look for them. You will not need to look far either, for unless you and your elderly parent live in a particularly isolated spot in the country, there may be any number of potential friends for you amongst your neighbours in the flats and houses in your own road: some living alone or caring for an elderly relative as you are and too afraid of revealing their loneliness to make the first overture. These may be people you have known by sight for years and met in the local shops or public library, but to whom you have never spoken. Well, speak to them now. Take it slowly; find out a little about them and tell them a little about yourself in casual conversation, and then, if you feel you are on the same wavelength, ask them home to a cup of tea or coffee – nothing formal in the way of an invitation at first, as you will both want to find out to begin with whether you wish to proceed from the stage of nodding acquaintances to that of friends. Many good, neighbourly friendships have started like this, but someone has to make the first move.

If you have very few friends amongst those living around you, could it be that you lack confidence in what you have to offer? If so, you are almost certainly being too modest in your opinion of yourself. Or could it be that you are just a little too choosy and have made the common mistake of thinking that even your outer circle of friends should be people who share all your own special interests and attitudes, as your close friends do? If so, you are missing a lot. Obviously vast differences in outlook on everything do not augur well for the establishment of an enjoyable friendship, but then neither do strongly held prejudices, and it is a pity to be put off people simply by discovering that they read a newspaper with a different political bias from your own, or have a different religion or skin colour. *All* people are interesting in some way, and many of them have hidden talents and absorbing hobbies which may add fresh colour to your life, as yours could to theirs if you take the trouble to get to know them. Friendships, even those at a fairly superficial level, can be great stress breakers, so make the development of a network of good relationships a matter of top priority in your battle against the effects of excessive stress. As you give, as well as take, you will be surprised to discover that you have provided yourself with a strong safety-net which will make you feel altogether more relaxed and secure in your present situation.

Stress and guilt feelings

The more loyal and conscientious a person you are, the more guilty you will feel when you think you may have failed in some small way in your care of your elderly parent. This is bound to happen sometimes, and when it does it is important for you to learn to forgive yourself with the same degree of generosity and understanding that you would show to others.

Feelings of guilt, anger, and even rejection can exist together with deep love in all close relationships, but they are often found in confusing abundance in the relationship of a caring relative and a dependent elderly parent. Guilt is not an unhealthy emotion, though. It helps to prevent us from becoming smug and too ready to judge the actions of others. It is one of the growing-pains we all experience in our emotional development, which is a process which continues as long as we live. We all hate some of our thoughts, words and actions from time to time. It is only when we cannot accept the fact that no one manages always to live up to the ideals they cherish, and when we refuse to forgive ourselves, that we get 'stuck'. Guilt can then become pathological, counter-productive, and a source of constant stress long after the event that gave birth to it.

Even Florence Nightingale, who endured all the horrors of nursing the wounded in the Crimean War, had her breaking-point and feelings of guilt. It came, not in the dirt and danger of that situation, but later, when she returned to her family home in 1872 to look after her aged parents. No adventure there, no excitement, no support from nursing colleagues: just a long, hard slog, and a life which, in her despair, she was reduced to describing as 'petty, stagnant and stifling'. Somehow it adds an element of love to our respect for this courageous woman to learn that she was human and vulnerable enough to react just like the rest of us when she was called upon to bear great stress in a lonely, undramatic situation in her parents' home. In the summer of 1872, she wrote in a letter 'I should hate myself (I do hate myself) but I should LOATHE myself, oh my God, if I could like it, find "rest" in it. Fortunately there is no rest in it, but ever increasing anxieties. *Il faut que la victime soit mise en pièces*. Oh my God!' And again in 1879, when her father was dead and she was still caring for her ninety-one-year-old mother, whose mind and sight were failing (and who died in the following year), in another letter she wrote, 'Why do you abuse me for being here? Do you think any part of my life is as I please? Do you know what have been the hardest years of my life? Not the Crimean War. Not the five years with Sidney Herbert at the War Office, when I some-times worked twenty-two hours a day, but the last five years and three-quarters since my father's death.'

Sometimes she obviously found life almost unbearable, but she never totally despaired; perhaps because, although she kept faith with her parents, she knew the value of diversion. She had the good sense to know that she could not and should not simply lie down and die with them. She had to extract something for herself from the years she gave to them: some satisfaction, and some achievement, apart from the rewards of doing what she considered to be her duty. It was during this period, against al-most impossible odds in her personal life, that she embarked upon organising the reconstruction of the Nightingale School of Nursing, which she founded at Saint Thomas's Hospital in London in 1860. Some of the work she could do only by correspondence, but she did it. Somehow she struck just the right balance between her own needs and the needs of the two old people who depended on her.

Florence Nightingale knew all about guilt feelings, frustration, and the strain of prolonged stress. She suffered, she faltered, and sometimes the weight of her home responsibilities almost broke her, but she was a very positive thinker. She stayed the course, looked to the future, and went on to contribute more than ever to the society in which she lived.

11
Nursing the elderly at home

When an elderly parent has to be nursed at home, whether for an acute illness lasting for a few weeks, or for a chronic one lasting for several months or years, careful planning of your resources can make life much easier.

Unless you have had nursing training, you should not attempt to become involved in any very complicated procedures in the sick-room. These should be left to the experts, but with the right information at your finger-tips, you can become proficient in the simple but all-important matters of keeping your parent clean, well-nourished and comfortable, and carrying out the instructions of the doctor and any visiting nurses to the letter.

In order to give a high standard of care, you need to remember that people of all ages react to illness according to their personality type, and that the elderly often worry a good deal about becoming a burden to others. This calls for constant reassurance that they are loved and wanted, which can be shown in numerous ways: the tenderness and respect with which their bodies are handled when they are being washed or moved; the occasional spontaneous kiss on the forehead when you settle them down for a rest, or wish them goodnight; the trouble you take with their hair and general appearance, which makes them feel cherished instead of merely 'maintained'; and, above all, your willingness to sit and talk to them whenever you can spare the time from your other family responsibilities. There are bound to be times when you are over-tired and tense, and fall short of these ideals – particularly if your parent is deaf, or slow to respond; and you may feel impatient and show it. But if you really care, and are trying to be much more to them than just an efficient life-support system, they will know it, and understand.

Your main areas of concern in home nursing (apart from your attitude towards the patient) should be:

1. to keep yourself mentally and physically fit;
2. to create the right conditions for caring for the patient;
3. to assemble the right equipment;
4. to acquire basic nursing skills; and
5. to avail yourself of all the supporting medical, nursing and social services in your area.

Putting your own health and well-being first on the list may sound a little selfish, but obviously it is in your parent's best interests that you should manage to keep fit enough to stand by her in her trouble. This means that you must not neglect your own diet and that somehow you must try to make time to get some outdoor exercise each day. A break away from the patient and her needs, as well as the occasional holiday, will also be essential, or you may become so tired that you will be unable to carry on.

Planning for comfort and efficiency in the sick-room needs much careful thought and organisation if the illness is likely to be a long-term one. A brief illness can usually be coped with quite well with just one or two additions to the basic equipment to be found in most homes, and these can easily be obtained 'on loan' from local organisations, such as the British Red Cross Society, or through the district nurse. There need be little rearrangement of the furniture in the bedroom, provided there is plenty of space to move around the bed, warmth, and a comfortable easy chair for the patient (if and when she is allowed to get up).

Dealing with an illness of longer duration is quite different. You should be prepared to make as many changes in the patient's room as are needed to make her more comfortable, and to make your task and that of the doctor and nurses as easy as possible. This will have to be done quietly, tactfully and with the patient's consent, keeping a homely, non-clinical atmosphere in the room, and not stripping it of all loved and familiar possessions.

The patient's comfort, as much space as possible to move around in, easily cleaned working surfaces, and furniture that moves on castors are what you should aim for. If it is not distressing to the patient, any larger items not in immediate use, such as wardrobes, should be moved to another room in the house, with a clear assurance given that this is only a temporary measure.

The sick-room may have to be your parent's whole world for the duration of her illness, so it should be made to look restful and attractive. It should also be kept spotlessly clean, well-ventilated but draught-free and, unless otherwise stated by the doctor, at a steady temperature of about 18° Centigrade. Bear in mind, too, that it is going to be more than just a bedroom; it is going to be a meeting place for visiting friends and relatives, and a working area for the medical team.

A rough guide to sick-room planning for long-term illness
Amongst any other items that can easily be fitted in, the room should contain:

1. A single bed (as high as possible) on castors.
2. A bedside table on castors, with a wipe-clean surface and several drawers.
3. A table-lamp with an extension switch that can easily be reached.
4. A folding, over-bed table on castors – for meals, writing or any craftwork.
5. A radio (and television set if obtainable and desirable).
6. A commode chair with padded lid, that can be camouflaged with cushions and used also as a visitors' chair.
7. A second chair for visitors (which will also be useful to put bedclothes on while the bed is being made).
8. A comfortable chair for the patient, high enough for easy rising, with padded arms, a good lumbar support and a 'wing' back, in which pillows can be arranged to support the head. If there is a tendency to incontinence, a chair covered with vinyl-type material is best, as these materials are wipe-clean.
9. A screen to protect the patient from draughts and to ensure privacy when necessary.
10. A large chest of drawers, the small drawers of which can be used for the patient's personal items such as brush, comb,

cosmetics, talc and cologne; and the larger ones for clean nightclothes, and fresh dressings or incontinence pads if necessary. The top should have a wipe-clean surface or be covered with a large washable tray and kept clear, so that it can be used as a working surface for the doctor or nurses.
11. A second chest of drawers will be useful, if there is room for one without overcrowding the room. The top can be used at one end for flower vases, with a tray at the other end on which to put medicines. When not in use, the tray should be kept locked in one of the drawers.
12. A clear-faced wall clock.
13. An easily reached hook on the bedroom door for the patient's dressing-gown.
14. An 'Engaged' notice to hang on the outside of the door to indicate to other members of the family that they should not enter, if the patient is being bathed or using the commode. (A bolt on the inside of the door is also necessary if there are young children in the house who may run in without warning at an inconvenient moment.)
15. A loud hand-bell on the bedside table which the patient can reach without strain.
16. A good bright central hanging light for use if the doctor wishes to examine the patient at night when the table lamp would be insufficient.
17. Fine plain white Terylene net curtains at the window (as well as the side curtains) for extra privacy if the patient is being nursed in a downstairs room.

The bed should not face the window, as light glaring continuously in the eyes can be very trying for a sick person, but the window should be close enough to the bed for the patient to have good light for reading, and to see out, if there is a garden, or some interesting activity to watch. However, plenty of space must be left around the bed for those attending the patient.

TYPES OF BEDS
The best type of bed on which to nurse an elderly person is a single one, and to avoid the possibility (which is a very real one)

of your developing a slipped disc or severe back strain it should be approximately twenty-eight inches high. If the patient is sleeping on an old-fashioned single bed, there will be no problem, as most of them tend to be fairly high, but if it is a modern divan type it will probably be much too low. Sometimes this difficulty can be solved simply by getting a handyman to buy and screw in a set of longer legs (with castors) or by adding a second deep mattress on the bed to raise its height, or again, by buying – quite cheaply – a good old-fashioned, high, second-hand single bed from a local salesroom or through the small ads in the local paper. Bed-blocks can also be used, and sometimes are the easiest solution (see Chapter 12).

Unless otherwise recommended by the doctor, a good-quality firm mattress (either Dunlopillo or interior sprung) will be most comfortable, as it gives the body the correct support. A plastic mattress cover is advisable too, for even if the patient is not incontinent there is always the chance of water being spilled when the patient is being bathed or having her hair washed in bed, and a wet mattress is a very difficult thing to cope with.

If the patient is completely bed-bound, and risks developing bed-sores, particularly when there is loss of movement following a stroke, you should ask the doctor's advice about getting a special type of mattress, known as a Ripple bed. This is a mattress made of Polythene that is electrically operated, with sections which inflate and deflate in turn continuously to relieve pressure. As it is waterproof it needs only to be covered with a sheet (and a drawsheet if required).

If the patient is allowed to sit up, an adjustable bed-rest is helpful, together with a number of good pillows filled with washable material such as Terylene or Dunlopillo.

BED LINEN, BLANKETS AND OTHER TOP COVERINGS

Sheets and pillowslips made of a mixture of cotton and Polyester are easy to wash and dry, crease less than 100% cotton and are more comfortable than nylon, but it is very important to see that they are wide and long enough to tuck in well; otherwise they will ruck up and cause discomfort.

Drawsheets should be of thick absorbent cotton, about a

yard wide and six feet long, and a plastic sheet placed underneath is a sensible safety measure, unless the whole mattress is in a plastic cover and fully protected, as the patient will feel less worried about a possible 'accident'. If the bed is properly made and suitable lightweight top coverings are used the patient will not be too hot or uncomfortable.

An underblanket should be provided to go over the mattress, under the bottom sheet (unless using a Ripple bed).

Elderly patients in particular need coverings that provide warmth without weight. If there is no incontinence, by far the best way of achieving this is to dispense with all top coverings (unless a bed-cradle is being used, in which case a top sheet that tucks in well will be needed) and use a large, very good quality continental quilt (duvet), preferably one guaranteed to contain 100% white goose down (which is expensive), or failing that, a mixture of goose down and feathers, or Dacron (the latter being washable). One of the best people to advise on this will be the buyer in the bedding department of the nearest reputable department store but, unless you can afford to buy a really good one, it is better to forget it, for the others will be useless for the purpose. On no account should you allow yourself to be persuaded to buy one that is less than five feet wide for a three foot bed, as anything narrower will not keep an elderly person warm all round. Two or more quilt covers in easily washed, drip-dry cotton and Polyester (not nylon) should be purchased at the same time.

If a continental quilt is not suitable for the patient for any reason, cellular cotton blankets are light, warm and fairly quick to wash and dry. Most types of woollen blankets are rather heavy for someone who is in bed all day, and much more difficult to wash.

If the patient wants to use his or her eiderdown on top of whatever blankets are being used, it is a good idea to buy two or three attractive continental quilt covers for it as these can be washed frequently so that the bed always looks fresh and clean.

SICK-ROOM EQUIPMENT
The type of equipment required will depend very much on the kind of illness the patient has and its likely duration and you should

not be tempted to install anything apart from the very basic items without first taking the advice of the doctor and visiting nurses. Too much equipment in a sick-room is like too much in a kitchen – it can sometimes be more of a hindrance than a help. It is useful, however, to know about the kind of things you may possibly need (many of which you can get on loan, as previously stated), and these may include:

Ripple bed mattress.
Plastic mattress cover if the normal type of mattress is being used.
Bed-rest.
Bed-cradle.
Bed-blocks.
Three rubber sheets.
Folding over-bed table.
Hot water bottle with a separate thick cover to encase it completely (and a spare washer).
Bedpan and disposable paper towels to cover.
Urinal (bottle) and disposable paper towels to cover.
Bedside commode chair and soft toilet tissues.
Airwick air-freshener.
Medicine measure glass.
Thermometer.
A watch with a second hand.
A Carters hair rinser (see Chapter 12).
Plastic wash bowl.
Hand hair-dryer.
Large plastic bucket.
Large enamel jug.
Incontinence pads for bed and chair if necessary.
A large single-size sleeping bag in quilted nylon, filled with 38 oz. Terylene, to zip the patient into if he or she sits out in a chair for any length of time. This is much warmer than a rug, and cannot slip off.
A hoist (free-standing and hand operated) for lifting a helpless patient from bed to chair, or to take him or her to the bathroom (see Chapter 12).

Disposable plastic gloves and finger-stalls.
Two 'receivers' (stainless steel or enamel dishes) for the doctor's or nurses' instruments.
A supply of cotton-wool, gauze, bandages and adhesive plaster.
Two *thin* face flannels.
Packet of 'J' cloths.
Mild lanolin-based toilet soap.
Talcum powder.
Mouthwash and beaker.
Tooth and denture brushes.
Denture cleaners and denture bath.
Nail-scissors and clippers for hands and feet.
Hand and bath towels.
Plastic linen basket.
Plastic waste-paper basket.
Dettol.
Savlon antiseptic cream.
Vaseline.
Barrier cream.
Glycerine suppositories.
Feeding cup with spout.
Child's plastic feeding cup with enclosed top, but with a lip with perforations – for the patient to drink from in the night more easily (obtainable from Boots the Chemists).
A plate holder and plate guard (see Chapter 12).
Combined knife and fork, for right or left hand (see Chapter 12).
A folding walking aid (see Chapter 12).
A 'Helping Hand', long-reach type – for picking up things from the floor (see Chapter 12).

Supporting services (medical, nursing, auxiliary and social)

Your general practitioner will be able to tell you what services are available in your locality, but you should also make an effort yourself to find out all about them, and a visit to the local authority Social Services Department, or the Citizens' Advice Bureau will be helpful in this respect. Every area in the country has a team of trained district nurses who co-operate with the local doctors, visiting patients in their own homes as often as is recommended. They will, when necessary, undertake to bathe the patient and deal with any treatments or dressings ordered by the doctor; and their advice and support is invaluable to relatives caring for a sick elderly person at home. In some parts of the country, night-sitters are also occasionally available to relieve relatives of some of the strain. In the case of serious illness, night-nurses are available.

Other services which may be obtainable through the local authority are visits from a physiotherapist, a chiropodist, an occupational therapist and social workers, as well as a laundry service for incontinent patients, the supply of special equipment for home nursing, a library service, home help, and any essential adaptations to the home (such as the provision of wheel-chair ramps or hand-rails) to increase the patient's mobility. Unfortunately in most areas there are shortages of both staff and money to supply all the needs of the many sick people who are entitled to this help, so what looks on paper to be a wonderful array of services may turn out to be disappointing in practice. This is no fault of the workers concerned, who put in long hours to try to meet the demand, but the more pressure the relatives of sick people as a whole can bring to bear on the government to release more funds for this sector, the more likely it will be that the situation will improve rapidly as the economy picks up. You may need to show determination and initiative in this matter, for naturally these specialist workers in the field of medicine, nursing and welfare will not all come flying to your aid as soon as an emergency arises. You have to make your needs, and those of your parent known to them, so that a good team of helpers can be assembled, with the assistance of the general practitioner. When this is done, you should no longer feel so alone in your troubles, but supported by skilled and friendly people whose visits to the home will strengthen you in your endeavours, as well as helping your parent.

There are many excellent voluntary organisations to which you can also turn for help – particularly the British Red Cross, who can let you have nursing equipment (such as bedpans, bedrests, etc.) on loan. Their officers are always willing to help and advise those who are nursing the elderly at home, as are those of the St John Ambulance Association, and the St Andrew's Ambulance Association. Numerous other voluntary social services exist in most parts of the country, and a social worker from the local authority Social Services Department can guide you towards those best suited to assist in your particular situation.

Simple nursing procedures

You will save yourself a lot of trouble and unnecessary physical strain if you decide from the outset to learn the correct way of doing things, to say nothing of the difference it will make to the patient's comfort. The best way of doing this is to learn by practical example from one of the area authority district nurses or someone fully trained in home nursing from one of the above mentioned associations and society. The purchase of the St John Ambulance book, *Nursing*, which is also the authorised manual of the St Andrew's Ambulance Association and the British Red Cross (available through local bookshops, or from the organisations themselves), is probably the best investment anyone can make if they find themselves faced with nursing a sick relative at home, as it gives simple, clear instructions and illustrations, plus much very useful information, and would be a good inexpensive reference book on this subject for any household to have. It was prepared by one of the country's leading experts on the subject, Miss J. Markham s.r.n., s.c.m., r.n.t., h.v., d.n. (London) and can be relied upon absolutely.

The following, however, may be some useful hints if you are completely inexperienced in nursing an old person at home and you are suddenly presented with this task, although it is not intended to be a substitute for the valuable practical demonstration and instruction that should be given by a trained nurse.

PATIENT MOBILITY

In many cases of illness in the elderly, doctors recommend that they should be encouraged to move around the room a little and sit out of bed in a comfortable chair for part of the day. This is because there are risks attached to total immobility in later life: muscles weaken, joints stiffen and sometimes tend to contract painfully. Bedsores may appear and bladder disfunction sometimes leads to incontinence. Constipation can also be a problem for bedridden patients, and serious circulatory difficulties may arise, which in some cases result in embolism, thrombosis, or the development of pneumonia.

Sometimes elderly patients will say that they would much rather stay in bed all the time and that there is no point in getting up. This is in many ways quite understandable, as the effort of getting out into a chair, even with help, can be considerable for the old and frail.

Clearly it is not suitable to explain all the most serious results of immobility to some elderly patients as this would make them very anxious, but since most of them worry about their bowels, they can truthfully be told that the doctor thinks that these will function better if they can move about a bit, and sit out in their chair for a while, and this often motivates them to do so. While they are out of bed, it can then be made freshly for them as follows (adapting the method to the patient's condition and type of illness):

BEDMAKING
1. Get someone to help you if possible, although this is not absolutely necessary.
2. Place an underblanket on the mattress (unless it is a Ripple bed mattress, when only a sheet is required).
3. Cover with a waterproof sheet of rubber or plastic.
4. Cover with the bottom sheet (making sure that it is central). Tuck in, but pay particular attention to the corners. Start at the head of the bed, as this can make all the difference to the comfort of the bed, and will help to prevent the sheet from wrinkling. Hospital nurses are taught to do what are known as 'hospital corners', which are neat and taut. This is quick and easy to learn by the following method: Pick up the edge of the sheet that is hanging over the side of the mattress (about 18–20 inches from the head of the bed). Hold it up, and tuck in the point of the sheet that is then hanging

down. Tuck in the side of the sheet very firmly, like an envelope. Tuck in all down the side of the bed. Do the same on the other side, starting at the head end. Finally, tuck in at the bottom end, making sure that the sheet is fitting over the mattress smoothly and firmly, and that it is neatly 'cornered'. That is all there is to it – a simple little trick, but one that makes a tidy and comfortable bed for the patient.

5. Next, place the drawsheet (with a waterproof drawsheet beneath it if necessary) on to the bed in the position where the patient's buttocks will be. Leave one end much longer than the other. Roll the long end up neatly and tuck it under the side of the mattress, then tuck in the shorter length on the other side.
6. Place the required number of pillows on the bed, positioning one each side for the patient to rest the arms on if she is to sit up.
7. Put the top sheet on, making sure that it is central and that about 20 inches of it is covering the pillows, for turning down later. Make a pleat in it near the foot of the bed to allow for free movement of the patient's feet. Tuck it in at the bottom (remembering to make 'hospital corners') and tuck it in at the sides.
8. Cover with the continental quilt or, if using blankets instead, put each one on and tuck in and 'corner' as you did with the sheets.
9. Put the bedcover on (if not using a continental quilt), tucked in at the bottom, but left to hang straight down the sides.
10. Turn the top sheet down neatly over the bedcover and make sure that the bed is warmed before the patient returns to it.

MAKING THE BED WITH THE PATIENT IN IT
1. Get someone to help if possible.
2. Make sure that the room is warm and that there are no draughts.
3. Assemble all you need: clean linen on a chair near the bed, a chair at the end of the bed for pillows and blankets and a linen box for any soiled linen.

4. Tell the patient just what you are going to do so that she will not feel disturbed and will co-operate as much as she can.
5. Loosen all the bedclothes and remove eiderdown, if any. Fold the bedcover, blankets and top sheet in three individually and remove them. Cover the patient immediately with a blanket to keep her warm.
6. Remove all the pillows (gently) except one, unless you have been instructed by the doctor to keep the patient's head and shoulders raised at all times.
7. Roll the patient gently away from you to the other side of the bed, where your helper can steady her, making sure first that this is the side where the short end of the drawsheet is tucked in.
8. Brush out any crumbs etc. with your hand.
9. Pull out the long end of the drawsheet which will be on your side of the bed and roll it up neatly until it rests against the patient's back.
10. Make sure that the bottom sheet and underblanket are smooth taut and well tucked in, and brush with the hand.
11. Tuck in the end of the roll of drawsheet on your side of the bed, still leaving a neat roll of 'spare' against the patient's back. Instruct your helper to roll the patient over towards you carefully so that she can pull on the freed drawsheet and tuck more of it in on her side, which will give the patient a clean section of it to lie on.
12. Roll the patient on to her back in the middle of the bed, seeing to it that the drawsheet is smooth and well tucked in now on both sides.
13. Replace the top bedclothes as previously instructed, using a clean top sheet and pillowslips if necessary.

Never appear to hurry or be impatient. Disturb the patient as little as possible, speaking gently and reassuringly to her. Never chat about other things to the person across the bed who is helping you, as this makes the patient feel like an object rather than a person.

If you find you have to make or change a bed with the patient in it, without a helper, seek a practical demonstration of the safest way to do this from a trained nurse, particularly if the patient is in a weak and helpless condition. If this is not possible, do the best you can by rolling the patient towards you, rather than away from you. Place a heavy upholstered chair or some other suitable piece of furniture (that you can move without damage to your back) on the side of the bed that is not within your control, to prevent the patient from falling off it.

CHANGING A BOTTOM SHEET OR DRAWSHEET
1. Roll the clean sheet lengthwise and place it on a chair.
2. Roll the patient over towards your helper.
3. Untuck the soiled bottom sheet on your side and roll it neatly towards the patient's back.
4. Place the clean bottom sheet that has been previously rolled lengthwise on to the bed at your side, tucking part of it well in, all down the side of the bed, unrolling the rest of it until it lies beside the roll of soiled sheet at the patient's back.
5. Roll the patient slowly back towards you over the two rolls of sheets and steady her, while your helper removes the soiled one, unrolls the rest of the clean one and tucks it in on her side.
6. Roll the patient on to her back in the middle of the bed.
7. Make sure that the sheet is taut and that you have made neat 'hospital corners'.
8. Replace the top bedclothes.

You can use a similar method for changing a drawsheet, rolling it up before you start.

TURNING A PATIENT IN BED
It is very important to learn to do this properly without hurting or distressing the patient, and if she is bedridden and weak the doctor may advise that she is turned at least every two hours to help to prevent the development of bedsores through pressure.

Here again, it is best to have someone to help you if possible, as the patient will need to be lifted into the centre of the bed, once she has been turned on to her side.

You should proceed as follows:

1. If the patient is to be turned from her back on to her left side, stand at the left side of the bed.

2. Place her left hand on the edge of the bed with the elbow relaxed.
3. Place the right arm across the body.
4. Turn her head very gently to the left (any sudden movement may cause severe neck pain).
5. Lift the right leg over the left one.
6. Holding her with one hand and arm supporting the shoulders and one supporting the hips, roll her over towards you, and then with the assistance of your helper, lift her into the centre of the bed so that she is lying comfortably on her side.

CORRECT LIFTING

You need to have a practical demonstration of the correct technique for this from a trained nurse, and it is essential for you to seek this, as lifting a helpless or even weak patient can be dangerous both for him or her and for you, unless you know exactly how to take the strain. The main thing to remember is to lift with your feet apart, knees bent, and your back straight, using your thigh muscles, and never attempt to lift a helpless patient quite alone. However strong you may feel, remember that many nurses have suffered permanent back injuries through lifting patients, and that not a few patients have been casualties of incorrect lifting, although the patients have suffered much less than the lifters.

Keeping the patient clean and comfortable

GIVING A BED BATH

A bed bath given by an inexperienced person, with no knowledge of the right method, can be a chilly and exhausting experience, but if it is done properly it can leave the patient feeling warm, comfortable and refreshed.

First, see that the room is warm and that there are no draughts. Hang the 'engaged' notice outside the bedroom door to ensure privacy for the patient. See that the patient is aware of what you are going to do, and that she passes water before you start. Assemble all the things you will need in the room before uncovering the patient, the requisites being as follows:

1. Full-length rubber sheet to cover the bottom sheet.
2. Three large, thick bath-towels (the largest made, which are usually sold under the name of 'bathsheets' in most linen stores or department stores).
3. One hand-towel.
4. Soap.
5. Two thin face-cloths (thick ones are difficult to rinse free of soap quickly).
6. Two 'J' cloths.
7. Warm mouth-wash, plastic beaker and dental cleaning equipment.
8. Talcum powder.
9. Any lotion or creams that have been recommended by the doctor or visiting home nurse, for application to pressure points: heels, buttocks, lower back, shoulders and elbows.
10. Nail-scissors and nail-clippers.
11. Large plastic washing bowl of hot water.
12. Large jug of hot water.
13. Large pail or plastic bucket to place on the floor.
14. The patient's overbed table, to be placed near the bed, with the washing bowl, soap and flannels on it.
15. The patient's clean, aired nightclothes, placed on a chair nearby.
16. Brush, comb and mirror.

METHOD
1. Remove the top bedclothes.
2. By using the method previously described, roll the patient gently on to her side and back on to the full-length rubber sheet covered by one of the bathsheets.
3. Cover the patient immediately with another bathsheet to keep her warm. An old, clean blanket can be used for this purpose if desired but, if the bedroom is warm, the feel of a towel on the patient's skin is more pleasant.
4. Remove her nightclothes, trying to keep her covered up as much as possible to prevent a chill.
5. Wash and thoroughly rinse and dry in turn the following parts: face, neck and ears, arms and hands (allowing her to

dip them into the washing bowl), chest and under her breasts, armpits, navel and abdomen, legs, and feet. Then turn her by the method previously described. Wash shoulders and back. Allow her to wash and rinse the gentital region with the 'J' cloths (which are softer than flannels). If she is too weak to do this herself, do it for her very gently. *Change the water several times.* When washing, never dab or wipe, as this is very irritating to the patient. Wash carefully but thoroughly. Make sure to rinse and dry well, and only uncover that part of the body that is actually being dealt with.

6. Attend to the pressure points, according to the instructions left by the doctor or home nurse.
7. Clean and cut the finger and toe-nails if necessary, making sure that none of the nail clippings get into the bed.
8. Allow her to clean her teeth. Help her if necessary.
9. Place a plastic bin-liner bag (or cloth) over the pillow and do her hair. Then remove the bag or cloth with the hairs on it.
10. Remove the bath-sheet and rubber sheet from under her and smooth the bottom sheet and drawsheet.
11. Gradually remove the top bathsheet, helping her into her clean nightclothes. Comb her hair very lightly again to tidy it.
12. Replace the top bedclothes and leave her to rest undisturbed for half-an-hour.

WASHING THE HAIR IN BED

There is a specially designed hair-washing bowl on the market for this, which is very helpful (see Chapter 12), but it can also be done as follows:

Requisites
1. Large deep plastic bowl of hot water (half full).
2. Large jug of hot water for rinsing.
3. Large plastic bucket.
4. Four large waterproof sheets (rubber or plastic).
5. Waterproof cape.
6. Two medium hand-towels and one small guest-towel (for the patient's eyes).
7. A one-pint jug.

8. Mild shampoo.
9. Hand-dryer.
10. Clean brush and comb (plus setting lotion and roller curlers if the patient wishes).

Method
See that the room is warm, and put the 'engaged' notice on the door. Decide whether the patient's condition and personal wishes make it more suitable for a front-wash or a back-wash. Surround the bed with old newspapers and waterproof sheets.

For front hair-wash
1. Turn down the bedclothes to below the waist.
2. Put the rubber cape on the patient.
3. Cover the front of her and the bed with waterproof sheets.
4. Hand the patient the guest-towel for her eyes.
5. Put the large bowl of hot water on to the overbed table in front of her and wash the hair into it as she bends forward. Massage very gently with the hand and use the water in the pint jug.
6. Rinse. Then rinse again with water from the large jug.
7. Remove bowl and dry the hair gently with hand-towels.
8. Remove rubber cape, rubber or plastic sheets, newspapers and all other equipment after covering the patient up.
9. Brush, comb (and set if desired) and dry with a hand-dryer.
10. Settle the patient down to rest for an hour in warmth and comfort.

For back hair-wash
1. If the mattress is thin, or of the type that can be rolled under at the top, do this. If it is a thick Dunlopillo or interior sprung mattress on a divan base (which is more usual), get a helper to assist you to position the patient comfortably first and then pull the mattress down, away from the headboard, leaving enough room on the divan base for the bowl of water.
2. Protect the floor, the patient, and the bed, as previously described, covering the head end of the mattress and divan base with a large waterproof sheet.

3. Place the large bowl half full of hot water on to the waterproof sheet on the exposed divan base.
4. Turn the bedclothes down to the patient's waist.
5. Place the rubber cape round her shoulders.
6. Give her the guest-towel for her eyes.
7. Get your helper to assist you to re-position the patient, with her neck well supported, but her head over the bowl, and proceed to wash, rinse and towel dry the hair.
8. Remove the bowl and all the protective materials and equipment speedily.
9. Keep the patient warm and put the mattress back into its normal position. Make her comfortable.
10. Dry the hair with the hand-dryer (setting it first if she wishes).
11. Settle her down to rest in warmth and comfort for an hour.

TREATMENT OF BEDSORES

Prevention, as always is better than cure, and this is most likely to be achieved by cleanliness, regular turning of the patient at least every two hours and, in many cases, nursing on a Ripple bed (see Chapter 12). If the latter is not suitable for some reason (if, for example, the patient needs continuous firm support for a spinal condition), then nursing on a sheepskin relieves pressure and allows for some circulation of air beneath the body. Constant attention to the various pressure points (according to the doctor's instructions) is also of the utmost importance. If a bedsore does develop, the doctor and home nurse will treat it, and will leave precise instructions for you to follow. These may vary according to the degree of the sore and the condition of the patient. If her condition is complicated by incontinence, every effort has to be made to keep the patient clean and dry, to create the right conditions for healing.

If the patient is bed-bound or chair-bound, you should carefully examine her skin when you wash her, for any sign of redness or cracking, and the doctor should be informed at once if such signs appear. Even quite bad pressure sores, which can appear with amazing rapidity, can be healed once the correct treatment is given, provided the patient's general condition is not too bad and she is well nourished on the right foods.

Caring for Elderly Parents

GIVING A BEDPAN

Everyone who has been bed-bound completely at any time in their life will know that one of the most distressing features of their helplessness was their total dependence on others for help with the intimate matter of their personal 'waste disposal'. Great gentleness and sensitivity are needed in this area of nursing. The three things the patient needs most, to reduce anxiety and embarrassment, are:

1. A kind and cheerful nurse.
2. *No* waiting *ever*.
3. Complete privacy.

The worst thing of all for a sick person is to be kept waiting when she wants to move her bowels or pass water. When she says that she wants a bedpan, she has often delayed asking for it until she thinks her nurse is reasonably free to attend to her, so, by then, her need is usually fairly urgent. Possibly more distress is caused to patients by those few words, 'All right, in a minute. I'll come as soon as I can', than by anything else in the whole experience of human sickness apart from pain. Obviously there are times when a serious emergency elsewhere must cause delay, but these are rare, and this particular request from a patient should, under normal circumstances, be given priority.

A stainless steel or plastic bedpan is better than an enamel one as it does not chip; a chipped bedpan easily harbours bacteria. When taken to the patient, it should be warm and dry and covered with a disposable paper towel. When it is removed, it should be covered again as it is taken from the room. After it has been emptied and rinsed out it should be disinfected with a mild solution of Dettol, or something similar, and left to dry upside down.

Method
1. Close the door and hang the 'engaged 'notice on it.
2. Make sure that the patient is warmly clothed round the chest and shoulders.
3. Turn down the bedclothes, and raise the nightdress.

Nursing the elderly at home

4. Slide the bedpan under her buttocks very carefully, remembering that any damage to the skin may cause a bedsore. If she is very weak, you may need a helper to assist you with lifting her on to the bedpan.
5. Give the patient a packet of soft good quality toilet paper to use, and if she is too ill to manage on her own clean her yourself, speaking gently and reassuringly to her as you do so. (Wash her after a bowel movement.)
6. Let her wash her hands in a bowl of warm water.
7. Take the bedpan away for cleansing and disinfecting.
8. Never forget to wash your own hands afterwards.

GIVING A URINAL

This should be taken to the patient covered with a disposable paper towel or cloth. If he is too weak to place it in position for himself, you should do this for him. When removed, it should be covered again before taking it from the room, emptied and rinsed with cold water. When disinfecting a urinal, it is most important to rinse it out very thoroughly several times afterwards.

If your elderly male relative is taken ill suddenly and unable to get out of bed, until a urinal can be obtained for him an instant coffee jar or even a jam jar can be used in an emergency.

Medicines and drugs

The most important things to remember when handling **drugs** or medicines are:

1. To keep them out of reach of children.
2. Only to give the patient what the doctor has prescribed or approved.
3. Check and double-check on the amount to be given each time, and make sure that it is the right drug.
4. Give it always at the correct time.
5. Have a pleasant drink for the patient to sip afterwards, or a boiled sweet if allowed; if not, a drink of water to wash the taste away.

Medicine bottles should be shaken well first and the dose

poured with the label bearing the name of the medicine and instructions uppermost, to prevent drips from obliterating it. (A broad strip of sellotape over the label and round the bottle is also a good idea.)

When giving tablets, shake the right number out of the bottle into an egg-cup and give them with a drink of water. Divide or crush them and give them in a spoonful of jam (if allowed) if the patient finds them difficult to swallow. Never hurry the patient, but stay with her until you have actually seen her taking the drug. Then remove bottles and tablet boxes right out of her reach, unless asked by the doctor to leave any beside her. Powders may be given in a spoonful of jam (if allowed). Capsules of course cannot be crushed, and must be swallowed whole with water. A hot drink after certain types of drugs, particularly the pain-killers, will often speed their action, but the doctor should be asked about this first.

Some patients who cannot swallow properly are prescribed special suppositories by the doctor. These are inserted gently into the rectum at the stated times, where they are retained by the patient and absorbed.

GIVING A SUPPOSITORY

The doctor may recommend that the patient be given one (or two) glycerine suppositories if the bowels do not move regularly and easily – which is often the case, if she has to spend much time in bed. Constipation can often be greatly helped by drinking plenty of fluids, eating a moderate amount of fresh fruit daily, and the addition to the diet of three dessert spoons of 100% bran breakfast cereal daily, but all this should be checked out first with the doctor in case there should be some special diet instead.

Method
1. Remove any foil or plastic covering from the suppository.
2. Have to hand the bedpan (or commode), soft toilet paper, a small bowl of warm water and a disposable plastic glove.
3. Wash your hands.
4. Make sure that the room is warm and that the door is closed with the 'engaged' sign on it.

5. Ask the patient first to pass water.
6. Turn down the bedclothes.
7. Ask her to lie on her left side with the knees drawn up.
8. Encourage her to relax and breathe gently through the mouth.
9. Put on the disposable plastic glove.
10. Dip the suppository into the bowl of warm water.
11. Push the suppository, very gently, well into the rectum, saying quietly to the patient: 'Just relax, that's fine. Just relax.'
12. Remove the finger from the rectum. Remove the glove.
13. Wash your hands.
14. Turn the patient on to her back and ask her to try to retain the suppository as long as she possibly can before she moves her bowels. But make sure you are around to help her on to the bedpan or commode quickly when she needs it. Afterwards, make her clean and comfortable again. Allow her to wash her genitals and her hands. Remove the bedpan from the room as soon as possible, covered with a disposable towel.

GIVING INJECTIONS

In some circumstances, you may be asked by the doctor if you feel able to undertake to give the patient injections. If so and you agree, he or the visiting nurse will show you exactly how to do this, and you should ask for several demonstrations and short sessions (just a few minutes) of instruction if you feel at all unsure about the method. The technique is actually quite simple – nothing to fear – and the disposable syringes now available make it easier than ever before.

TAKING THE TEMPERATURE BY MOUTH

You will normally only be expected to take the temperature by mouth, although in some circumstances the doctor may ask you to take it in the rectum or the armpit, but in these cases he or the nurse will show you just how to do it.

Many thermometers have Fahrenheit and Centigrade markings. The normal temperature is 98.4° Fahrenheit and 36.9° Centigrade but this can vary slightly at different times of the day. You should not allow yourself to become an anxious slave of the thermometer, remembering that it is only one of the many pieces of equipment for diagnosing and monitoring illness. Your object should be to use it as often as the doctor wishes and make a careful note of the daily readings, so that these can be reported to him. If, however, there is any significant variation he should be notified at once.

The thermometer should be kept, bulb down, in a small glass of mild antiseptic, and it should be rinsed well under running water before it is given to the patient. It should also be rinsed again after the temperature has been taken and put back into the antiseptic. The temperature should not be taken if the patient has just had a hot drink or a hot bath, and she should always be sitting (or resting on her bed).

Method
1. Shake the mercury down into the bulb at the end of the thermometer.
2. Place it under the patient's tongue, telling her to close her lips but not to bite upon it.
3. Leave it for two minutes.
4. Remove it. Make a note of the temperature.
5. Rinse it well and return it to the glass of antiseptic.

TAKING THE PULSE
The doctor or nurse will instruct you on how to do this if it is necessary. You will need a watch with a second hand.

Method
1. Make sure that the patient is sitting or lying down.
2. Adopt a quietly casual attitude, so that she does not become anxious about it.
3. Place the tips of the first three fingers on the artery on the inner side of the wrist, with your thumb behind it.
4. With the watch in your other hand, count the pulse rate for one minute and note it in writing for the doctor. The average pulse rate in an adult is seventy-two beats to the minute, sometimes a little less or a little more. The rate is of course often altered in certain types of illnesses.

Nursing the elderly at home

NOTING THE RESPIRATION RATE
Patients sometimes become worried and tend to over-breathe if they know that their respiration rate is being counted, so it is best, if possible, to do this when they are not aware of it. One way of achieving this is to do it while still holding the wrist after the pulse has been taken. The normal rate is 15–20 times per minute, and one breath in and one breath out equals one respiration. Always make a written note of the respiration rate for the doctor (but not in front of the patient).

OBSERVATION OF THE PATIENT
The patient's mood, behaviour, colour, quality of sleep, changes in temperature and respiration, and any abnormalities in motions or urine or other changes should be recorded and reported to the doctor.

The use of hot water bottles or electric blankets

The advice of the visiting home nurse should be sought on the best method of heating the patient's bed, as this may vary according to her illness and condition. In some cases, if a patient is paralysed, incontinent, or unconscious, you may be advised to rely entirely on keeping the whole room very warm instead of putting extra heat into the bed.

Electric blankets and rubber or stone hot water bottles all have their advantages and disadvantages, which have to be weighed carefully. Even the best electric blanket can develop a fault, and of course, it would not be suitable for an incontinent patient. Good quality, new rubber hot water bottles have been known, on rare occasions, to burst in the bed, and stone hot water bottles are so hot when first filled that unless they are very well covered they could easily burn the leg or foot of an elderly person, who may have lost some sensation.

If a rubber bottle is to be used, buy a good one (with a spare washer) *without* an integral all-over cover, as it is difficult to keep a check on these for slight cracks which may lead to leakage. Buy or make a cover for it, which buttons right over the top. Never fill the bottle with boiling water, or more than three-quarters full.

One of the safest types of heating is the stone hot water bottle, *provided* all the following precautions are taken. It keeps hot longer than a rubber one, and also has the added advantage of lifting the bedclothes up a little at the foot of the bed, giving more freedom of movement for the patient's feet. Make several very thick bags for it, out of double towelling, with a fine zip, lengthwise, along the top. These can easily be washed and are soft and comfortable to the touch. Buy two spare washers for the bottle, as the only place where a leak could possibly occur would be where it is screwed up. If necessary, write to the manufacturers for these if they cannot be supplied by the shop from which you purchase it. When placing it in the patient's bed, in its bag, put it at the bottom, to one side, well away from her feet so that she can feel the benefit of the heat without actually touching it. Remember that hot water bottle burns can be very serious for any sick person but particularly for the elderly, so great care should be taken in their choice, handling and maintenance.

Incontinence
This problem has already been mentioned in previous chapters, but we should now consider some of the practical ways of dealing with it, although it is a very big subject upon which whole books have been written, so we cannot hope to cover every aspect of it. Much of the information you may need will come from the patient's doctor and any visiting home nurses, but if your parent becomes incontinent and you wish to obtain literature and details of the large number of different aids for coping with it you would be well advised to write to:

> The Disabled Living Foundation,
> 346, Kensington High Street,
> London W14 8NS.

You should also read *Incontinence* by Dorothy Mandelstam, MCSP, DIP.SOC.SC., published by William Heinemann Ltd. It cannot be emphasised too strongly what a distressing and humiliating experience incontinence can be for a patient (as well as an exhausting one for the relative) unless the problem is handled with much kindness, sensitivity and patience and an attitude quite free of any blame. Many old people are reduced to tears and near-despair every day by such thoughtless and unfeeling remarks as, 'So we've been a dirty girl again, have we?' Even when this is followed up by, 'Oh, well, never mind,' it is a wound and an insult to a grown person, and just as cruel and pointless as boxing a small child's ears for wetting the bed. Those who are cared for by kind and imaginative people, who try to cut the problem down to size for them and understand their feelings, have much less to endure in the course of their illness.

No one likes to lie in a wet bed or a dirty one, and then to be dependent upon others to clean up after them. Occasionally there may be a psychological reason for these accidents if a patient is emotionally disturbed and feels anxious, depressed and rejected, but usually the cause is purely a physical one: an unfortunate symptom, for all concerned, of a very real illness.

If you encounter this in the elderly parent you are nursing at home, tell the doctor at once, and get all the help you can in tackling it right away, before it begins to wear you down. Help *is* available, more now than at any other time in medical and nursing history. Sometimes the trouble can be cured or greatly improved by surgery or a special type of physiotherapy, and sometimes drugs can be prescribed that will help. The right kind of timing and routine for the malfunctioning bladder may also ease things considerably, so the patient should be given a bedpan or urinal regularly at intervals suggested by the doctor or nurse. Washing and drying the patient frequently, and the use of a barrier cream, an incontinence sheet, and disposable pads in the bed or chair can also help. Use should be made of the local authority laundry service too, if there is one in the area.

You may be told that because of the existence of brain damage or the seriousness of the illness, improvement cannot be hoped for. If so, try as far as possible to accept this sad fact and settle down into a routine of dealing with it, rather as a mother does with a young baby, without resentment (and without restricting the fluid intake). There is, of course, a very big difference between infant and geriatric incontinence. With a child, we know that bladder control will gradually come; but both are human beings needing our care perhaps for quite a long time – and the attitude we take to their helplessness can either make or mar their lives and ours during this difficult period.

The preparation and presentation of food

The doctor's instructions on the question of diet should be followed carefully, and whatever the patient is allowed to eat should be presented as attractively as possible to stimulate the appetite. If the diet has to be a rather colourless one, it can be made to look more tempting by garnishing it with sprigs of parsley, a lettuce leaf or small slivers of tomato, even if these cannot actually be eaten. Dull food often looks better served on a white plate with some kind of green leaf design round the edge, and crisply clean and colourful traycloths and napkins. A rose, or other flower from the garden, with the stem cut off near the bloom, placed in water in a small shallow dish on the meal-tray is also pleasing evidence of extra care and affection which encourages the patient. Vases on trays should be avoided as they are too easily knocked over.

The main consideration will be to see that the patient takes plenty of fluids, and as much nourishing food of the right kind as possible. A liquidiser can be a boon to those looking after an invalid, as some foods which are not easy to eat may be much more acceptable as a drink or in the form of soup.

If the doctor recommends that your parent drink plenty of milk, and she happens to dislike it, it can be given in the form of various sweet and savoury sauces and soups, or flavoured to taste. Flavoured or unflavoured Complan (a nutritious powder obtainable from all chemists that is made up into a drink with milk or water) can also provide a balanced meal occasionally when the patient does not feel like eating normally.

When feeding a conscious but helpless patient, gentleness, time and patience are required and she should never be hurried.

A life worth living

For most of us, life is only worth living so long as we feel loved and wanted by those around us. If this feeling is taken from us, we can soon become depressed. So if we are nursing our elderly parent, we should try to make sure that life still has some meaning for her. This will mean giving her love as well as the work of our hands, and providing her with every kind of mental stimulation she can still enjoy: visits from relatives and old friends, books, magazines, newspapers, radio and television, as well as the opportunity to do any sort of creative work she likes, such as knitting, sewing, sketching or writing.

There will come a time, of course, when she becomes very ill, and her interest in many things and even in people will wane, but if we do all we can for as long as we can, however hard it may be, we shall never regret it.

12
Clothing and aids for the disabled elderly

Clothing

Few elderly people fail to get a lift from being able to cover an ageing frame with a well-cut suit or dress which to some extent appears to restore lost muscle or contours, and wearing a colour they know suits them well can give a considerable boost to their morale. So those who are caring for elderly parents can do much to preserve their self-respect and enjoyment of life by making it possible for them to feel better by looking good and well-groomed.

The younger elderly are, of course, quite able to care for their clothing and appearance themselves, but those who are very old or disabled, either mentally or physically, will need some assistance. We should never assume, however old or 'fey' they are, that they cannot feel some small pleasure in wearing clean, comfortable and attractive clothing.

If a stage is reached when your elderly mother can no longer choose and maintain her clothing in a state of cleanliness and good repair, the situation may sometimes be further complicated by such problems as her inability to eat or drink with a steady hand, so that her clothes soon become marked and stained, or some degree of incontinence may exist, with all its attendant difficulties. At this point, all concerned will find life much easier if she can happily be persuaded to wear well-styled, casual outer clothing in man-made fibres, such as Polyester, which can be washed frequently and drip-dried quickly. The acrylics should be avoided though, as they are inflammable, and the elderly who smoke, or who sit near to a fire for long periods in winter, are at some risk if they wear or are wrapped in materials in this group.

Clothing and aids for the disabled elderly

Unless there is obesity, or some preference for a certain type of dress, often the most comfortable and convenient garments for women, as well as men, in their later years are warm, quick-drying Thermolactyl underwear, man-made fibre slacks, well-cut tunic blouses or leisure shirts of cotton and Polyester (or 100% Polyester) in attractive colours, and long (but never tight) Polyester socks, with well-fitting shoes, or slippers, that are washable both inside and out.

Bibs and pinafores to protect clothing should be avoided whenever possible (except at meal-times if an old person has to be fed and has difficulty in eating normally) as these childish extras tend to be very humiliating. On no account should she be made to look foolish either by tying coloured ribbons in her hair – which is done occasionally and unwisely, but with kind intentions, by those caring for elderly women, who sometimes find it easier to accept their problems if they treat them like children. If your elderly mother agrees, a short, manageable hair-style is often more becoming, and once the hair has been styled by a hairdresser, you may learn how to maintain this for her yourself, using one of the inexpensive hair-cutters obtainable from all branches of Boots the Chemists and many other stores.

For nightwear, cotton and Polyester nightdresses or pyjamas are ideal, as they wash and dry quickly and need no ironing, and are much more comfortable in bed than nylon, which is non-absorbent. A short- or long-sleeved Thermolactyl vest can be worn next to the skin for extra warmth if necessary, and bedsocks of the same material are comfortable and easy to care for.

Good quality, quilted, man-made fibre dressing-gowns are an excellent choice for both sexes as they are warm and easily washed and dried. The following are the addresses of some of the firms who supply specially designed clothing for elderly and disabled people. There are many more, whose addresses, together with details of their products, can be obtained from the Disabled Living Foundation, Information Service for the Disabled, 346 Kensington High Street, London W14 (telephone 01-602-2491). Advice can be obtained also from this organisation on how to cope with any special problem connected with clothing and aids for the elderly infirm. It should be remembered, though, that much help is also available from the local authority social services departments and local voluntary social service organisations in these matters.

Day clothes

NB For those elderly people who are not badly disabled and merely need well-cut, easy-care casual clothing, in attractive styles and colours, what they want can often be found in most branches of Marks & Spencer; and the same applies to nightwear.

DRESSES

J. H. Bounds Ltd, 68 Sackville Street, Manchester M1 3WJ. (Washable button-through dresses and washable dresses with Velcro-button fastenings and open backs in a range of styles).
County Textiles Ltd, 61 Charles Street, Cardiff CF1 4RW. (Suppliers of similar types of clothing.)

WRAPOVER SKIRTS (WASHABLE) AND WOMEN'S TWO-PIECE SUITS WITH WRAPOVER SKIRTS (WASHABLE)
J. H. Bounds Ltd (address as above).
Jennings and Leeson Ltd, Yeoman Lane, Leicester LE1 1UT.

TROUSERS (WASHABLE)

For women
J. H. Bounds Ltd (address above).
Carita House, Stapeley, Nantwich, Cheshire.

For men (washable, with elasticated waist or Velcro fly fastening)
J. H. Bounds Ltd (address above).
Carita House (address above).
County Textiles Ltd (address above).

For incontinent men
'Edgware' trousers, with extra deep Velcro fastened front, for urine bottle, for use while sitting down.
D. Ransome Ltd, Abbey Mills, St Albans, Herts A13 4HQ.

Clothing and aids for the disabled elderly

Men's suits (washable)
D. Ransome Ltd (address above).
Tilco Men's Wear, 156a Arkwright St, Nottingham.
D. B. Thomas and Co., 14 Andrew St, London E14.

OUTSIZE CLOTHING (FULL RANGE)

For women
Evans Outsizes Ltd, 4 Bilton Road, Greenford, Middlesex.
Whitfords (Bury) Ltd, Brandlesholme Rd, Bury, Lancs BL8 1BQ.

For men
High and Mighty, 86 Prospect St, Hull HU2 8PG.

Night clothes

NIGHTDRESSES AND NIGHTSHIRTS (BUTTON-FRONTED, OPEN AND CLOSED BACKS)
J. H. Bounds Ltd (address above).
Crompton Manuf. Co., Ltd, P.O. Box A32, Lockwood, Huddersfield.

PYJAMAS
J. H. Bounds Ltd (address above).

DRESSING-GOWNS (DIFFERENT DESIGNS, SOME WITH OPEN BACKS)
J. H. Bounds Ltd (address above).
Milan Gowns Ltd, Riverpark Road, London N22.

Underwear for summer and winter and for men and women
Damart Thermawear (Bradford) Ltd, P.O. Box 23, Bingley, Yorkshire BD16 4BH.
Whitfords (Bury) Ltd (address above).
J. H. Bounds Ltd (address above).

STOCKINGS AND TIGHTS (WARM AND EASY TO MANAGE FOR THE ELDERLY, WITH SOME OUTSIZES)
Damart Thermawear (Bradford) Ltd (address above).

Brettle Sales, P.O. Box 5, Belper, Derby DE5 1AS.
Elbeo Ltd, Lenton Lane, Nottingham NG7 2NS.
Tytex Hosiery Ltd, Hamilton Rd, London SW19. (Separate stocking legs on their own waistbands, like open crotch tights).
Yellow Top Hosiery Co., 93 High St, Boston, Lincs. (Open crotch tights up to 70" hips).
Pretty Polly Ltd (Stockings and tights 60 denier. Obtainable from major department stores).

WASHABLE SLIPPERS FOR MEN AND WOMEN
Dunlop Footwear Ltd, Rice Lane, Walton, Liverpool.
Carita House (address above) ('Plast-sok' washable plastic-footed socks).

Outdoor clothing for men and women

Light weight, but warm quilted coats, or jackets are easy to wear and to put on, and Gannex Raincoats (wool-lined), obtainable from major department stores, are lighter than overcoats; very warm and wind and rainproof.

FOR WHEEL-CHAIR USERS
A waterproof leg and lap cover can be supplied for outdoor use by the Department of Health and Social Security.

Zip quilted leg covers can be obtain from Comfy Products, Comfort House, Marshall Ave, Bridlington and Simplantex Ltd, Willow Road, Eastbourne, Sussex, who also supply a heavy waterproof apron and nylon waterproof cover, known as 'Wheelymac', which completely protects the wheel-chair and the patient.

All the firms mentioned above will be glad to send particulars of their products on request.

Aids for the elderly infirm

Although information on aids of every kind can be obtained from the Disabled Living Foundation (address already given), it can be very helpful first for an elderly person to be visited at home by a social worker, physiotherapist and occupational therapist from the local authority social services department, who may be needed to advise upon what aids and equipment should be chosen to meet specific needs. Much of what is required may be supplied 'on loan', and the British Red Cross Society and others may also be of assistance in this respect.

For those, however, who prefer and can afford to purchase their own aids, the following is a list of some of the most useful ones. The firms concerned will supply price lists, and often brochures as well, giving photographs or illustrations, with exact measurements and detailed descriptions of the products.

WALKING

Zimmer lightweight walking aid, adult adjustable model, made in aluminium alloy tubing, fitted with four heavy-duty non-slip rubber tips. Strong and stable. (Zimmer Orthopaedic Ltd, Bridgend, Glamorgan.)

Zimmer reciprocal folding lightweight walking aid (each side is moved forward alternately). Extension legs model, height adjustable. (Zimmer Orthopaedic Ltd, address above.)

Zimmer adjustable quadruped walking aid (to be used singly or in pairs). A very stable walking stick of aluminium alloy and chrome-plated steel, with contoured hand-grip and four legs with non-slip rubber tips. Height adjustable. (Zimmer Orthopaedic Ltd, address above.)

Zimmer adjustable walking stick, adjustable height, lightweight and strong. Aluminium alloy, with plastic hand-grip moulded to fit the contours of the fingers. (Zimmer Orthopaedic Ltd, address above.)

SITTING

High-seat and high-back armchairs
Parker-Knoll high-seat, 'Highworth'. Padded arms, optional open sides. (Parker-Knoll Ltd, The Courtyard, Frogmore, High Wycombe, Bucks. Also many department stores and furniture shops.)

Parker-Knoll 'High-Wing', as above, plus wings. (Parker-Knoll Ltd, address above.)

Thanet Orthopaedic chair. Wooden framed chair with vinyl or

soft cover and padded arms. Extras include wings, filled-in sides, head roll, lumbar pad, seat board. Alterations can be made to order, e.g., to slope of back and extra seat height. (A. Rye & Sons Ltd, 107/109 High St, Whitstable, Kent CT5 1AY.)

High-seat chairs and High-seat kingsize, with matching footstools available (Shackletons (Carlinghow), 501 Bradford Rd, Batley, Yorks WF17 8LL.)

Wide selection of high-back chairs with or without wings or padded armrests. Wood and metal frames, vinyl covers, flame retardent, various seat heights. (James Spencer and Co. Ltd, Moor Road Works, Leeds LS6 4BH.)

Special chairs made to order to meet requirements. (A. J. Way and Co., Spring Gardens Road, High Wycombe, Bucks HP13 7AG.)

Reclining chairs

Norton Recliner, upholstered and with leg rest. (Parker-Knoll Ltd, address above.)

Apollo Super chair, upholstered with leg rest. (James Spencer & Co. Ltd, address above.)

Mobile chairs

Mobile lounge chair, with four castors, braked at the rear. Tubular framed, vinyl covered, with padded arms. Adjustable large tray and retractable footrest. Fixed back or semi-reclining model. (Zimmer Orthopaedic Ltd, address above.)

Self-lifting chairs

May Wing Chair, upholstered easy chair with wings. Counter-balanced mechanism operates lifting seat. Side lever permits seat to be locked in horizontal position. (May Wing Chair Co. Ltd, 26 High Street, Malmesbury, Wilts SN16 9AU.)

Lifting chair. Wooden framed, infilled sides, wings, various coverings. Spring-activated lifting seat. Give user's weight when ordering. Carlton Mills (High-Seat) Ltd, Dept L, Hirst Road, Dewsbury, W. Yorks WF13 2AE.

Spring-lift seat. A seat to place in any chair. Takes up to twelve stones. (Carters (J. and A.) Ltd, Alfred St, Westbury, Wilts.)

Raising blocks for chairs
Three-way wooden blocks, with holes for the legs of chairs. Different sizes, to raise the chairs to various heights. (Homecraft Supplies Ltd, 27 Trinity Rd, London SW17 7SF.)
Four-way blocks, with optional heights and different sized holes for chair-legs. (Phoenix Supply Ltd, 28 Sanderstead Rd, Croydon, Surrey.)

Footstools
Three heights, upholstered stools. (Shackletons (Carlinghow) Ltd, address above.)
Carters footstool. A hard wearing footstool with chrome legs and rubber feet. (Carters (J. and A.) Ltd, address above.)

Leg-rests
'Trueze' foot and leg rest. PVC covered. Rocking tubular metal base. (Carters (J. and A.) Ltd, address above.)
Anton, wooden frame. Padded Vynide top. Cantilever design. (James Spencer and Co. Ltd, address above.)

Cushions
Posture-Curve for support of the lumbar spine, transportable. A shaped lumbar support cushion, with removable zip covers. Can be used in any chair or in a car. (F. Ashton Ltd, 15 Groton Road, London SW18 4EP.)
Mandarin neck pillow, for gentle support of the neck. Down-filled. Cover extra. (Army and Navy Stores (Linen Dept), Victoria St, London SW1.)
Geriatric chair cushions. A range of foam cushions of varying shapes and sizes, including one which is wedge shaped. The thickest part of the wedge is placed at the front of the chair to prevent the user from sliding out. (Surgicgoods Ltd, 26 Tenter Rd, Moulton Park Ind. Estate, Northampton NN3 1PZ.)
Li-Lo small square inflatable cushions. For use in any chair or car. (Milletts Camping Stores.)

Folding table
Very table. A folding table that can be used for the infirm who cannot sit up to a dining table for their meals. Also useful for disabled people in wheel-chairs or as an overbed table for meals, reading, writing, or craftwork. Consists of two working surfaces, adjustable in height. The main table can be adjusted to any angle. The side table is for items needed close at hand. The table feet can be folded under the lower tube for storage and are fitted with castors. Chromium-plated frame and washable surfaces. (Carters (J. and A.) Ltd, address above.)

Wheel-chairs
A number of firms make these, and there are wheel-chairs to suit every type of disability. Carters (J. and A.) Ltd, address above will supply a list on request, together with details of measurements and prices etc., as well as illustrations. The long list of models includes attendant-type chairs giving a comfortable ride over all surfaces, with four pneumatic tyres.
Car transit chair, attendant type, designed to pack easily.
'Compact' chair. Self-propelling, folding and portable, combining swinging detachable foot-rests.
'Premier' chair. For indoor and outdoor use. Rolls easily over rough or uneven ground or rugs. Self-propelled or attendant-controlled.
'Detachable arms' chair. The arms are removable to facilitate sliding in and out from the side, and close approach to a table or desk. Self-propelled or attendant-controlled.
'One-arm drive' chair. Guided and propelled with one hand (left or right) the chair is easily controlled. Can also be attendant-controlled when necessary.
'Semi-reclining' chair, with high back. The back can be adjusted up to 30° angle to allow for a change of posture.

BEDS AND BED-AIDS

Ripple bed
An air-bed (placed on top of the existing bed) for the prevention of bedsores. Electrically operated. Alternating pressure. Hire

or purchase. (Talley Surgical Instruments Ltd, 47 Theobald St, Borehamwood, Herts.)

Bed-rest
Chrome-plated tubular steel frame. Gives comfortable and reliable support and yields to the body's contours. Adjusts to four positions. (Carters (J. and A.) Ltd, address above.)

Bed cradle (folding)
Chromium plated. Choice of four sizes. (Carters (J. and A.) Ltd, address above.)

Bed blocks
To raise the height of the bed, with holes for the bed legs. (Homecraft Supplies Ltd, address above. Phoenix Supply Ltd, address above.)

Protective bedcovers
For the elderly bedridden who enjoy reading the newspapers, but dislike soiling the sheets, eiderdown, or Continental quilt with newsprint, a Marks & Spencer single Polyester and cotton bed-sheet in a dark colour that tones with the colour scheme of their bedroom, will, if cut in half and hemmed, make two excellent, lightweight, crease-resistant, washable and drip-dry covers for the top of the bed when required. For incontinence equipment, the doctor and home nurse should be consulted.

BATHROOM AND TOILET AIDS

Swedish bath seat. Chromium-plated steel tubing, with plastic coated open-mesh seat, with a bar to support the back. The support arms and seat-bearing rails are rubber-protected to prevent marking of the bath sides. (Carters (J. and A.) Ltd, address above.)

Adjustable bath rail. An easily fixed rail which gives support when entering or leaving the bath. Made in chrome-plated steel tubing to fit any bath. Height adjustable. (Carters (J. and A.) Ltd, address above.)

Non-slip bath mat: Croydex bath mat, with suction caps beneath it. (Boots the Chemists.)

Mobile shower chair. On wheels. Arms and back provide secure support. (Carters (J. and A.) Ltd, address above.)

Hair rinser

Simplair hair rinser, for chair-bound patients. Fits any wash-basin. Contoured to the shape of the neck and designed to back-wash the hair. (Carters (J. and A.) Ltd, address above.)

Hair rinser, for washing the hair of a bed patient when lying flat. Supports the head and neck when the hair is being washed and has deep sides to prevent the water from wetting the bedclothes. The water is channelled into a bucket placed in position by the bed. (Carters (J. and A.) Ltd, address above.)

Toilet-roll holder

Toilock toilet roll holder. Suitable for those with the use of only one hand. Permits only one sheet of paper to be taken at a time. (Burn Bros (London) Ltd, Cray Avenue, St Mary Cray, Orpington, Kent BR5 3RH.)

Raised toilet seat

Raised toilet seat, suitable for most toilet pedestals. Can be lifted off when not in use. Polypropylene. Can be washed and cleaned with boiling water if needed. (Carters (J. and A.) Ltd, address above.)

Adjustable raised toilet seat, fitted with brackets all round to enable it to be used on most toilet seats. Height adjustable. Strong white polypropylene seat and sanitary shield are washable. Secure and comfortable support. (Carters (J. and A.) Ltd, address above.)

Toilet aid (free-standing.) This is placed round the toilet to assist patients to lower and raise themselves. Fits all standard toilets. Made in aluminium tubing with plastic armrests. Fitted with four non-slip rubber tips. Gives reliable support. Floor fixing flanges available if desired. (Carters (J. and A.) Ltd, address above.)

Commode. Commode and visitors' bedside chair combined.

Part padded backrest. Upholstered, removable seat cover, toilet seat, small front castors, front skirting. Takes 'Perfection' bedpan. (Thackray Ltd, P.O. Box 171, Park Street, Leeds LS1 1RQ.)

Mayfair bedside commode, made in chrome-plated steel tubing. Fitted with non-slip rubber tips. Overseat covered in PVC and padded with foam rubber. Square plastic pan. Good support for arms and back. (Carters (J. and A.) Ltd, address above.)

Traditional armchair-type commode. Good range of seat heights from which to choose. (Shackletons (Carlinghow) Ltd, address above.)

Adjustable commode, lightweight, with no back rest. Made in aluminium alloy tubing with white armrests and white polypropylene seat. Fitted four, non-slip rubber feet. Plastic pan extra. Strong and stable. (Carters (J. and A.) Ltd, address above.)

Plastic bidet. Lightweight. To be used over toilet pedestal. Can be ordered through local chemists who sell medical aids, or from Bodycare, 155 High Rd, Willesden Green, London NW10 2SG.

Bedpans and urinals (male and female). A selection of male and female standard-type bedpans and urinals in plastic or steel. (James Spencer & Co., address above. Thackray Ltd, address above.)

Slipper bedpans. Plastic female urinal, wedge-shaped with handle at one end. To slide under a recumbent patient, e.g. someone suffering from slipped disc who cannot move easily. Sometimes known as fracture bedpans. (Home Nursing Supplies, Headquarters Rd, West Wilts Trading Estate, Westbury, Wilts.)

Chamber pots

Plastic chambers, round. (Home Nursing Supplies Ltd, address above.)

Steel chambers, round, with side handle. Two sizes. (A. C. Daniels, 41 New Cavendish St, London W1.)

Footstool, for use in bathroom, bedroom, or kitchen. With

chromium-plated legs with rubber feet and a chromium-plated handrail attached to give support when getting into the bath, into bed, or reaching to shelves in the kitchen. Sturdy and secure. A two-step stool is also available with handrail. (Carters (J. and A.) Ltd, address above.)

Medi-hoist. A versatile lifter, which is easy to use and manoeuvre in a confined area. This hoist enables a patient up to 127 Kg (20 stone) in weight to be moved or lifted single-handed and with the minimum of effort. The lifter glides easily through narrow doorways on sturdy castors. Complete with fitted spreader bar and brake castors. Seat and backrest with snap-on chain. (Carters (J. and A.) Ltd, address above.)

SELF-HELP

Stocking aid. Long handled. Fastens to the stocking top with suspenders and has a rigid handle, to be used in reverse as a shoe horn. (Homecraft Supplies Ltd, 27 Trinity Rd, London SW17 7SF.)

Sock puller. Steel and perspex stick with cross bar to hold sock. (Mecanaids Ltd, St Catherine Street, Gloucester.)

Long-handled shoe horn. This has a smooth blade mounted with a spring on to a rigid shaft, allowing the shoe horn to flex. Lengths from 15 to 25 inches. (Homecraft Supplies Ltd, address above.)

Rigid shoe horn. Metal. Lengths 22 to 24 inches. (British Red Cross Society Medical Aid Dept, 157 Cavendish Road, Leicester.)

Dressing sticks. Long handled, with a small hook end to assist in dressing. (British Red Cross Society Medical Aid Dept, address above.)

Trouser pull-on. Clips to the waist of trousers and has tapes to allow it to be lowered and pulled up over the feet without bending. (Llewellyn and Co. Ltd, South East Princes St, St Nicholas Place, Liverpool L3 OAZ.)

Helping hand. A reacher for those who have difficulty in bending. Grips articles, which are picked up by means of a simple trigger action. Magnet attached for small metal objects. Various lengths. Tall people often find the long-reach model most helpful.

There is also a folding model. (Carters (J. and A.) Ltd, address above.)

Nelson knife. Combined knife and fork. A rocking motion on the curve of the blade cuts food, using only one hand. Useful for stroke patients. (Carters (J. and A.) Ltd, address above.)

Plateholder. Holds a plate firmly and securely in position by means of suction pads made in resilient rubber. Useful for stroke patients and others. (Carters (J. and A.) Ltd, address above.)

Food guard. Clips round the side of the plate, providing opposition to spoon or fork. Useful for stroke patients and anyone who has the use of only one hand. (Carters (J. and A.) Ltd, address above.)

These are only some of the vast number of aids available. The Disabled Living Foundation (address previously given) can supply on request a list of others and of publications on various subjects of interest to those caring for the elderly.

13
Admission to hospital

Emergency admission
As people grow older, there is always the possibility of sudden illness which may necessitate urgent admission to hospital. It is sensible to be prepared for this by having a small case packed ready for them in an easily accessible place in their bedroom (as mentioned in Chapter 3). It can also be a considerable help to the hospital staff to place in this case a large white envelope addressed to 'The Medical Officer in Charge' with the words underneath, 'Report on: (patient's full name and age)', containing a brief but full history of her previous illnesses and operations, details of present medication, any allergies known and particulars of any special diets. If you are able to accompany the patient into hospital in the ambulance you can hand this to the Ward Sister immediately on arrival. This information could be not only time-saving, but life-saving as well in some circumstances.

Unless you have had proper nursing or first-aid training, you should not attempt to take any complicated or heroic measures if your parent suffers a sudden collapse, as you may do more harm than good. The important things to do are:

1. To keep her breathing (or to help to start breathing again if she has stopped).
2. To stop bleeding.
3. To treat for shock.
4. To get the doctor and ambulance.

Unconscious but still breathing
Lay the patient down on her side with the leg that is against the ground stretched out. Bend the other leg at the knee. Position

Admission to hospital

the shoulders so that the lower arm is behind her and the upper arm bent at the elbow, with the hand resting on the ground, level with the face, which should be turned towards the hand. This is called the recovery position, and will stop the tongue dropping back into the throat and causing obstruction of breathing. Loosen the clothing. Cover with a warm blanket, but do not give anything to drink, and do not use hot water bottles to keep her warm. Call the doctor or ambulance at once. If however there are any broken bones or other obvious complications which would make movement dangerous, just try to keep her airway clear until help arrives.

Unconscious and not breathing
Take action at once. Any delay, even for a few moments, could be fatal. Supporting the neck, tilt the head back and push the chin up. This will keep the tongue clear of the throat. If she starts to breathe again immediately, place her in the recovery position previously described, on the ground, and cover her with a blanket. If this measure has not started her breathing again, roll her on to her back, tilt the head back, holding the nostrils; squeeze her nose, take a good breath in yourself, put your mouth right over her mouth and blow your breath into her; remove your mouth when you see her chest rise (which will mean that you have successfully inflated her lungs). When the chest falls do the same thing again, at the normal intervals of your own breathing. Continue this mouth-to-mouth breathing until she can breathe normally on her own. Then place her in the recovery position, covered with a blanket, and call the doctor or ambulance at once. Try to keep your head, and follow these instructions step by step, but if you panic and find yourself unable to remember what to do, concentrate all your efforts on getting medical help after you have placed her in the recovery position. Whoever you speak to on the telephone (e.g., doctor's secretary) make it clear that the patient has stopped breathing and is in a very serious condition, needing help at once.

To stop bleeding
Lay the patient down. If the bleeding is from one of the limbs,

raise it. Place a tightly folded clean handkerchief or clean small cloth over the wound and press firmly, holding it there for ten minutes if necessary, to give the blood a chance to clot and the bleeding to stop. Then cover with a dressing and a thick pad of cotton wool (even a sanitary towel can be used for this, if available). Bandage the pad firmly to the wound. If you have no bandages, cut a strip lengthwise from an old clean sheet, or failing that from a large clean bath towel. Get medical aid and keep the patient warm, but give nothing to drink in case an anaesthetic is necessary on arrival at hospital. Although the important thing is always to stop serious bleeding, great care must be taken in handling a patient who also has a fracture, or something in the wound.

Sudden acute abdominal pains
There can be many reasons for this, such as strangulated hernia, obstruction of the bowel, appendicitis or retention of urine. Allow the patient to sit or lie in the position found to be most comfortable. Call the doctor at once. Keep the patient warm, but give nothing by mouth until the doctor has seen her. If her mouth is very dry, just moisten inside the lips only. Observe her carefully so that you can report to the doctor exactly what has happened, for example, any vomit or bleeding from the mouth, nose, bladder or rectum.

Burns
Elderly people who are unsteady on their feet have been known to suffer bad burns from falling on to an electric fire, or scalding themselves while cooking or filling hot water bottles, because their hands shake, or they are arthritic and their grip is lessened.

Do not put anything at all on a burn. Just run it under cold water for some minutes until the pain eases. Many people still think that oil or antiseptic creams should be applied to burns, but this will only make matters worse. Cover the burn with a clean dry dressing of some kind and let the patient lie down until the doctor arrives. If the burns are extensive instead of local this can be a serious emergency, and the patient must be got to hospital as soon as possible for treatment which cannot be given at home.

Fractures

If an elderly person falls and breaks a bone, do not attempt to apply bandages, splints or slings unless you are fully trained in First Aid. Concentrate on treating her for shock. Do not move her, just make her as comfortable as possible under the circumstances, cover her with a warm blanket, but do not give her anything to drink. Get the doctor at once.

Heart attacks

The main signs may be severe chest pains, breathlessness, pallor, sweating and collapse, sometimes with loss of consciousness and complete failure of breathing. If this happens, loosen the clothing. Never try to get the patient upstairs to her bed, for movement can be dangerous. Lay her down just where she is and raise her slightly on two or three cushions or pillows. Reassure her as much as you can. If she has stopped breathing keep her airway clear and start mouth-to-mouth resuscitation. Get the doctor immediately.

Stroke

If an elderly person suddenly develops a weakness or paralysis in a limb, or appears confused and has difficulty in forming words properly, sounding almost as though drunk, it will be quite likely that she has had a stroke. She should be reassured, and rested in bed or on a couch, and not given anything to drink until the doctor arrives as her swallowing might also have been affected.

If the stroke is a major one and she loses consciousness, she should be placed in the recovery position (previously described).

The collapse of a diabetic

If an elderly person goes into a coma and it is known that she suffers from diabetes, it is often difficult for anyone but a doctor or trained nurse to know whether the coma has been caused by too much insulin or too little insulin, either of which can be the result of a fault in the type of food she has eaten, the interval between meals, or an accidental overdose of insulin. Because of this, it is best to get medical help very quickly if you can. If this is not possible, you should remember that if she has not had enough insulin she will probably be breathing deeply and sighing, with a flushed face, and will go into coma slowly; whereas if she has had too much insulin she will be breathing lightly, sweating and pale in the face, will seem 'muddled' mentally, and will go into coma quickly. If she is still conscious, give her about eight lumps of sugar to eat, or preferably the equivalent amount of granulated sugar stirred into water to drink (four dessertspoons). If this revives her, you will know that she has taken too much insulin, but if it makes no difference you will not have made her condition any worse, and the doctor will take over as soon as he arrives. If she is already unconscious, do not give anything by mouth. Simply place her in the recovery position (previously described) and call the doctor at once, as this is a serious emergency.

Admission to hospital for mental illness (See also Chapter 9)

Most people who enter psychiatric hospitals for treatment these days do so on a purely voluntary (informal) basis, just as they would enter a general hospital of their own free will. Some are admitted to the psychiatric wing or hospital in the grounds of a general hospital. However, there are many large psychiatric hospitals catering exclusively for those with mental illness (sometimes of a long-term nature) where excellent work is still being done, and it is often to the geriatric wards of these hospitals that old people are admitted.

Some of the many circumstances which can arise that could make it necessary for your elderly parent to be admitted to hospital for a mental condition have been discussed in Chapter 9. The methods of assessment and treatment are now so good that if you have to allow your parent to go into one of these hospitals, you can feel optimistic that she may be helped and stabilised on the correct drug therapy. She may hope to return home in a few weeks or months much improved, and able to cope with life again on a maintenance dose of the drugs which have been found helpful. Others may need treatment for a longer period, or indefinitely.

The sudden onset of a confusional state in an elderly parent should be reported to the doctor at once, as this may well be

Admission to hospital

caused by some physical condition which can be treated at home, and it is no kindness to your parent to delay in seeking medical advice. If the doctor thinks that admission to hospital is necessary for assessment, this should not be feared. The pressure on hospital beds is so great that you can be sure that your parent will not remain there longer than is absolutely necessary.

As described in Chapter 9, it may be advanced arteriosclerotic or senile dementia, depression, or a paranoid state that brings matters to a head and makes it impossible for you to manage your parent at home any longer, and you should always seek the advice of the doctor if things seem to be getting past the point of no return. The sooner you get help if there are signs of mental disturbance, the greater are the chances of a good recovery. The doctor, who may also call in a social worker trained in dealing with mental health problems from the local social services department, may suggest hospital treatment (some of the provisions of the Mental Health Act are described in Chapter 9). Every attempt will be made to persuade your parent to enter hospital informally, but if it is necessary for reasons of safety to compel her to do so, you will be consulted at every turn, and your objections (if any) will be given the proper consideration. A few elderly people who are quite ill mentally can be treated at home, if there is plenty of room and there are plenty of people to keep an eye on them; but in many modern homes, where all the adults are out at work, and conditions are somewhat cramped, it can be quite impossible to leave an old person alone for any part of the day if she is disorientated and likely to turn gas taps on, or wander out into the traffic in the street, unaware of what she is doing, or who she is.

It is important that you follow the advice of the doctor as to the best course to take, and to dispel any bizarre thoughts from your mind that your parent has 'gone mad' – remembering that the brain, like any other part of the body, can be subject to illness, and that often there is a chance of total or partial recovery.

Planned admission to hospital
If your elderly parent has to enter hospital for an operation or some course of treatment, there is much that you can do before-

hand to make the whole experience less traumatic. First of all, you should help to prepare her emotionally for it, by listening patiently to any expression of fear or apprehension, giving reassurance, and taking a positive and optimistic attitude towards the outcome of the proposed treatment. You should also assure her that her home and her possessions (and her cat or dog if she has one) will be well looked after during her absence. You should offer to attend to her business affairs for her if she wishes. Then you should make it clear that you will be looking forward to welcoming her back when she is discharged.

If necessary, you should help her to bathe, to wash her hair and set it into an easily manageable style, and to trim her finger and toe nails.

If you pack her case for her, you should see that all her nightclothes are clearly marked with her name, that there are two thin face flannels packed with the other things in her toilet bag, also a small torch and a small travelling clock with a very clear face to place on the bedside locker, so that she can see the time in the night. A box of paper handkerchiefs, a paperback by her favourite author and a tin of barley sugar or fruit drops to take after any unpleasant tasting medicine will also be appreciated! If your parent is able to write letters, and may want to do so in hospital, a box of notelets with envelopes already stamped, and a pen, should also be included. Remember, too, to pack her reading glasses which she may need as well as her bifocals.

Flowers sent or delivered to the hospital to be there on her arrival are always a helpful gesture, and you, some other member of the family, or a close friend, should go with her on the day of her admission. You should make immediate contact with the ward sister, and the doctor in charge if he is available. If not, you can make an appointment to see him within the next few days to discuss your parent's illness and the prognosis when this is known.

Visit the hospital as soon as possible after admission, and regularly thereafter. If you know that she would welcome other visitors, you should notify friends, and other relatives, and encourage them also to write and to visit. It is better to agree, though, that one particular member of the family should be the person to have close contact with the medical and nursing staff regarding her progress, in order to avoid everyone else constantly telephoning the hospital for news.

While your parent is in hospital, check regularly on supplies of clean nightclothes and the fruit juices she is allowed (one of the most refreshing drinks being well diluted lime juice). Make sure that her spectacles are within easy reach, and that her dentures are being kept clean. This latter would be normal good nursing practice, but in an under-staffed ward it can sometimes be over-looked, and a patient can develop an infected mouth and glands.

Check with the ward sister to see what kind of food, drink or sweets you may bring in with you, and what fruit will be suitable. Homemade cakes and biscuits, which are usually very welcome gifts, should be in easily handled airtight containers. There is nothing worse than stale, lavender-scented sponge-cake that has been kept in a tin with an ill-fitting lid in a hospital locker next to the talcum powder. Magazines and easily held books are appreciated too, as well as flowering plants – rather than too many gifts of cut flowers which add to the work of the ward.

Day hospital support on discharge

With the success of modern methods of treatment of illness in the elderly, many patients can be discharged and return home even when they still need a certain amount of medical and nursing supervision, which is sometimes arranged at a day hospital.

Transport to and from the day hospital can be provided if necessary, and patients can have their meals there. Help can be given with bathing, chiropody, nursing attention, occupational therapy, stroke rehabilitation, physiotherapy, and many types of occupation and recreation in a sociable atmosphere. Arrangements are also made for patients to have regular check-ups with the geriatric physician at the main hospital's out-patient department. Hospital-based and Community-based social workers play an important part as members of the therapeutic team.

Patients with psychiatric illnesses usually attend separate day hospitals, when necessary, where their progress can be observed and out-patient treatment and care continued. They have all the same facilities as patients recovering from physical illnesses.

Day hospitals exist not only for those who have recently been discharged from hospital and need further care. If your elderly parent is suffering from an illness or disability which could be helped by out-patient therapy, daily or once or twice a week, she may be referred through the general practitioner, following assessment by a geriatric or psychiatric consultant, to one of these hospitals. Social workers and others connected with the local authority health and social welfare services may also be involved in arranging this, and keeping contact with them may be a great help to you.

What care hospitals can provide for the elderly

There are long waiting lists for hospital treatment for people of all ages under the National Health Service, but the shortage of beds for old people is particularly acute (although there is an emergency bed service which doctors can use for very urgent cases). Apart from this, however, most doctors prefer their elderly patients to be treated at home if possible, because of their lowered resistance to infections and the fact that some of those in the older age groups become upset and temporarily confused when they are removed from familiar surroundings. But sometimes admission to hospital is the only answer if the patient requires constant care, attention and observation by day and night, or if the nature of the illness makes home nursing impossible even with the help of all the statutory and voluntary nursing and social services.

If you are facing this situation with your elderly parent, although you may wish that it were possible to continue to look after her at home, you will no doubt be relieved if the doctor can arrange admission to hospital, where you role can still be a caring one by giving emotional support and co-operating fully with nursing and medical staff.

The decision regarding the type of hospital to which your parent will be admitted will be primarily a matter for medical judgement, but it will also depend to some extent on the bed situation at the time, and facilities vary too in different parts of the country. But broadly speaking, those suffering from physical or mental illness of an acute type which may respond fairly quickly to active treatment, or who need a brief period in hospital for special diagnostic investigations, are admitted to hospitals which cater mainly for short-stay patients. Those with chronic physical or mental illness are more likely to be sent to long-stay hospitals. Fortunately, more interest than ever before is now being taken in geriatric medicine, and there is a trend towards the provision of more specially trained staff and better accommodation for the elderly sick, but anyone trying to get an elderly parent admitted to hospital, or visiting them in one, will know that there is still much to be done in this field.

Medical geriatric units

These are sometimes part of a large general hospital and provide a very high standard of treatment, but more often they are in smaller hospitals. Sadly, much of the long-stay accommodation for geriatric patients is still substandard, and frequently there is a shortage of efficient modern equipment and aids which could make life so much easier for both patients and staff.

These wards for the care and treatment of these sick old people, whose only 'home' in their last months or years is a hospital, are too often situated in Dickensian buildings, quite unsuitable for the purpose for which they are now being used. There are invariably staff shortages too, though the devotion of the nursing and medical staff, who have innumerable difficulties to surmount in bad working conditions, is often remarkable.

In certain circumstances you may have no option but to allow your parent to enter one of these hospitals when she cannot remain at home, but you also have every right to do all you can to improve the service that is being offered to your own and other people's elderly parents who rely upon the National Health Service in time of sickness. If you are of a crusading nature, you can bring their plight to the notice of your Member of Parliament, your local Community Health Council and other bodies; if not, you may still be able to do much to help them, and the staff who are caring for them, by joining the Hospital League of Friends, in which you can begin at once to do something positive for their welfare in small ways by helping in various fund-raising activities to provide extra comforts. This will also give you a valuable opportunity to meet and talk with members of the senior nursing and administrative staff.

If your elderly parent in a long-stay geriatric unit seems constantly distressed, or obviously badly cared for, spare no effort to put the matter right, but reserve judgement until you are quite sure of your facts. It needs courage to complain, but do so if necessary, for to ignore a plea for help from someone who can no longer fight for herself is always a betrayal of trust, and not an easy thing to live with in later years. If you feel that a complaint is justified an approach should first be made quietly and without aggression to the ward sister, who can often iron out a difficulty quite quickly. If this fails, ask for an interview with the doctor in charge. If this brings no results, the next step is to put your complaint in writing (keeping a copy) to the hospital secretary. By then, it will be most likely that the matter will have been investigated and rectified, but if not it should be pursued with determination, through the hospital group secretary, and if necessary the local Community Health Council and the Area Health Authority. But it would be very unusual to have to go as far as this to obtain satisfaction. Most hospitals are anxious to investigate any complaints thoroughly, and are as aware as we are that, however old patients may be, they are still entitled to their share of the full range of medical, nursing and other services available, and entitled to be treated with kindness and respect by those who are paid to serve them.

Long-stay psycho-geriatric wards

These wards are mainly for elderly patients suffering from one of the various forms of brain damage and senile psychosis. They are usually part of a large psychiatric hospital, and since many of the National Health Service psychiatric hospitals are rambling Victorian buildings, not planned for today's methods of treatment and care, and most are under-staffed, these long-stay wards often leave much to be desired. As mentioned in Chapter 9, your first visit to your parent, who will be with a group of old people in various stages of mental deterioration (some of them perhaps noisy and restless), may be rather distressing for you. You should be as vigilant regarding the standard of care your parent is receiving as you would be if she were in a medical geriatric ward, but it is important to remember that some elderly dementing patients relate appalling stories about the nursing staff, which are usually only paranoid fantasies. With very few exceptions, psychiatric nurses do an extremely tiring and exacting job remarkably well, try their best to create a bright and homely atmosphere and go to endless trouble to encourage mobility, interest and occupation, often achieving a great deal for their patients.

Visiting

Much of the depression experienced by those visiting an elderly parent in a medical or psycho-geriatric ward is due to feelings of guilt. You may feel that you have let your parent down because you are not the one who is feeding, washing, and caring for her now that she is in need of such help, even though you realise that you could not possibly have provided adequate nursing at home. Some of these very painful feelings have been discussed in other chapters, but it may help you to remember that you are not alone in having them. Most relatives experience guilt feelings in this situation, just as the bereaved do when they so often plague themselves with the question 'Could I have done more?', when the true answer is usually 'No'. When serious illness strikes both the patient and their close relatives become wounded, vulnerable people. You will most probably find that when you have absorbed the first shock of what has happened you will gradually be able to come to terms with your feelings of guilt and get things more into perspective, but if you are severely disturbed by them you should not hesitate to seek help by discussing them with your parent's doctor or the hospital social worker, who are trained to understand and support relatives through this difficult period. According to your personality, your previous life experiences, and many other factors, you may react with depression, extreme anxiety or anger against yourself, your parent, or the hospital staff, but they will accept this and help you to talk it out in an atmosphere of uncritical confidentiality. Your parent's ward sister may be a great help to you also, for she will have dealt with hundreds of relatives who have felt very much as you do.

You may also feel distressed if, after making what is perhaps a long and difficult journey to the hospital you are sometimes greeted by apathy, indifference, or even irritability by your parent. Try to remember that illness of mind or body, or both, can alter a person's response even to those they love most, and sick people often save up all their 'grumbles' for those visitors in whose love they feel secure, and who they know will not reject them. So, hard as it may be, you will be doing your parent a very real service if you are prepared to listen patiently to her descriptions of the discomforts of hospital life, as well as the pain or discomfort connected with her illness.

Long-stay elderly patients usually want to do either all the talking or all the listening, and it is best to fall in with their wishes on this willingly. Those in medical wards often want to tell their visitors the life history and medical details of everyone around them, and although this may hold very little interest for you, try to listen attentively, remembering that this is their whole world now; these are their new life-companions, and this is their way of trying to adjust to it. If your parent appears to be more interested in the patient in the next bed than in any special news you may have to tell of her grandson's success in his examinations, though it may sadden you a little, it will be evidence that she is trying to identify more with those with whom she is sharing what may be her last 'home'. If your parent is unable to let go of some of her emotional involvement with people and places outside the hospital, there will be much less chance of her settling down in a long-stay ward with even a moderate degree of contentment, so although you should always be ready to give her news of home and family you should show as much interest as possible in everything and everyone connected with her new environment. Sustained conversation with most patients in long-stay psycho-geriatric wards is usually out of the question, although a few of them do have their lucid moments, but it is just as important to visit them regularly, however 'difficult' or uninterested they may seem, for most visits from affectionate family and friends have value and meaning for even quite disorientated patients.

Regular visiting of an elderly parent in a long-stay ward also makes it possible to build up good relationships with the nursing staff, which is very important. They are often interested to hear a little of what their patient was like in his, or her younger days. One daughter, longing for those who were nursing her paralysed stroke-stricken mother to know how she had looked, and the kind of person she was before her illness, brought in a small unframed photograph of her as a beautiful elegant woman in her thirties, with her name and age written on the back. She asked the ward sister, who was a kind and understanding woman, if it could be placed in the folder containing her mother's medical notes. This was done, and the idea was so well received that the geriatrician in charge asked other relatives to do the same, as the nurses found it very helpful in their efforts to relate to some of their old patients whose minds and/or bodies had become pathetic wrecks. This is just one example of what can be achieved by relatives who visit frequently and are on good terms with the hospital staff and appreciative of all their efforts.

Making friends with other visiting relatives may help you too, particularly if there is an opportunity for you to have a cup of tea together in the hospital after visiting hours, so that you can share your feelings and anxieties if you are returning to an empty house.

The question of the reduction of your parent's State pension after eight weeks in hospital and its further reduction after a year in hospital to a few pounds for pocket money is explained in Chapter 5. Full details can be found in the Department of Social Security leaflet NI9. You should make sure that she is receiving pocket money and is able to spend it if she wishes on the small luxuries which are often available from a hospital trolley or hospital shop. But what she will want and need more than anything else will be to see you as often as possible; to know that she is loved and not forgotten.

14

Coping with terminal illness

The strain of coping with the terminally ill at home can be considerable, and even when the patient has lived for a normal span of life, children who care deeply naturally find it very hard to face death with them. The fact that they are old and have had their life does not make the prospect of parting any easier, and it is a situation in which those involved need all the help they can get, both practically and emotionally, from family, friends and neighbours, as well as from the doctor and visiting nurses.

Although the life of the household must go on, and the usual routines observed for the sake of the whole family, every effort should be made to see that the dying person is as comfortable, pain-free and relaxed as possible, and undisturbed by noise or family wrangles, which often tend to erupt quite violently under this sort of stress, and can be bitterly regretted later.

The question of whether the elderly person is to be told of approaching death, is bound to arise, and should be discussed with the doctor, although this is an issue patients usually decide for themselves by either indicating their wish to be told the truth, or their need to be protected from it. It is necessary to be quite certain of the patient's wishes in this matter before informing them of a truth which can sometimes prove to be intolerable and impossible to handle, and which may create a hopeless state of depression during the last few weeks of life in some people. So a reply to a 'one-off' remark (which may, indeed, be just a remark, and not a question) of 'I'm not going to die, am I?' has to be weighed very carefully. We may imagine that a person who has had a very strong, forthright character would definitely want to be told if he or she were dying, and that someone more gentle and submissive might shrink from the knowledge, but often the opposite is true. The strong ego may rage against the prospect of death, while the seemingly weaker personality sometimes finds it easier to accept. It is never possible to predict accurately how any individual may react to the awareness of the approach of death. Most people die much as they have lived, facing this last event as they have faced all the other important ones in their lives – although there are always the 'Sidney Cartons' who surprise everyone at the end by the contrast between the courage and dignity of their death, compared with the apparent muddle and failure of their life. The type of last illness, too, can in some cases alter a person's previously stated feelings towards the taking of this last hurdle, when it is in sight. So, whatever our own views happen to be on the desirability or otherwise of telling a dying person the truth, they should not be imposed on others. The choice must be the patient's, and our task is to discover his or her wishes, bearing in mind that we have no right, ever, to rob someone totally of hope, for there is always the one chance in a million that both we and the doctors could be wrong.

A dying person will often swing from one mood to another. There may be disbelief and denial of the reality of what is happening to her, anger, despair, and finally acceptance. Those who are told the truth on one of their 'good' days, by a well-meaning but incautious relative, may be found to be in a state of uncontrollable anxiety or depression when their mood changes. A good doctor and sensitive relatives will usually be able to interpret the signals in the patient's conversations over a period of time, and discover whether she wants to know everything, a little, or nothing at all. We must let her make the running and follow her lead, however hard it may be.

Unless there is incontinence or severe brain damage, the physical comfort of a clean, warm bed and gentle handling are not so difficult to provide if there are no other family responsibilities, but in this situation we need all the help and support we can get from family and friends to enable us to stand up to the strain.

The control of pain is quite another matter, and an extremely important one. The object should be not just to control it but to anticipate it and to see that the patient is given the right drugs in the right amount before it becomes fully established. There is no need for any terminal patient to be in severe pain, for research in recent years has brought tremendous advances in this area of medicine, particularly through the work of 'pain' clinics, such as the one at St Christopher's Hospice in South London. Modern tranquillisers and anti-depressants can help as well to relieve distress of mind, although not every unpleasant symptom can be controlled.

Most general practitioners and hospital doctors give great help and support to the dying, but if your parent is terminally ill and appears to be suffering great pain, you should press for this to be relieved, and continue to do so, politely, but with real determination, until some action is taken. For this is the last battle you will ever be able to fight for her, and one which you have a right to win. In most cases, though, battle does not come into it, for there are very few doctors who are not just as anxious as relatives are that a dying person should be able to end his or her days peacefully.

The weeks or months preceding the death of someone we love can be full of strange and unexpected emotions. Perfectly natural but seemingly very odd things can happen in the relationship of the dying and those closest to them, for illness and stress can have a profound effect on both of them. It is a time when old wounds can be opened – or healed – and almost anything must be expected, and borne somehow. Sometimes the patient will draw nearer to those caring for her, but sometimes she can appear to reject them. If this happens it can be very painful, but it helps if you can understand that it is the total life and the total love that matters – all the years shared together – not some brief crossing of swords at the last, under the intolerable strain of grave illness.

It can be very distressing too, if your dying parent seems apathetic and remote from you, especially if you have been close all your lives, but you need to accept that this is not evidence of a sudden withdrawal of love, but simply that she is inwardly very busy with the business of dying – which, like being born, is one of the great events of life. She is packing her bags and disengaging, and this is something she needs to do alone.

If she becomes comatose, it is always wise for those around her to be careful in their conversation, and safer to act as though she can hear and understand all that is being said, since hearing is the last sense to go in the dying. So to talk to her softly and lovingly as you attend to her bodily needs can be comforting to you, and in some cases to her also.

In this harrowing time those who fare best are undoubtedly people with a religious faith that enables them to believe that there is life after death, which turns the dreaded 'Goodbye' into the hopeful 'Au revoir'. But those who have no such belief can, and do, come through the experience equally well – if more painfully.

Many relatives fear being present at the moment of death of someone they love, but afterwards they will often be heard to say things such as, 'I was terrified of facing it. I thought it would be horrible, but it wasn't. When it finally came, it was beautiful, and I just felt so happy for her.'

If, when your parent dies, there is, for some reason, a considerable delay before the arrival of the doctor and nurse, it is important to know just what to do. It is very unusual for relatives to have to undertake the 'last offices' themselves, but of those who have done it, almost all say that they were surprised to find that it did not distress them half so much as they imagined it would, and some, not at all. As one daughter put it, 'I loved her in life, why should I fear her in death?'

If we ever find ourselves in this position, the following things should be done:

1. Close her eyes and inform the doctor and nurse.
2. If they are going to be delayed, proceed to wash the body all over, having first emptied the bladder by pressing on the lower half of the abdomen, while holding a small bowl between the legs.
3. If you feel able to do so, plug the rectum and the vagina. If not, do not worry about it, and in any case place a thick wad of cotton wool or two sanitary towels between the legs and up under the buttocks.
4. See that the mouth is closed by tying a broad bandage

(or strip of material cut from a pillow case) under the jaw and in a knot at the top of the head.
5. Re-dress any wounds or open sores.
6. Put on clean nightclothes.
7. Comb the hair.
8. Remove all pillows.
9. Straighten the body and limbs, with the hands by the side.
10. Tidy the bed, cover the body with a sheet. Tidy the room and draw the curtains.

When the doctor comes, he will write the death certificate (unless there are any unusual circumstances which he wishes to report to the Coroner). The death certificate has to be taken by the next-of-kin to the Registrar at the local office within five days for the death to be registered. The deceased's pension book and medical card also have to be taken to the Registrar.

Contact should be made with a funeral director (undertaker) who will, if you wish, take the body away to carry out the 'last offices' and then place it in his chapel of rest, where you can visit before the funeral. It is unusual these days for the body to remain at home until the funeral, although this is a matter for the family to decide.

Terminal illness in hospital

It may not be possible for your elderly parent to die at home, if there are no suitable facilities for heavy nursing and night-care, or he or she requires special pain-relieving techniques, which you cannot be expected to supervise. In some circumstances you will just have to be prepared to stand back and let the experts take over.

Your role then will be to visit the hospital (or home) at every opportunity to give comfort and support, and, even if unconsciousness supervenes to keep up the regular visits holding your parent's hand and speaking softly and reassuringly to her, in case there is the slightest spark of awareness still left. This constancy, to the end may just possibly be of help to your parent, and it will certainly help you, and be appreciated by the nursing staff in the hospital as well, who will see how much their patient is loved and valued.

15
The women who care

Some of the most courageous women in every generation are those who give generously of themselves and their time to caring for elderly parents. Unlike people who are involved in single acts of heroism, they rarely make the headlines, but to meet them is to meet with courage and constancy of a very high order.

Theirs is the quiet day-to-day courage that just keeps on going in the face of every difficulty without benefit of applause, and theirs the constancy of one of life's hardest commitments: that of standing by another human being in his or her need; not just during a temporary crisis, but perhaps for years and seeing it through to the end. Women like this – perhaps you are one of them – can be found in every city, town and village in the country: people who have taken on the task of caring, sometimes carrying heavy burdens alone, with none of the advantages of companionship when the going is rough. Some of them too, after struggling for a very long time to keep their elderly parent out of hospital, suffer deeply under a false sense of failure if her condition finally requires special treatment or nursing care which cannot be given in the home. But most of them, by then, have been through so much, and have become such seasoned emotional steeple-chasers in the care of the elderly that they manage somehow to clear even this high fence with courage, if they are completely convinced that it is in their parent's best interests to go into hospital, and that they will still be able, by frequent visiting, to give her what she needs most: the assurance that she is loved.

Society rarely sees more than the tip of the iceberg of the problem of elderly people whose health or circumstances have made it necessary for them to turn to their children for help during their last years. When we look closely, we become aware not only of the size of the problem, but that right at its heart are often just two women: one old, frail, and more than a little sad, who is no stranger to loss of almost every kind: and the other middle-aged, menopausal, and apprehensive about the future as she copes with all the anxieties of the present. Sometimes there is shared love and devotion, sometimes hostility, and sometimes just toleration. But both are prisoners of circumstance, washed up together for a while on one of life's desert islands; and what they make of the time they spend there depends not always so much on their feelings for one another, as upon their willingness to act towards each other with kindness, understanding and respect, and to try to build a good relationship on this foundation. And some of them manage to make a remarkably good job of it against extremely heavy odds.

Many women who can look back on such an experience and are willing to discuss their feelings about it with honesty often infer that for them, 'it was the best of times – it was the worst of times', but not a time they regret. They do not pretend that they did not occasionally feel a loss of freedom and opportunity, and they remember all the loneliness, the physical exhaustion, and the stretched nerves. But they also recall how completely 'alive' and 'real' they felt during that period of their lives when they were giving (and, in some cases, giving up) so much: a feeling of living dangerously once they had decided not to cut and run, but to stand and face a difficult and demanding situation with long-term courage. Every day was a challenge to their powers of endurance, but they remember the good times, too: the moments of shared laughter and tenderness and the rewarding realisation that, tough as it was, they were doing something really worth while. Some were under great strain due to the emotional instability or brain damage of the old person in their care, and wondered, looking back, just how they got through it, but were pleased that they had. Others, who were more fortunate, often remember not only their own struggles, but the fortitude shown by their parents as they faced the gradual loss of their strength and independence, their anxiety about always being on the receiving end after a lifetime of looking after others, and the concern they felt for those who were caring for them.

They all dealt with their commitment in their own way. Some did so in a highly efficient and well organised fashion. Some simply muddled through, but just as successfully, 'playing it by ear' with intuition and a warm and willing heart. Others, whose nature it was, in all close relationships in their lives, to think the world well lost for love, chose, against all the advice of their friends and the carping of their critics, to put their own health and prospects at risk in order to care for an elderly parent, sometimes in appalling circumstances: not as martyrs, not as masochists, but just as loving people exercising their right to do it 'their way' in order to be true to themselves, which makes them equally deserving of respect.

And so they stand in every generation, these millions of ordinary women of extraordinary courage, loyally caring for and protecting those who once protected them.

Index

abdominal pains, sudden acute, 262
Age Concern, 45, 96
aids for the disabled, 250–9
  bathroom and toilet, 255–8
  bed and bed-aids, 254–5
  self-help, 58–9, 258–9
  sitting, 251–4
  walking, 251
alcohol, alcoholism, 23, 186–7, 196–7
alimentary canal, diseases and
    disorders of, 139–42
anaemia, 151–2
angina, 128
animals, 52, 103
annuities, 81, 84
anxiety, 14, 15, 125, 184–6
Area Health Authority, 43, 270
armchairs, high-seat and high-back,
    251–2
arteriosclerotic dementia, 175, 176–7,
    265
arteriosclerotic Parkinsonism, 154
Arthritis and Rheumatism Council,
    158
assaults on elderly women, 115–18
Attendance Allowance (leaflet NI
    205), 73, 75–6, 82

bath mat, non-slip, 59, 256
bathroom:
  aids, 255–6
  improvements and adaptations in,
    59–60
bath safety rail, 59, 255
bath seat, 59, 255

bed(s) for elderly patients, 220–1
  changing bottom sheet or
    drawsheet, 230
  correct lifting of patient, 231
  making, 227–8
  making, with patient in it, 228–30
  ripple, 221, 223, 254–5
  turning a patient in, 230–1
  use of hot water bottles or electric
    blankets in, 241–2
bed bath, 231–3
bed-blocks, 221, 223, 255
bedcovers, protective, 255
bed cradle, folding, 222, 255
bed linen, 221–2
bedpan, 257
  giving a, 236–7
  slipper, 257
bed-rest, 221, 223, 255
bedsores:
  ripple bed for patient with, 221
  treatment of, 235
bereavement, 5, 7–29
  emotional support, 25–8
  funeral, 21–2
  immediate help, 20–1
  practical help, 23–5
  safeguarding her health, 22–3
  widow, whose marriage was
    unhappy, 15–17
  widower, 17–20
*Bereavement. Studies of grief in adult
  life* (Parkes), 28
Bergman, Dr K., 172
bidets, 60, 257

283

Index

birthdays, 38
blankets, 222
bleeding, stopping, 261–2
blood pressure, 136
bodily changes, 2
British Red Cross Society, 168, 218, 225–6, 251
brittle bones, 2
bronchitis, 137
building societies, 24
    tax on interest on money in, 82
burns, 262–3
business affairs, helping the bereaved in her, 23–5

cancer, 164–9
    home care of, 167–8
    services of Marie Curie Foundation, 168–9
carbohydrates, 64
cardiac neurosis, 130
Caring for the widow and her family (CRUSE), 24
carpets, fitted, 55, 57, 58
cataract, 148–9
chairs (for disabled):
    high-seat and high-back, 251–2
    mobile, 252
    raising blocks for, 253
    reclining, 252
    self-lifting, 252
chamber pots, 257
children *see* grandchildren
chiropodists, 44, 137, 225
chronic emphysema, 138
Chronically Sick and Disabled Persons Act (1970), 49
circulatory disorders, 126–8
Citizens' Advice Bureau, 45, 53, 224
clothing, 246–50
    day clothes, 248–9
    night clothes, 249
    outdoor, 250
    underwear, 249–50
commodes, 256–7

communication, old people's means of, 48–52
Community Health Council, 43, 269, 270
Community Service Volunteers, 45
compulsive eating, 197
confusion in elderly people, 173–5
constipation, 140–1, 142, 238
continental quilts (duvets), 222
coronary heart disease, 128–31
cramp, 131–2
CRUSE (National Organisation for Widows and their Children), 24, 27
cushions, 253
cystitis, 146–7

day hospitals, 267–8
deafness, stress and, 205–8
death:
    elderly people's need to talk about, 104
    last offices after, 277–8
    pensions and, 78–9
    registration of, 21, 278
    see also bereavement
death certificate (form BD8), 79, 278
death grant, 24, 73, 79
delusions, 179–82
dentists, 44
Department of Health and Social Security, 24, 82
    state pensions and benefits available from, 73–8
    see also social services
depression, 36, 63, 125, 131, 184–6, 265
    bereavement and, 10–11, 15, 18, 26
    see also stress
diabetes, 152–3, 263–4
diarrhoea, 141, 142
diet/nutrition, 63–71
    basic constituents of food, 64–5
    for bereaved, 23

Index

for constipation, 141
for coronary patients, 129, 130
for elderly patients at home, 244
for elderly people living alone, 46–8
menus for a seven-day period, 66–70
vitamins, 65
Disabled Living Foundation, 242, 247, 250, 259
disabled people, 39, 53
aids for, 250–9
attendance allowance, 75–6
clothing for, 247
free telephones, 49
home improvement grants, 53, 54
invalid care allowance, 76–7
loss of sight, 149–50
district home nurses, 44, 225
diversion, to reduce stress, 208–9
diverticulitis, 141–2
domestic chores, 40–2
domiciliary medical and social services, 42–5
double-glazing, 55–6
draught-strip, copper or plastic, 55
dressing sticks, 258
drinking *see* alcohol

Easy cooking for one or two (Davies), 70
Elderly Invalids' Fund, 96
electric blankets, 61, 241
emotional immaturity, 14
emotional support for bereaved, 20–1, 25–8
emotionally disturbed parent, living with, 115–18
errands, for old people living alone, 45
exercise for coronary patients, 129, 130
eye diseases, 148–50

falls, 124, 157

father or father-in-law, living with, 111–15
fats, 64
financial problems, 4, 5, 72–85, 96–7
death of the parent, 78–9
income tax, 79–83
management of finances of seriously ill, 84–5
occupational pensions, 79
people living alone, 47–8
rent and rate rebates, 83
safe investment of capital, 83–4
state pensions and benefits, 73–8
floor coverings, safety of, 57–8
food, preparation and presentation of, 244
see also diet
food guard, 259
footstools, 253, 257–8
one-step, with handrail, 58
two-step, with handrail, 258
foot troubles, 137
fractures, 263
frozen shoulder, 159–60
funeral, 21–2
furniture, easy moving of, 58

gall bladder, diseases of the, 153
gangrene, 132
garden planning, 61
gastric ulcers, 140
general practitioners (GPs), 42–4
genito-urinary organs, diseases and disorders of, 142–8
geriatric units/wards:
medical, 269–70
psycho-, 270–1
visiting patients in, 271–3
gifts for elderly people living alone, 38
glaucoma, 149
good relationships and stress, 212–14
grandchildren, elderly people's relations with, 109–11

Index

'granny-bashing', 115–18
grants for home improvements, 52–4
Grief and how to live with it (Morris), 28
A grief observed (Lewis), 28
guilt feelings and stress, 214–16
gynaecological illnesses, 147–8

hair, loss of and loss of colour, 2
hair rinser, 256
hair-washing in bed, 233–5
halls, safety of, 60–1
hallucinations, 182–4
handicapped people, help for (Dept of Health leaflet HB1), 73
Health Food shops, 70
heart attacks, 263
heartburn, 140
heart disease, 126–8
    coronary, 128–31
heating, 56–7
height, shrinkage in, 2
Help the Aged, 24, 45
Helping Hand aid, 58–9, 224, 258
hernia:
    hiatus, 140
    strangulated, 141
hoist, 223
Home Help, 41–2, 225
home improvements and alterations, 52–61
    bathroom and lavatory, 59–60
    easy moving of furniture, 58
    garden planning, 61
    grants for, 52–4
    heating, 56–7
    insulation, 55–6
    kitchen, 58–9
    lighting, 57
    safety and functioning of equipment, 61
    safety of floor coverings, 57–8
    safety of halls and stairways, 60–1
    security measures against intruders, 55

home nursing procedures, 226–44
    bed bath, 231–3
    bedmaking, 227–30
    bedpan, giving a, 236–7
    bedsores, treatment of, 235
    hair-washing, 233–5
    incontinence, dealing with, 242–4
    injections, giving, 239
    medicines and drugs, 237–9
    patient mobility, 226–7
    pulse, taking, 240–1
    suppository, giving a, 238–9
    temperature, taking, 239–40
    turning and lifting patient, 230–1
    urinal, giving a, 237
Home Responsibilities Protection Regulations (1978), 76
hospital:
    day support on discharge from, 267–8
    intensive care unit, 129
    long-stay psycho-geriatric wards, 270–1
    medical geriatric units, 269–70
    provisions for care of elderly by, 268–9
    terminal illness in, 278
    visiting, 271–3
hospital, admission to, 260–73
    benefits affected by, 76–8
    emergency, 260–4
    for mental illness, 264–5
    planned, 265–7
    preparation for possible urgent, 61–2
    under Mental Health Act, 190–2
hot water bottles, 241–2
house tax, 81
housekeepers and nurses, 96
Housing Corporation Head Office, 97
Housing grants and allowances for disabled people, 54
How to pay less rates (leaflet), 83

Index

hygiene, personal, 59, 60
hypochondriasis, 124–5
hypothermia, 57, 150–1
hysterectomy, 148

illusions, 182–4
income tax, 24, 79–83
  age allowance, 82–3
  on annuities, 81
  house tax, 81
  on interest of money in building society, 82
  on occupational pensions, 80
  on retirement pensions, 80
  on savings invested with local authority, 81
  tax codes, 80
  for wife who also has a pension, 81
Income tax and the elderly, 79, 82
incontinence, 144–6, 225, 242–4, 248–9, 275
Incontinence (Mandelstam), 242
indigestion, 140
injections, giving, 239
insulation, 55–6
insurance, 24
Invalid Care Allowance (leaflet NI 212), 73, 76–7
investment of capital, 83–4

jaundice, 153

kidney disease and urinary tract infections, 143–7
kitchen, improvements and adaptations in, 58–9

laundry service for incontinent patients, 225
lavatory improvements and adaptations, 59–60
leg and lap covers (for wheel-chair users), 250
leg-rests, 253

leg ulcers, 136
library service, 225
lighting, 57
  emergency kit, 57
living alone (elderly parents), 30–62
  birthdays, 38
  communication, 48–52
  domestic chores, 40–2
  domiciliary medical and social services, 42–5
  diet, 46–7
  errands, 45
  financial problems, 47–8
  gifts, 38
  improvements and alterations in the home, 52–61
  pet animals, 52
  preparation for possible urgent admission to hospital, 61–2
  social life, 38–40
  visiting, 32–8
living with elderly parent in her own home, 87–97
living with elderly parent in your home, 97–119
  life with emotionally disturbed parent, 115–18
  life with father or father-in-law, 111–15
  life with mother or mother-in-law, 104–11
  making plans, 98–102
  settling in, 102–4
locks and bolts (on front and back doors), 55
lung diseases, 137–9

Mandelstam, Dorothy, 242
Marie Curie Memorial Foundation, cancer services of, 168–9
Markham, J., 226
Martin, Dr Ian, 183
mattresses, 221
Meals-on-wheels, 46
Medical Social Worker, 77, 78

Index

medicines and drugs, 237–9
medi-hoist, 258
memory, loss of, 2, 172, 174, 176, 177
Mental Health Act (1959), admission to hospital under, 190–2, 265
mental illness and impairment, 170–92
   admission to hospital, 190–2, 264–5
   alcoholism, 186–7
   changes in personality and behaviour, accepting, 187–90
   confusion, 173–5
   day hospitals for, 267–8
   delusions, hallucinations and illusions, 179–84
   depression and anxiety states, 184–6
   organic dementia, 175–9
   psycho-geriatric wards, 270–1
milkman, social role of, 48–9
minerals, 64
mobile chairs, 252
mobile shower chair, 256
Mobility Allowance, 73
mortgage payments, 24
mother-in-law:
   daughter-in-law's relations with, 105–8
   son-in-law's relations with, 108–9
mouth ulcers, 139–40
muscles, wastage of, 2

National Association of Citizens' Advice Bureaux, 45
National Council for the Single Woman and her Dependants, 92–3, 96
National Council of Social Service, 45, 95–6
National Health Service, 44, 170, 268, 270
National Insurance (Industrial Injuries), Acts, 82

National Savings Bank, 82, 84
National Savings Certificates, 82, 84
Nelson knife, 259
Nightingale, Florence, 215–16
Nursing (Markham), 226
nursing the elderly at home, 167–8, 217–45
   food preparation and presentation, 244
   hot water bottles and electric blankets, 241–2
   incontinence, 242–4
   keeping patient clean and comfortable, 231–7
   medicines and drugs, 237–41
   nursing procedures, simple, 226–31
   sick-room planning for long-term illness, 219–24
   supporting services, 224–6
   see also home nursing procedures
nutrition *see* diet

occupational pensions, 79, 80
occupational therapists, 44, 156, 225
'old age rickets', 65
old people's homes, 77
organic dementia, 175–9
osteo-arthritis, 156–9
   frozen shoulder, 159–60
   of the spine, 160–1
osteomalacia, 40
osteoporosis, 164

paraffin oil heaters, 56
paralysis agitans, 154
paraphrenia *see* delusions
Parkinson's disease, 154–5
part-time jobs, 113–14, 131
patient mobility, 226–7
pensions and benefits (state), 73–9
   admission to hospital and, 77–8, 273
   attendance allowance, 75–6
   death of parent and, 78–9
   graduated, 80

Index

invalid care allowance, 76–7
leaflets published by DHSS, 73
  occupational, 79, 80
  retirement, 73, 77–8, 80
  supplementary, 73–5
  widow's, 24
personality and behavioural changes, 135, 187–90
physiotherapists, 44, 134, 136, 155, 225
piles (haemorrhoids), 142
Pitter, Ruth, 72
plateholder, 259
positive thinking and stress, 198–201
Power of Attorney, 84–5
prostate gland enlargement, 146
proteins, 64
pulse, taking the, 240
pyelitis, 147

raised toilet seat, 256
raising blocks for chairs, 253
relaxation and stress, 209–12
reminiscences of elderly people, listening to, 34–5
Rent and rate rebates, 83
retirement, 3–4
  see also pensions and benefits
Retirement Certificates, government index-linked, 83–4
rheumatism, 155–64
rheumatoid arthritis, 155–6
ripple bed mattress, 221, 223, 254–5
roller blinds, 59
Royal National Institute for the Blind, 150

safety:
  of equipment, 61
  of floor coverings, 57–8
  of halls and stairways, 60–1
St Andrew's Ambulance Association, 226
St Christopher's Hospice, 276

St John Ambulance Brigade, 168, 226
savings, 47–8
  invested with local authority, 81
security measures against intruders, 55
self-help aids, 258–9
self-lifting chairs, 252
senile dementia, 176, 177–9, 265
share dividends, tax on, 82
shoe horn, long-handled, 258
shower, 59–60
shower chair, mobile, 256
sick-room planning for long-term illness, 219–24
  bed linen, blankets, etc., 221–2
  equipment, 222–4
  furniture and other items needed in, 219–20
  type of beds, 220–1
  see also nursing elderly at home
sight, partial or complete loss of, 149–50
  see also eye diseases
'silent' illnesses, 123
single women living with elderly parents, 87–97
sitting aids, 251–3
skin, thinning and wrinkling of, 2
sleeping bag, 223
slipped disc, 162–4
social life of elderly people living alone, 38–40
social services/workers, 224, 225
  domiciliary, 44
  Home Helps provided by, 41–2
  provision of telephone by, 49–50
  visits from, 44, 51–2
  see also voluntary services
Social services year book, 45
sock puller, 258
spinal illnesses, 160–4
stairways, safety of, 60–1
State Retirement Pension *see* pensions

Index

status, change from 'wife' to 'widow', 11–12
steps, step-stools, 58, 258
stocking aid, 258
strangulated hernia, 141
stress, 115, 117, 193–216
   adaptation method of control, 197–8
   avoidance of stress triggers, 201–5
   deafness and, 205–8
   diversion and, 208–9
   guilt feelings and, 214–16
   high-risk methods of control, 196–7
   a network of good relationships and, 212–14
   positive thinking and, 198–201
   relaxation and, 209–12
   see also anxiety
stroke, 132–6, 263
Stroke Rehabilitation Centres, 136
'successful' grieving, 10
Supplementary Benefits Act 1966, 74
supplementary pensions and allowances (leaflet SB1), 73–5, 80
supporting services, 224–6
suppositories, giving, 238–9
Swedish bath seat, 255

table, folding, 254
telephone, 49–51
temperature, taking the, 239–40
terminal illness, 12, 20, 166–7, 274–8
   in hospital, 278
There's money off your rent, 83
thyroid gland, diseases of, 153–4
toilet aids, 256–8
toilet-roll holder, 256
tranquillisers, 23, 117, 197, 276
trouser pull-on, 258
Trustee Savings Bank, 82, 84
tuberculosis, 138–9

ulcers:
   gastric or duodenal, 140
   leg, 136
   mouth, 139–40
unconscious person, first-aid for, 260–1
uraemia, 142–3
urinal, 257
   giving a, 237
urine, abnormalities of, 143–4
   incontinence, 144–6, 242–4
   retention of, 144

varicose veins, 136
visiting, visits:
   elderly persons in hospital, 271–3
   elderly persons living alone at home, 32–8
   by social workers, 51–2
vitamins, 65
voluntary services, 44, 225–6

walking aids, 224, 251
wheel-chairs, 254
wheel-chair users, outdoor clothing for, 250
'Wheelymac', 250
widow whose marriage was unhappy, 15–17
widowers, 17–20
widowhood *see* bereavement
widow's pension/benefits, 24, 73
Will, 23
Women's Royal Voluntary Service (WRVS), 24, 95
   Meals-on-wheels service, 46

Your guide to house renovation grants, 53
Your home and your rheumatism, 159

Zimmer walking aids, 251